EVEREST
A TREKKER'S GUIDE
7 TREKS IN THE EVEREST REGION

Dedication

This book is dedicated to the volunteer doctors at the HRA health post in Pheriche, in gratitude for lives saved – known and unknown.

About the Author

Kev Reynolds has trekked in many different regions of Nepal, from Api in the farthest west to Kangchenjunga in the northeastern corner of the country, and to many magnificent places in between. He has organised and led treks in remote districts and written guides to five of Nepal's most popular trekking regions. A freelance writer, photojournalist and lecturer, he has published more than 40 books to date which, besides his Nepal trekking guides, include the Pyrenees, a series on the Alps and, nearer to home, several books on walking in southern England. Check him out on **www.kevreynolds.co.uk**

Trekker's Guides to Nepal by the same author, also published by Cicerone Press:

Annapurna
Langtang, Gosainkund & Helambu

Kangchenjunga
Manaslu

In addition, Kev has written over 25 further guides to walking and trekking in the Alps and British Isles.

EVEREST
A TREKKER'S GUIDE
7 TREKS IN THE EVEREST REGION

by
Kev Reynolds

With additional material by Joe Williams

2 POLICE SQUARE, MILNTHORPE, CUMBRIA LA7 7PY
www.cicerone.co.uk

© Kev Reynolds 1995, 2000, 2005
1st Edition 1995
2nd Edition 2000
3rd Edition 2005, reprinted 2008 (with updates)
ISBN-10: 1 85284 418 3
ISBN-13: 978 1 85284 418 9
A catalogue record for this book is available from the British Library.
All photos by the author except where credited otherwise

WARNING

All mountain activities contain an element of danger, with a risk of personal injury or death. Treks described in this guidebook are no exception. Under normal conditions, wandering the trails towards Everest will be neither more nor less hazardous than walking among big mountains anywhere in the world, but trekking involves physically demanding exercise in a challenging landscape, where caution is advised and a degree of stamina is often required, and it should be undertaken only by those with a full and proper understanding of the risks involved, and with the training and experience to evaluate them. Trekkers should be properly equipped for the routes undertaken. Whilst every care and effort has been taken in the preparation of this guide, the user should be aware that conditions can be highly variable and change rapidly. Rockfall, landslide and crumbling paths can alter the character of the route, and the presence of snow and the possibility of avalanche must be carefully considered, for these can materially affect the seriousness of a trek.

Therefore, except for any liability which cannot be excluded by law, neither Cicerone Press nor the author accepts liability for damage of any nature (including damage to property, personal injury or death) arising directly or indirectly from information given in this guide.

Readers are warned that trekkers are sometimes badly injured by passing yaks; a few unfortunates die of hypothermia or acute mountain sickness; while some simply lose their balance and fall from the trail due to a momentary loss of concentration. Since there is no organised mountain rescue service in Nepal, such as exists in some mountain regions of Europe, if an accident occurs self-help may be the only option. Note too, that where it is possible to summon a rescue helicopter, the cost of doing so is very high and guarantee of payment essential. Make sure your insurance includes such costs, and carry a credit card with sufficient funds to back its use for the initial call-out.

Everyone trekking in the Everest region should assume responsibility for their own safety and look to the needs of those with them. This includes especially porters and members of a trek crew, as well as fellow trekkers.

Front cover: The North face of Everest from the Rongbuk Monastery (Joe Williams)

CONTENTS

Map Key

~~	ridge
••••••	trekking route
••••••	alternative route
≈≈≈	road
~~	river
⬭	lake
▨	glacier
⬭	national park
~ ~ ~	national boundary
■	habitation
●	town
▲	summit
⛰	gompa
⛺	camp
)(	col
⋈	bridge

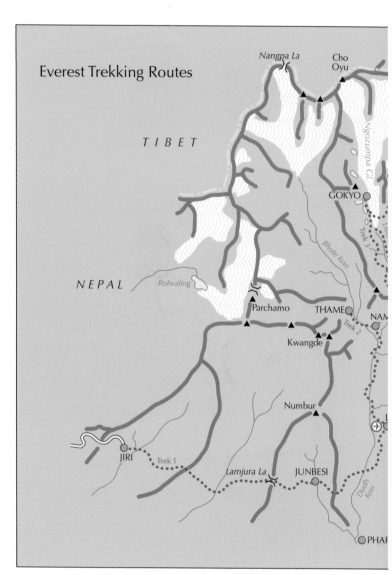

Everest Trekking Routes

TIBET

Nangpa La

Cho Oyu

Ngozumpa Gl.

GOKYO

Bhote Kosi

Trek 3

NEPAL

Rolwaling

Parchamo

THAME

Trek 2

NAM

Kwangde

Numbur

JIRI · Trek 1

Lamjura La

JUNBESI

Dudh Kosi

PHA

8

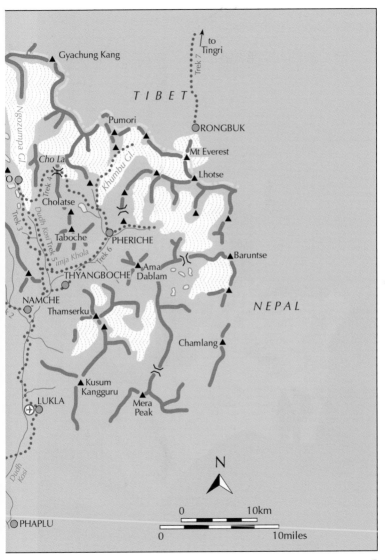

to
Tingri

Trek 7

T I B E T

▲ Gyachung Kang

Ngozumpa Gl.

▲ Pumori

○ RONGBUK

Cho La

Khumbu Gl.

▲ Mt Everest

Trek 4

▲ Cholatse

Dudh Kosi Trek 5

Trek 3

▲ Lhotse

▲ Taboche

○ PHERICHE

Imja Khola

Trek 6

▲ Baruntse

▲ Ama
Dablam

THYANGBOCHE

N E P A L

○ NAMCHE

▲ Thamserku

▲ Chamlang

2

▲ Kusum
Kangguru

▲ Mera
Peak

⊕ LUKLA

Dudh
Kosi

N

0   10km

0   10miles

○ PHAPLU

Thamserku, one of the finest peaks on the Dudh Kosi's east wall, is seen to dramatic effect from a trail linking Khunde with Khumjung

PREFACE TO THE THIRD EDITION

The Himalayan Kingdom of Nepal is a trekker's dream world. The dramatic beauty of its mountains is legendary, its people among the most warm-hearted, gentle and openly friendly that you could possibly wish to meet. From the lush foothills stepped with immaculate terracing, to the stark upper regions of snow, ice and towering walls of rock, a series of unfolding landscapes impress all who wander through. None who are lured along its trails need fear disappointment.

This book is a guide to just one region of this magical land – the district known as Solu-Khumbu, home of the legendary Sherpas – and its northern neighbour in Tibet. Among its

mountains Cho Oyu, Ama Dablam, Kangtega, Thamserku, Nuptse and Lhotse all present powerful images, as do many others with less familiar names. But it is Mount Everest that naturally provides the magnet for the vast majority of trekkers and all who love the high, wild places.

Traditionally known among both Khumbu Sherpas and Tibetans to the north as Chomolungma, 'Goddess Mother of the World', the highest mountain on Earth is Sagarmatha to the people of Nepal. Chomolungma, Sagarmatha, Everest, the mountain is the lure.

Each of the trekking routes described in the following pages will open the eyes of the sensitive traveller

The classic view: Everest and Nuptse from Kala Pattar

to scenes of unbelievable grandeur. Whether your plan is to study Mount Everest in some detail from the crown of Kala Pattar, or to gaze at it from Thyangboche's rhododendron-clad slopes; whether you aim to explore the lake-gemmed delights of Gokyo or the raw beauties of the valley of the Imja Khola below the huge wall of Lhotse, rewards will be plentiful. As they will be for trekkers on the northern side of the mountain in Tibet.

Trekking through Solu-Khumbu provides an opportunity to build a relationship with people of a different culture, a vastly different background, a different outlook on life; people who seem largely content and unencumbered by possessions, many of whom live free from the drive of competition, and among whom the passage of time has an entirely different meaning to ours. The strong Buddhist faith of the Sherpas has manifested itself not only in the way they live, but also in the landscapes in which they live; nature, environment and human activity balanced by the pivot of this faith. We, as trekkers from an alien culture, need to be aware of that balance and determine not to upset it.

How you interact with both the country and its inhabitants will depend on the degree of sensitivity carried with you. The riches you will harvest there will be measured by your willingness, or otherwise, to put Western values in abeyance and submit yourself to the multiple experiences waiting. Trekking in the shadow of Mount Everest can be a feast. There's no need to go hungry.

Trail information contained in this book reflects as accurately as possible the routes as found during research. However, each monsoon adds its own signature to the landscape. Trails and bridges may be washed away and replaced elsewhere. Villages expand, teahouses and lodges multiply, and paths are re-routed when landslips reshape a hillside. In order to improve and update future editions of this guide, I'd appreciate the assistance of any reader who would provide a note of changes found on trek. I'd also welcome comments or suggestions that might be of benefit to future trekkers. All notes and corrections sent to me via the publisher will be gratefully received.

This third edition owes much to a number of people. First of all my good friend Kirken Sherpa, of Himalayan Paradise Trekking & Mountaineering in Kathmandu, not only provides the logistical support for my treks, but also often acts as sirdar. The crew often give valuable insights in unsuspected ways; so my thanks go to Tsewang Sherpa, Pasang, Choden, Phuri, Dawa, Lhakpa, Phurba, Dines, Bhadru and the porters who are the real heroes of trekking in Nepal. Allan Brown, Graham Muirhead, John Robertson, Janette Whittle, Norman and Elaine Wright, Steve Neville and Jonathan Williams made my latest trek one of my best ever, and I thank them once more for their humour and excellent company. On previous treks in the

The small village of Bupsa is perched among terraced fields above Kharikhola (Trek 1)

Everest region I've benefited from the company of Krishna Bahadur Tamang, Alan Payne, and of course, my wife. Though she was not with me on the latest trek, her support at home made it possible. This edition of the guide is enhanced by the description of the trek to Rongbuk in Tibet, for which I am extremely grateful to Joe Williams, and for the inclusion of his superb photographs of that trek.

Once again I am indebted to the staff at Cicerone Press for putting their skills and talents at my disposal in the design and production of this book. And finally, I thank the countless unnamed lodge keepers, villagers, porters and yak herders of the Everest region whose broad smiles and greetings of *Namaste* are every bit as important as the mountains that form a dramatic backdrop to our travels. It is they who will ensure my return to Nepal – again and again.

Kev Reynolds, 2005

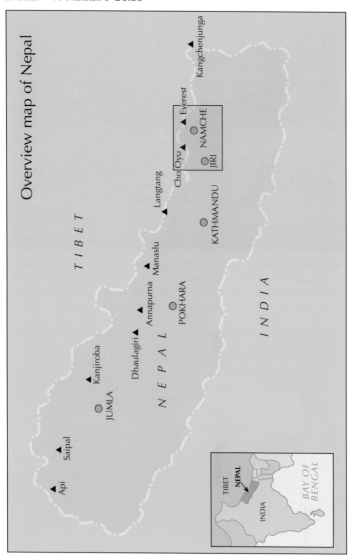

Overview map of Nepal

INTRODUCTION

Mountains are fountains, not only of rivers and fertile soil, but of men. Therefore we are all, in some sense, mountaineers, and going to the mountains is going home.

John Muir

For all its great bulk and a height of 8848m (29,028ft) Mount Everest is remarkably shy, and for many days successfully eludes the gaze of trekkers approaching from the south. On the walk-in from Jiri there is one memorable stretch of trail between Junbesi and Sallung where for a few glorious minutes an amazing line of snowpeaks, including Everest, marks the far horizon. Then it's gone, not to appear again for several days until a bend on the final slope leading to Namche Bazaar grants but a brief, tantalising glimpse.

Beyond Namche, however, the summit pyramid, often devoid of snow, appears from a variety of viewpoints as a black crown perched on the Nuptse–Lhotse ridge. All around other peaks, of varying altitudes and degrees of grandeur, jostle for attention while Everest impresses, as has been said, not so much by its great height 'but by the suggestion ... of the immensity of its unseen mass'.

The trail to Sallung gives a tantalising view of Everest on the horizon

For most trekkers following the trails in this book a clear view of the world's highest mountain will be the lure. That is understandable. But Everest is merely one among dozens of stunning peaks that crowd each day in Khumbu. Stand on the summit of Gokyo Ri and a truly remarkable panorama displays rank upon rank of snow, ice and rock peak, each carved with its own savage profile, while far below shines a turquoise lake and beyond its walling moraine the longest glacier in Nepal stretches grey, bleak and rubble-strewn.

At the head of Gokyo's valley, Cho Oyu – one of the first 'eight thousanders' ever to be climbed – presents an almost featureless white face, a vast wall of snow-covered ice, while neighbouring Gyachung Kang provides a neatly sculpted contrast, appealing yet formidable with its bare-rock buttresses rising steeply from the glaciers.

Then there are the ice-crusted walls and pinnacles of Kangtega and Thamserku soaring above Namche, and nearby Ama Dablam, as easily recognised and as eternally memorable as Machhapuchhare (the 'fish-tail' peak) in the Annapurna Himal. From the trail above Namche, as from Khumjung and Thyangboche (or Tengboche), graceful Ama Dablam dominates views along the valley of the Imja Khola. Yet if you trek farther upvalley and view it from the north, the mountain is transformed entirely, and still it remains handsome, aloof and seemingly unattainable.

From Kala Pattar below stately Pumori, directly opposite Everest itself,

Gokyo Ri overlooks Nepal's longest glacier

Nuptse soars above Gorak Shep

the impressive west flank of Nuptse with its fluted peak, its great daubs of meringue-like snow and hanging glaciers, shames its more illustrious neighbour with startling beauty. If ever there were a crystal mountain Nuptse, seen from this view, would be it.

These, and other magnificent peaks, provide all the visual drama for which Nepal is so justly famed.

Nepal claims 8 of the 10 highest mountains in the world. Of these, three are Khumbu mountains (Everest, Lhotse and Cho Oyu), while a fourth (Makalu) is seen from specific viewpoints on and above the trail. Not without good reason did the much-travelled Bill Tilman call this 'the grandest 30 miles of the Himalaya'.

Yet trekking in Solu-Khumbu is more than a simple adoration of mountains, for there are other aspects of the region that will enhance the whole experience of travel there. Villages along the trail, for example, reflect a way of life long forgotten by the developed world. Men and women still work the land either with the aid of water buffalo (in the foothills), or simply by hand (in the higher regions). As there are no roads there are no wheeled vehicles and all goods must be transported on the backs of porters or by strings of ponies or yaks. Along the trail prayer flags, prayer wheels, *mani* walls, *chortens* and gold-topped *gompas* all symbolise a tranquillity of spirit ignored by our industrialised society.

For many, trekking in the Khumbu can become almost a spiritual experience, a communion with both nature and man. Along the trails described in

17

Inquisitive children at Junbesi

the following pages one has an opportunity to touch heaven every day.

EVEREST AND THE SOLU-KHUMBU REGION

The pull of Everest was stronger for me than any force on earth.

Tenzing Norgay

Tucked away among a bevy of huge mountains in northeastern Nepal, Mount Everest forms a pyramid with three great ridges, along two of which runs the border with Tibet. The most southerly of these drops to the South Col, then rises to the summit of Lhotse (8501m: 27,890ft), from which other ridges stretch out to the west and east. An enormous horseshoe, known as the Western Cwm, is created by the linking of Everest, Lhotse and Nuptse, out

18

of which the Khumbu glacier cascades in an immense frozen cataract.

It is the river which springs from this glacier, and other tributary glaciers feeding into it, that waters the Solu-Khumbu region on its tumultuous journey south – out through the middle hills and foothills of Nepal, out to the steamy, low-lying Terai and the Gangetic plain of India.

Khumbu is the mountainous Sherpa-inhabited region fanning southward from Mount Everest to the junction of the Bhote Kosi and Dudh Kosi rivers below Namche Bazaar; Solu, the middle hills that drain into the Solu Khola west of the Dudh Kosi. Linking the Solu district with that of Khumbu is the region known as Pharak – 'the area that connects'.

South of the Nuptse–Lhotse wall a tributary valley joins that of the

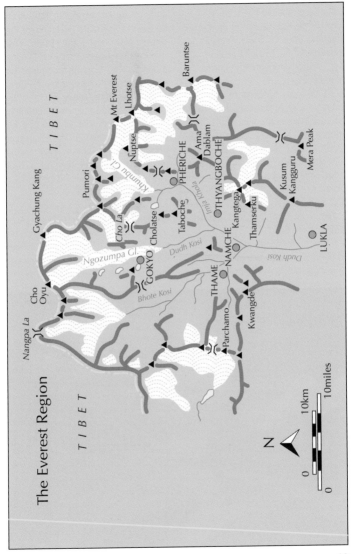

The Everest Region

Khumbu just below Pheriche, bringing with it the meltwater of numerous glaciers, three of which form an icy moat round the trekking peak of Imja Tse, more descriptively known as Island Peak.

Below the junction of these two valleys the river flows southwestward and is known as the Imja Khola, but it soon trades this name for that of the Dudh Kosi at Thyangboche. For it is here that another major tributary flows from the frontier mountains – the Dudh Kosi, born in the Ngozumpa glacier that noses through the Gokyo valley from Cho Oyo and a host of stunning peaks.

Once the Dudh Kosi and Imja Khola rivers merge the valley narrows with huge walls rising on either side,

and south of Namche Bazaar it becomes a veritable gorge. Then the Bhote Kosi swells the Dudh Kosi immediately below Namche, having drained more frontier mountains on the ridge continuing west of Cho Oyu. At the head of the Bhote Kosi's valley lies the Nangpa La, a pass traditionally used by generations of Tibetans for cross-border trade with the Sherpas of Khumbu, while above Thame, the main village in the valley, the pass of Trashi Labtsa provides a potentially dangerous route into Rolwaling.

The Dudh Kosi gorge begins to open out at Mondzo, a trailside village on the edge of the Sagarmatha National Park. Some 1200 square kilometres (463 square miles) of mountainous country north of Mondzo – in

Approaching Gorak Shep the trail overlooks the Khumbu glacier

The bridge spanning the Dudh Kosi's gorge brings trekkers to the final long climb that leads to Namche

effect all of Khumbu except the villages which are excluded from its authority – were incorporated into the National Park in 1976, and the Park declared a World Heritage Site three years later.

South of Mondzo the Dudh Kosi ploughs a long straight furrow and its valley remains narrow, squeezed in places by mountain spurs pushing from either side, and only on rare occasions flat-bedded and broad enough to encourage villagers to turn its banks to agriculture. However, from Kharikhola down, the hillsides have been immaculately terraced and a variety of crops flourish in the lower altitudes and more benevolent climate.

All the main river valleys hereabouts run roughly southward between long foothill (or middle hill) ridges, several of which are connected by ancient passes. West of the Dudh Kosi the Beni Khola joins the Junbesi Khola above Phaplu to become the Solu Khola. The headwaters of the first of these rise in the snowfields and glaciers of Numbur and Khatang, then flow between pine-clad hills and orchards of apples, peaches and apricots. From the ridge crests, as from Sallung, long views north show an immaculate row of white teeth etched upon the horizon – Khumbu peaks rising over a succession of intervening ridges.

This is Solu-Khumbu, a magical land full of charm and grace; a trekker's dream world.

EVEREST TREKS

I felt I could go on like this for ever, that life had little better to offer than to march day after day in an unknown country to an ... unattainable goal.

H. W. Tilman

Considering the number of trekkers and mountaineers who have followed these trails over the past half-century, the route to Everest is no longer unknown country, even if, for the vast majority of those who go to seek its inspiration, the mountain itself remains an unattainable goal. But the spirit of Tilman's statement is one which many trekkers will echo with feeling.

Whether you choose to trek from Jiri in the foothills, or fly to Lukla and begin there, with Everest being the focus, all trek routes automatically converge on the Sherpa capital of Namche Bazaar, situated about 45km (28 miles) southwest of the mountain above the confluence of the Bhote Kosi and Dudh Kosi rivers. Above Namche further options become possible.

As set out in the following pages, the trek to Everest is described in several different sections. **Trek 1** deals with the walk-in from **Jiri to Namche Bazaar**, and includes the most heavily trekked section from **Lukla**. At Namche it will be necessary to take a rest day or two in order to aid acclimatisation, and suggested walks are given for this. The route to

Thame in the valley of the Bhote Kosi makes a particularly rewarding acclimatisation trek and is described as **Trek 2**.

There follows a description of **Trek 3** which branches away from the main Everest trail to visit the sparkling **Gokyo lakes** that lie in the ablation trough beside Nepal's longest glacier. The ascent of **Gokyo Ri** is included; from this vantage point the summit panorama includes four of the world's highest mountains.

Then comes a crossing of the **Cho La** to **Lobuche** (**Trek 4**), and a 'low-level' alternative trek (**Trek 5**) from **Gokyo** that also goes to **Lobuche** via **Phortse, Pangboche** and **Pheriche**.

After this the trek through the Sherpa heartland of Khumbu from **Namche to Lobuche, Gorak Shep, Kala Pattar** and **Everest Base Camp** is described as **Trek 6**, with a side trip via **Dingboche to Chhukhung** below the great wall of Lhotse.

Trek 7 provides information about the **northern approach to Everest via Tingri in Tibet**, and describes the **Rongbuk Base Camp** area.

As approximate timings for the various stages are frequently given in the following pages, as well as a note of villages where accommodation is available throughout, you should be able to create an itinerary to suit your own plans. On an organised group trek, of course, the sirdar and leader will have their own favoured places to halt for the night.

Since the choice of route will depend largely on the amount of time available, an indication of the length of each trek is given below, but remember to add acclimatisation days once you reach Namche.

Trek 1: Jiri to Namche Bazaar (7–9 days)

This is the classic walk-in which largely follows the trail used by the first successful expedition to climb Mount Everest in 1953, and which was adopted by just about every subsequent mountaineering expedition destined for the Khumbu until regular flights to Lukla offered a short cut. Rich in contrasts, it provides the best possible introduction to the area. There are plenty of teahouses and lodges along the way, thus making it an ideal route for independent trekkers as well as those in organised groups choosing to camp overnight. As the trail has been regularly used by Westerners for many years, it is not surprising to find that some of the lodges here are among the best in all Nepal.

Jiri lies in the foothills just west of the valley of the Khimti Khola, and may be reached from Kathmandu following a long day's journey by public bus. Leaving Jiri the trek heads roughly eastwards across the grain of the land, and by way of a series of high ridges meets the major valley of the Dudh Kosi after three or four days. (An alternative start, which avoids the long road journey to Jiri, makes use of the STOL airstrip at Phaplu in the valley of the Solu Khola below

Junbesi. By this option it is possible to reach Namche in about four to five days.)

As far as the Dudh Kosi this first part of the trek is reasonably strenuous with much height gain and loss. Vegetation is lush and varied with the hillsides either forested, or terraced for agriculture. Views of distant mountains tease day after day, and the highest point reached is the pass of the Lamjura La at 3530m (11,581ft), which comes after four or five days of trekking. This is even higher than Namche Bazaar. After crossing the Dudh Kosi below Manidingma (also known as Nuntala), the route heads north to rise steadily over successive mountain spurs, passing below Lukla to be met by the Lukla trail at Choplung, and reaching Namche at last with big snowpeaks rising all around.

Trek 1, Section 4: Lukla to Namche Bazaar (1½ days)

Flying in to Lukla has become the most popular approach, and is the choice of those with only a limited amount of time to devote to a trek. During the main trekking seasons flights from Kathmandu are scheduled daily, but these rely on clear, settled conditions. Low-lying clouds at any time of year can and do cause delays. Once safely landed at Lukla (2850m: 9350ft) it is important not to rush upvalley ignoring the need to acclimatise, but take an easy 1½-day hike to Namche, on the way joining the main trail from Jiri at Choplung.

Trek 2: Namche Bazaar to Thame (2 days – there-and-back acclimatisation trek)

Northwest of Namche, the Bhote Kosi's valley leads to Tibet via the Nangpa La. The first major tributary of this valley above Namche is the Thame Khola, which drains down from a glaciated ridge crossed by the Trashi Labtsa pass. A short way into this tributary lies the village of Thame, an unspoilt collection of traditional Sherpa houses and yak pastures at 3820m (12,533ft), with a wonderful view through the main valley to Thamserku. Since it is more than 350m (1150ft) higher than Namche, as an aid to acclimatisation before moving on to Gokyo or Lobuche, a visit to Thame makes a lot of sense, especially if you spend at least two nights there. A few lodges and campgrounds are nicely situated in and on the edge of the village.

Trek 3: Namche Bazaar (or Khumjung) to Gokyo (3–4 days)

Although Gokyo is not very far from Namche in linear distance, the advanced altitude demands short stages to get there. There are two alternatives for the first stage: one goes via Khumjung; the other takes the main Thyangboche trail as far as Kyangjuma before climbing the hillside to join the path from Khumjung on the way to Mong.

The Gokyo valley lies north of Namche, and the trail to the Gokyo settlement keeps on the west side of the Dudh Kosi valley, crosses one or two tributary glens and passes a few lodge 'villages' before reaching the snout of Nepal's largest glacier, the Ngozumpa. A string of lakes lie in the ablation valley below the glacier's moraine wall, and the lodges of Gokyo overlook the third of these, with Gokyo Ri rising above its northern shore. A climb to this tremendous viewpoint is highly recommended, while other places of interest upvalley would repay several days based here.

Trek 4: Gokyo to Lobuche via the Cho La (3 days)

In good conditions experienced trekkers could cross the Cho La (5420m: 17,782ft) to reach Lobuche in the upper Khumbu valley in a three-day trek from Gokyo. On the way to the Cho La the route crosses the Ngozumpa glacier, and there's another glacier to negotiate on the eastern side of the pass, followed by a steep descent into the glorious Chola valley.

Trek 5: Gokyo to Lobuche via Phortse, Pangboche and Pheriche (3–4 days)

An alternative and very scenic route to Lobuche descends the east side of Gokyo's valley to Phortse, then takes a high and exposed trail to Pangboche, a two-part village with the oldest *gompa* in the Khumbu located in the upper village. From Pangboche the route continues to Pheriche or Dingboche, where a day should be given to help acclimatise, before heading up to Lobuche.

Trek 6: Namche Bazaar (or Khumjung) to Lobuche, Gorak Shep, Kala Pattar and Everest Base Camp (5–7 days)

The nearest lodge accommodation to the base of Mount Everest is at Gorak Shep on the west bank of the Khumbu glacier, just beyond the point where it is joined by the Changri glacier. Everest Base Camp is about 2hr further upvalley, while directly above Gorak Shep rises the ever-popular viewpoint of Kala Pattar. About 6km (4 miles) downvalley, and set in a wide ablation trough, are the lodges and campgrounds of Lobuche where most independent trekkers prefer to stay. Both Lobuche and Gorak Shep are bitterly cold sites, and few choose to stay there longer than necessary.

The trail from Namche to Everest Base Camp and Kala Pattar is well trodden and visually spectacular. Because of the altitude it is important to advance in easy stages, and at least two nights should be spent in Namche (or at one or other of its neighbouring villages) before moving on. Another acclimatisation rest at Pheriche or Dingboche should be built into your schedule.

Above Namche the valley forks. While the left branch leads to Gokyo and the headwaters of the Dudh Kosi, the right-hand option entices with the summit of Everest seen peering over the huge Lhotse–Nuptse wall that appears to block the valley of the Imja Khola. The Thyangboche Monastery is located on a wooded ridge near the junction of these two valleys, a day's walk from

Taboche and the Chola valley, seen from the trail to Duglha

Namche. It's a wonderful site, but from there the trail goes to Pangboche, beyond which there's only one more village (Shomare), and a few scattered lodges before the next fork in the valley.

Here the right branch is the Imja Khola's valley, with lodges at Dingboche and Chhukhung. The main trail takes the left fork below Dingboche and leads to Pheriche, Lobuche and Gorak Shep. An alternative trail links Dingboche with Pheriche, and yet another takes a higher route across the slopes of Pokalde to join the main trail near the simple lodges of Duglha about 1½–2hr below Lobuche. At least two nights should be spent at either Lobuche or Gorak Shep in order to have time to visit Kala Pattar or Everest Base Camp.

Ways out

Whether you walked in from Jiri in the foothills, or flew in to Phaplu or Lukla to begin the trek, you'll no doubt join the vast majority of visitors to the Khumbu who return to Kathmandu by flying out of Lukla. Lukla is a day's hike from Namche; Phaplu is about three days from Namche, while to trek back to Jiri takes about five or six days.

Trek 7: Everest from Tibet: Tingri to Rongbuk Base Camp (3–4 days)

Included in this guide is a short trek on the northern side of the mountain which leads to the historic Rongbuk Monastery, and the Base Camp area used by pre-war Everest expeditions.

By contrast with the Nepalese side, the view of Mount Everest from here is uninterrupted; a stunning spectacle. The trek from Tingri is short and uncomplicated, but the advanced altitude makes it a tougher proposition than might be imagined. It is essential to go through an acclimatisation programme before setting out for the Rongbuk Base Camp.

TREKKING AND TREKKING STYLES

The art of Himalayan travel ... is the art of being bold enough to enjoy life now.

W. H. Murray

Trekking is the simplest and most rewarding way to travel in mountain country; a journey on foot through an unfamiliar land, moving on day after day as though on pilgrimage. And in common with the pilgrim those who gain most from it are those who have managed to cast off the anxieties of their everyday life, who readily absorb each new experience, and live in every moment of the present.

Wandering the trails of Nepal can – and should – be a life-enriching experience. Since the rate of progress through each day is self-governing, opportunities abound for observing the intricacies of the trail, of fellow travellers (trekkers, porters and local Nepalis going about their daily business); flowers, trees and shrubs; animals, birds and butterflies; village life; the changing light on a distant mountain; the roar of a river, dull clonk of a yak bell, the welcoming call of *Namaste*. There are scents, too, to draw upon. In the foothills they're often heavy with sun-drenched vegetation, while at altitude the crisp fragrance of morning is a tonic that sharpens all the senses. There's the taste of dust that fills the air after a yak train has passed by; the smell of woodsmoke drifting over the rooftops of Sherpa houses; or the more acrid, eye-smarting effects of a yak-dung fire in a remote trekkers' lodge.

Although you'll turn your back on most of the trappings of Western society, trekking towards Everest – though far from any road – could not be considered a true wilderness experience. There are many villages or hamlets liberally spaced along the valleys described in this guide, and a tourist infrastructure has developed which caters to the needs of thousands of visitors who annually flock there. This enables a choice of trekking styles to be enjoyed.

There are several different ways to trek in Nepal. There's the organised variety, where a group of people travel under the auspices of a commercial trekking agent or adventure travel company. There's independent trekking, where two or three friends forsake the company of porters or guides, travel light and use teahouses and lodges throughout – often referred to as 'teahouse trekking'. And there's a third course, a cross between independent and group travel, where a porter-guide is employed both to carry some of the trekker's gear and to lead him along the trail using lodges for overnight accommodation. Few regions of the Himalaya provide better facilities to accommodate trekkers of all persuasions than does that of Solu-Khumbu.

The particular trekking style to suit each individual will depend upon such considerations as cost, personal experience of mountain travel, availability of like-minded friends with whom to undertake the journey, amount of time required to organise and carry out the trek, the choice of route, etc. The following paragraphs, written with particular regard to the Everest region, may help you decide which option is most appropriate for you.

Trekking with an adventure travel company

This is the obvious choice for those with more money than time, who dislike the hassles of organisation, who get frustrated with bureaucracy, or who have limited mountain experience and want a degree of security. Trekking with a reputable adventure travel company does away with all pre-departure worries and trek concerns. Read the brochures and all dossiers carefully, sign the form, make out your cheque and let someone else take care of the arrangements. One of the most important things you are paying for is expertise.

A product of this expertise is pre-departure advice with regard to

inoculations, visa requirements and a suggested kit list. All flights to and from Kathmandu, and transfers and other travel arrangements within Nepal, will be taken care of, as will hotel accommodation and the provision of entry permits for the Sagarmatha National Park. Some companies also hire out items of equipment that would otherwise be expensive to buy, like a good-quality sleeping bag or a down jacket suitable for high altitudes.

On a group trek in Solu-Khumbu porters or yaks carry all camping equipment, food, kitchen stores and personal baggage, leaving the trekker free to shoulder just a light rucksack containing a few items likely to be required during the day, such as water bottle, spare film, fleece or down jacket.

Nights are usually spent in tents. All meals are prepared and served by a staff of trained Nepalese cooks and kitchen boys; latrines are dug by the trek crew, tents erected and dismantled for you, and Sherpa guides ensure that you do not get lost along the trail. A sirdar takes overall responsibility for the smooth running of the trek, but usually a Western leader also accompanies the group to liaise between trekkers and local staff. This leader often has an understanding of any medical problems likely to be encountered, and is in charge of a comprehensive first aid kit. Some companies based in the UK offer financial incentives to qualified medical personnel who accompany groups on a particular route.

A well-organised group trek can be a very sociable way to travel. Daily you will be walking, and sharing experiences, with people you may never have met before, and lasting relationships sometimes develop from on-trek introductions. On the downside, the disparate make-up of a group can lead to a clash of personalities (at altitude sometimes the best of friends can become tetchy), although groups are usually of a sufficient size (10–14 is normal) to make it possible to avoid too much contact with someone you don't get on with.

Organised groups, of course, generally need to keep to a predetermined route and maintain a fairly strict schedule, which can be a little frustrating if you pass an enticing side valley you'd like to visit. On the other hand, since each day's stage is limited by the distance a laden porter can cover, the journey is made at a leisurely pace, thus allowing plenty of time to enjoy the scenery, visit an occasional monastery, study the flowers or indulge in photography along the trail.

Although group travel tends to insulate its members from interaction with local people, trekking for two or more weeks in the company of Nepalese guides, cook and porters presents lots of opportunities – for those so inclined – to build a relationship that can be immensely rewarding for all concerned.

The group trekker's day begins with a mug of tea brought to the tent at around 6.00am, closely followed by a bowl of hot water for washing. Breakfast is served soon after. In the foothills this will be eaten outdoors with views of distant mountains and hills warming to the new day. In higher, colder country, a mess tent will be used.

The day's trek starts early, around 7.30am when the light is pure, the air cool and (in the foothills and middle hills) the birds active. The trek crew will break camp as porters either pack their *dokos* (large conical baskets in which goods are carried) or tie kitbags and tents together, and set off along the trail. During the morning's walk the kitchen crew will rattle past and select a lunch spot, often with a fine view. Lunch is eaten any time between 11.00am and 1.00pm, and is usually a hot meal with plenty of liquids.

The afternoon's walk will normally end at around 4.00pm, giving the chance to write journal notes, read, or chat with other members of the group while camp is being set up and the evening meal prepared. This is usually finished by 6.30 or 7.00pm allowing plenty of time to rest, read, talk or listen to the songs of the crew beneath a starlit sky.

One of the many positive aspects of trekking with a group is that with trained cook and kitchen staff as part of the crew, the standard of food hygiene can be controlled – an important matter over which independent teahouse

Dole enjoys spectacular views of Kangtega and Thamserku

trekkers have little influence in the lodges. A skilled Nepali cook will often provide a surprising variety of meals using just basic portable equipment, and is rightly seen in the hierarchy of the trek crew as number two after the sirdar.

Most companies are well aware of the need to adopt conservation practices, particularly with regard to cooking by kerosene or gas and never by wood fire; in fact it is a requirement of entry to the Sagarmatha National Park that no timber is cut for firewood. It is also important to ensure that all waste materials are disposed of in a suitable manner, and not to the detriment of the environment. The trek leader should make himself responsible for ensuring that his party leaves nothing but footprints.

Adventure travel companies regularly advertise in the outdoor press, and a number of these organise promotional slide shows during the winter months which provide an ideal opportunity for potential clients to meet and question trek leaders and assess what's on offer.

Independent teahouse trekking – the lodge option

For experienced travellers who either enjoy (or are not averse to) making all arrangements – organising visas, booking long-haul flights and hotels in Kathmandu, buying bus tickets to Jiri or arranging a flight to Lukla, route-finding on trek, and choosing meals and lodges – independent teahouse trekking is the answer. It can be extremely rewarding, as well as the cheapest option, but to be successful it is essential to adopt a flexible attitude of mind and be ready to adapt to a wide variety of circumstances. The only predictable element of travel in a country such as Nepal is the certainty that the unpredictable will happen!

Teahouse trekking is understandably popular in Solu-Khumbu, not least because the quality of some of the lodges there is equalled only by the very best Thakali-run establishments in the Annapurna region. Lodges and/or teahouses occur with great frequency most of the way from Jiri to Namche, while even above Namche it's possible to get accommodation right to the very foot of the biggest mountain of them all, thus enabling the trekker to travel with a minimum of equipment.

As far as this guidebook is concerned, a teahouse is a trailside building that offers basic refreshment for travellers; a lodge is a simple hotel (*bhatti*) where both food and shelter are provided. These *bhatti* are variously advertised as guesthouses, hotels, inns or lodges; but whatever the sign says outside, accommodation facilities are by Western standards fairly basic – although some offer degrees of luxury (in Nepalese terms) undreamed of until recently.

Most *bhatti* consist of a simple building (sometimes an adaptation of a private home, sometimes purpose-built) comprising kitchen, dining area and sleeping quarters. Washing facilities (where they exist) are fairly

primitive, but most lodge owners will provide a small bowl of warm water on request. Hot showers are often advertised; but if you imagine neat, tiled cubicles and abundant hot water, forget it. Often the 'shower' will consist of an outside shed with a hose of lukewarm water. Just occasionally you'll be pleasantly surprised, but don't bank on it, and as most outside the National Park are heated by dwindling stocks of firewood, you should seriously consider taking a shower only in those lodges using solar or kerosene-powered water heating. Toilets usually consist of a simple outbuilding with a hole in the floor over a pit. On my first trek in the Khumbu many years ago, one memorable *charpi* at a Dingboche lodge had just three low walls and neither roof nor door. But it did have a magnificent view of the South Face of Lhotse – a true loo with a view! It is worth stressing, however, that standards are improving, and the majority of toilets should be quite acceptable. Just a few make you yearn for constipation. Whatever the general condition of lodge toilets, their use is preferable to treating the countryside as an open-air latrine.

Dormitories may accommodate as many as 20 trekkers, but they're usually more spacious than, say, those of mountain huts in the European Alps. Twin-bedded rooms are often no more than a small bare 'cell' furnished with two firm but adequate beds. Each bed has a thin foam-rubber mattress and a pillow.

Blankets are rarely supplied. There will often be no floor covering, and as the walls consist of little more than thin wooden planks, there's no soundproofing. Rarely will there be so much as a hook from which to hang a few items of clothing or a towel, so it's worth carrying a length of string and a couple of small screw-hooks to make your own portable clothes line. Bedrooms (other than dormitories) are usually made secure with a padlock.

A growing number of villages now boast electricity generated by small hydro schemes. Their lodges (and others with solar panels) will then have modest electric lighting. Even so, dining rooms are often poorly lit, but in the best of them a convivial atmosphere is easily created. Since the hill people of Nepal have little concept of privacy, none should be expected. The children of lodge owners will often join you at table, pick up your books or camera, study your clothes and anything else left lying around. If you find this curiosity annoying don't provide temptation; set firm limits, but don't lose your temper. This is their home, their country, and you are the guest who walked through an open door. Patience and understanding may sometimes be needed, but on completion of a teahouse trek you'll probably discover that some of your happiest memories will centre on the lodges in which you stayed.

Lodges offer a surprising choice of meals. First-time trekkers who arrive expecting to exist on a diet of *daal bhat*

Simple teahouse beside the Gokyo valley's east bank trail near Thare

32

three times a day will be pleasantly surprised by the variety of meals available. On the trail to Everest it's easy to vary your diet between Western and local food. It is important to remember that since most lodge meals are cooked over a single fire, if several trekkers order a number of different dishes, it follows that some will have to wait a very long time before being served. Not only can this prove irksome (especially if you're hungry after a long day's trek), it also means that more fuel than necessary is being consumed. Assess what your fellow trekkers are ordering, and follow their lead. The majority of lodges have a few luxury items for sale: bottled drinks, biscuits, chocolate and sometimes tinned fruit.

Lodge owners often display certificates to show they've completed a course in lodge management. This should lead to improved hygiene in food preparation, but a few common-sense precautions will help minimise the risk of stomach upsets:

- Always wash your hands before meals.
- Make sure the crockery and cutlery provided is both clean and dry.
- Exercise caution in your choice of food and drinks.

The standard procedure on arrival at a lodge is to enquire of the owner if there are vacancies. After being allocated a room, secure it with a padlock. Before darkness falls seek

DAAL BHAT AND POTATOES

The staple diet of most of Nepal is *daal bhat*, a rice-based meal usually eaten twice a day; in mid-morning and early evening. *Daal bhat* consists of a huge amount of cooked rice (*bhat*) flavoured with a small bowl of lentil soup (*daal*) and, where available, a few curried vegetables (*tarkari*). Many Nepalis also chew uncooked chillies with their meal. Unless prepared and served by the same cook at an identical time, it would appear that no two *daal bhats* are alike. Order *daal bhat* in the same lodge on two consecutive days, and you're likely to receive two very different but equally tasty meals. However, in the Khumbu, which is too high and cold for rice to be grown, potatoes form the main ingredient of Sherpa meals. From Namche on potatoes appear with increased frequency on lodge menues in various guises: as chips (French fries), boiled, sliced and fried, hash-brown and *rösti*. A traditional Swiss dish, *rösti* is par-boiled potatoes, grated and fried, with perhaps onion added – a very popular item on Khumbu menus. But if you spend time in a Sherpa home, you're almost certain to be offered a plate of potatoes cooked in their jackets, and eaten dipped in a very hot chilli sauce. It's enough to keep both the cold and the yeti away.

out the washing and toilet facilities, for although electric lighting is provided in most village lodges, the lights don't always work. You'll need your torch. All food and drinks ordered should be entered in a notebook provided by the lodge keeper, and payment made prior to departure. Often you'll be trusted to add up the cost of each item ordered (listed on the house menu). Prices are exceedingly modest by Western standards, and the cost of accommodation so low that the lodge keeper relies on selling meals and drinks to make a reasonable living. It is unacceptable to book a bed in one lodge and eat elsewhere. Remember that prices increase in proportion to the lodge's distance from the roadhead.

Independent teahouse trekkers are able to enjoy a much more flexible routine than those on an organised trek, and can vary their route at will. Although there is a danger of mixing only with fellow Westerners, those who wish to learn more about local people, customs and the life of villages along the route will find that opportunities abound. However, the best way to enjoy cultural interaction is via the third method of trekking, that is, with a porter-guide.

Trekking with a porter-guide

The best porter-guides become your trusty friends and companions who provide a daily insight into the ways of the people whose country you're travelling through. The cameraderie and comradeship can hugely increase the pleasures of your trek, and the opportunity for regular cultural exchange can be a highlight of experience. A porter-guide will carry some of your gear, make sure you keep on the correct trail, and act as a link between yourself and locals met on the path. If he's a Khumbu Sherpa, you will no doubt be invited into his home to meet other members of his family. He may suggest alternative trails and take you to sites of interest well off the normal route of most trekkers.

A good porter-guide can teach you much of value and, if you're sensitive, eager to learn and prepared to treat your companion as a friend rather than a servant, your experience will be the more profound as a result. There's the additional assurance that you're providing useful employment too. Porter-guides may be hired in Kathmandu through one of the many trekking agencies based there, but insist on meeting him first before agreeing a contract. It's a good idea to go out for a meal together, to discuss the trek before setting off.

Of course, in such a well-trekked and documented region as Solu-Khumbu, it's not essential to have a guide simply to keep you on the correct trail. However, on occasion you may feel the need to have someone carry your rucksack for you. In this case a porter is all you need, and it's often possible to hire one along the route at short notice – either for just a

After a short day's carry, porters enjoy a rest at Machhermo

day or two, or for the duration of the trek. Enquire of your lodge keeper for a reputable local – preferably one who speaks a few words of English. Payment is usually based on a daily rate, inclusive of food and lodging, or a higher wage with the requirement that the porter provides his own food. Make sure that he understands and agrees the arrangement before you set out. It is worth remembering that the role of a porter is by no means a demeaning one, for portering has long formed a major source of employment throughout the hill regions of Nepal.

Once you hire a porter or porter-guide you assume employer's responsibility for his well-being. Nepalese law states that all trekking porters must be insured, have provision for security, personal protective equipment including clothing and footwear adequate for the weather conditions, and that the employer is responsible for the rescue of porter(s) when required.

So far as the Everest region is concerned your employee must be clothed and equipped to be able to cope with below-freezing temperatures if your proposed route reaches high altitudes (as at Gokyo, Lobuche or Gorak Shep, for example). Don't forget to supply sunglasses too, should your route take you across snow or glaciers. While a porter-guide hired from a reputable Kathmandu agency may be expected to be well equipped (but you need to check first), if you take on a porter from the lowlands he is unlikely to

35

YOU AND YOUR PORTER

Whether you're an independent trekker hiring a porter or porter-guide, or a member of an organised group, try to build a relationship with your porter(s). Keep in mind that, like you, they have their own limitations, but coming from a different culture they are carrying loads to earn money; very few choose to visit the high, cold places for the fun of it. The wage you pay should be realistic and in line with local law and custom, and tipping is an essential part of the deal. Consider giving a day's pay for each week on trek.

Porters are not super-human. Though they may carry what seem impossible loads, they too can be affected by the altitude, suffering from acute mountain sickness and, like you, be vulnerable to sub-zero temperatures. In fact Nepalese porters suffer four times as many accidents and illnesses than Western trekkers, and some appalling incidents of exploitation and abandonment by employers have been reported. Don't let your porters add to the statistics.

What can you do as a trekker?

Independent trekkers who hire a porter should adhere to the following recommendations:

- Ensure adequate clothing is available for their protection in bad weather and at altitude: footwear, gloves, windproof jacket and trousers, sunglasses and access to a blanket or sleeping bag (and mat if camping) above the snowline.
- Provide the same standard of medical care for porters as you would expect for yourself.
- Never send sick crew members down alone. Have someone go with them who understands the problem and speaks their language.
- Provide sufficient funds to cover the cost of a porter's rescue and treatment.

Members of a group trek can do the following:

- Before booking your trek ask the tour operator what policies they have in regard to porters' working conditions, and let them know it is important to you that your trek does not exploit its staff.
- Travel only with an operator that has policies on porters' rights (Tourism Concern publishes a list of UK trekking agencies with such policies: **www.tourismconcern.org.uk**).

- While on trek note the treatment of porters, their clothing, size of loads, where they sleep at night, etc.
- On return from Nepal, tell your operator if you thought they were treated badly – and report this to Tourism Concern.
- Just as importantly, tell your operator if the porters were treated fairly, and let them know that it was crucial to your enjoyment of the trek. If every trekker were to show their concerns for the treatment of porters and other trek staff, the trekking industry would be forced to define and improve its policies.

have anything more than the clothes he stands up in. It will be up to you to provide him with warm clothing once you get high. It is worth noting that down jackets, boots and other gear can be rented in Namche Bazaar.

In Kathmandu decent wind- and water-resistant clothing for porters can be borrowed through the Porter Assistance Project run by the Himalayan Explorers Connection (HEC) in association with the International Porter Protection Group (IPPG), whose clothing bank is located next to the KEEP information centre in Jyatha on the edge of Thamel. Clothing for porters is supplied to independent trekkers and small trekking agencies on payment of a modest refundable deposit. For more information about HEC visit **www.hec.org** (email: members@hec.org). IPPG details can be found on **www.ippg.net** (email: info@ippg.net).

The easiest, most lightweight and inexpensive form of trekking with a porter-guide relies on the use of lodges for accommodation. Once you decide to camp, of course, you enter a more complicated style, with a leaning towards an organised trek. The more equipment taken, the more porters you'll require to carry it. In Kathmandu there are plenty of trekking agents who, within a few days of arrival, can supply all the manpower and equipment needed.

One final point: **for safety purposes trekking alone is not recommended**. In the event of an accident, a companion can be invaluable in providing immediate help or summoning assistance. Sadly, although the populated hill-country remains virtually crime-free, Nepal has not escaped certain less-welcome aspects of Western 'civilisation' and theft is no longer unknown in the hills – if it ever was. Regrettably, trekkers are known to have been mugged, and one or two have even disappeared on lonely sections of even the busiest of trails. If you'd rather not travel with an organised group and have no friend to trek with, do consider hiring a porter-guide.

No one ever travelled far during the monsoon if he could help it.
Eric Shipton

Whilst trekking may be possible at any time of year in Solu-Khumbu there are generally considered to be two main seasons: the spring, pre-monsoon period, and the more popular post-monsoon months before winter sets in. Few would argue with Shipton in regard to trekking during the monsoon, while winter can be numbingly cold but still accessible for the hardiest of trekkers in the higher reaches of the Khumbu.

Spring (pre-monsoon): March–May
The spring trekking season runs from late March to May. Early March above Namche can be colder than December, but from mid-March on temperatures in the lower hills rise considerably, and by May the first few days of a trek from Jiri will be uncomfortably humid – especially for independent travellers carrying large rucksacks. Clouds often build up during the afternoons, while heat haze throughout the day can spoil distant views in the foothills and middle hills, although at higher elevations the atmosphere is generally clear and temperatures moderate. This is the season for the keen botanist, for numerous wild flower varieties add a riot of colour throughout the region. Rhododendrons will be blooming at lower elevations as early as late February, but coming into flower during March and April at higher levels.

Summer (monsoon): June–September
From June to September Nepal is affected by the monsoon. During this time paths can be treacherous with mud, rivers and streams become raging torrents, torrential rain and mist deny views for much of the day, while trees, shrubs and undergrowth are infested with leeches except in the highest valleys. However, the countryside is then green and lush, wild flowers are impressive, and when clouds shred and momentarily part the mountains reveal an undeniable drama. There are very few trekkers along the trails, and village life resumes its age-old pattern. Anyone tempted to trek during the monsoon, though, should be aware that paths may be re-routed, some bridges could be washed away and lengthy diversions become necessary. That being said, when conditions allow flights to Lukla still operate, so determined trekkers with sufficient time to wait for a window of opportunity could avoid the worst effects of the monsoon and begin there.

Autumn (post-monsoon): October–late November
The post-monsoon period, which begins in October and continues until the arrival of winter in December, is the most popular. Trails and lodges

Gentians on the trail to Kyangjuma in the post-monsoon season

will then be at their busiest, the weather is generally settled, but when rain does fall it is usually short-lived. Above 3000m an occasional dump of snow is not unusual, however, and when prolonged can have an effect on plans to cross high passes. Mostly, though, days are blessed with clear, often cloud-free skies with a magical light ideal for photography. Daytime temperatures are very pleasant. Above Namche nights can be chilly in October, while at Gokyo, Thyangboche and beyond heavy frosts should be expected. By mid-November night-time temperatures will have dropped to well below freezing, although views by day have a lustre unrivalled at any other time of the year.

Winter: December–February

December is statistically the driest month of the year, and as long as you've good down clothing and sleeping bag, trekking right up to Christmas can be magnificent. In mid-winter (January) the intense cold experienced above Namche Bazaar can make nights especially uncomfortable, and in some years heavy snowfall in the higher regions can make travel difficult or even impossible. In addition some of the lodges may be closed, thus putting a few areas effectively out of bounds to independent trekkers. Late winter (February–March) is sometimes disrupted by snowstorms. Not only can these cause severe trail problems, but on occasion flights are unable to land at Lukla for several days at a time.

PRE-DEPARTURE PREPARATIONS

The journey should be carefully planned beforehand, especial study being given to the matter of gradients.
Karl Baedeker

This guidebook has not been produced to encourage more trekkers to explore the trails of Solu-Khumbu, but hopefully to add something to the experience of those already committed to going there. Since it is better to be forewarned than to walk blindly into disappointment, this particular section should strip away the veneer of romance and expose the bare reality for those considering their first trek.

The highest mountains in the world attract numerous trekkers to their valleys, many of whom have neither undertaken a multi-day walk before, nor had any previous mountain experience. Mount Everest becomes a collector's item for world travellers, alongside the Pyramids of Egypt and the Taj Mahal. That so many survive the experience to return for more says as much for the spell cast by the fabled Himalaya as for the care and attention devoted to them by their trek organisers and crew.

Successful trekking may be described as the art of gaining most from the multitude of experiences on offer. But to achieve that requires as much mental preparation as physical fitness. Tackling a Himalayan journey that will demand two or three weeks of

effort is a far different proposition to that of a fortnight's holiday based in a comfortable resort hotel from which to set out on day walks whenever the mood arises. As a member of an organised group trek to Everest you will be expected to walk day after day, rain or shine, whether you feel up to it or not. Naturally, real infirmity is excluded, but trail weariness is not. So get yourself both mentally and physically fit before boarding the plane to Kathmandu.

Consider the following scenario: of waking one morning weary from past excesses and feeling queasy from a stomach upset. Consider a cold wind and falling rain and a trek leader cajoling you to start walking. You have about eight hours of uphill trail ahead of you before the next camp is set up – and there's no alternative but to pull on your boots and waterproofs and start moving.

In certain seasons and in parts of the Khumbu region there may well be extended periods of intense cold, of days without being able to have a decent wash, or several nights in a row when you've not been able to enjoy restful sleep. Perhaps you're slow to adapt to the altitude; maybe the diet is not to your liking or, if you're new to camping, you've discovered you don't like sleeping in a tent. (It happens, so do try a night or two camping out before you commit yourself to a trek that uses tents.) On a teahouse trek you could be dismayed by the standard of accommodation provided, or by the

The suspension bridge at Phakding

lack of hygiene. There will be times of confusion, times when your Western sensibilities are appalled by the different values accepted by those whose country you are wandering through.

Successful trekking demands an ability to adapt to a whole range of ever-changing circumstances, to put Western values on hold and be prepared to accept that there could be much to learn about living from the culture of Nepali hillfolk. Learning to respect unfamiliar ways is in itself sometimes a shock to the system.

But if you're convinced that wandering among the most dramatic scenery on earth, of mingling daily with people of an entirely foreign culture, and that a sense of achievement at the end of the trek offer sufficient rewards for the odd day of misery and discomfort – then trekking is for you. If you have doubts, forget it. Five or six days into a long walk is not the time to decide that trekking is too alien an exercise for enjoyment. The financial outlay required to undertake a trek in Nepal should be sufficient spur to ensure that you enjoy every moment of your time there. Don't waste it on doubts or inadequate preparation.

As a member of an organised trek you have a duty to your fellow group members and to the leader to arrive in good shape, with fitness to match your enthusiasm. Trails are uncompromisingly steep in places, and there's only one real way to get physically fit for trekking in the Himalaya, and that is by

walking up and down hills carrying a rucksack. Jogging will help build stamina and endurance, swimming and cycling are also beneficial, but uphill walking with a rucksack is the best possible preparation. If hills are in short supply near your home, just walk as far and as often as you can wherever is convenient. Once you arrive in Nepal and the trail winds ahead as far as the eye can see, you'll be glad you put in some effort at home.

Having decided to go trekking towards Everest, put most of your preconceived ideas behind you, open your eyes, heart and mind to all that Nepal has to offer, and set off with a determination to see and to understand. You'll soon discover that the mountains are only part of the charm. As has been pointed out by a number of experienced trekkers, few will be content with just one Himalayan journey. 'The trek of a lifetime' is likely to be the first of many.

GETTING THERE

For many people distant places have a peculiar form of magnetism which grows as the distance increases.

H. W. Tilman

Travel information is particularly vulnerable to change, as airlines come and go (no pun intended), schedules change, and routes are introduced and dropped a year or two later. Please read this section as a rough guide only and check the current situation with your local travel agent. If you plan to book an organised group trek that offers 'Land Only' prices, your tour operator should be able to give advice as to which airlines fly to Kathmandu. The following information is correct at the time of writing.

By Air

Several international airlines currently operate services from the UK to Tribhuvan International Airport in Kathmandu. These include Aeroflot, Biman Bangladesh, Gulf Air, Jet Airways, Pakistan International (PIA) and Qatar Air.

Biman flights involve a change at Dhaka; Gulf Air at either Bahrain or Abu Dhabi; Jet Airways at Delhi; PIA at Karachi and Qatar at Doha.

Other flights can be arranged that require connections in Delhi, but be warned that the bureacracy involved in organising transit at Delhi Airport can be extremely tedious.

There are direct scheduled flights between Kathmandu and Lhasa (Tibet).

Flights out of Kathmandu are nearly always completely booked during the main trekking seasons, and it is essential to reconfirm homeward flights at least 72 hours before departure time. Failure to do so may lead to your name being deleted from the passenger list. Before going on trek make a point of visiting the airline office in Kathmandu to reconfirm – for it may be too late when you get back from trek. While reconfirming your flight home, check the amount of departure tax that will need to be paid at the airport, and put this money aside before spending the last of your rupees.

Travel within Nepal

Domestic flights are operated by RNAC and a number of independent airlines with varying degrees of efficiency. All flights by foreign nationals must be paid for in US dollars. Of particular interest to trekkers planning to visit Solu-Khumbu are the STOL (Short Take-Off and Landing) airstrips at Phaplu and Lukla.

Lukla is far and away the busiest STOL airstrip in Nepal, with a mixed reputation. Some love the excitement of flying into (or out of) this short, sloping strip of hillside above the Dudh Kosi, while others are terrified both with the prospect and the reality. In the past pieces of wrecked fuselage scattered alongside the runway did little to inspire confidence, but debris has now been cleared away and the runway surfaced with tarmac. With regular use of helicopters as well as fixed-wing aircraft, flights are more predictable than was previously the case, but stories still abound of angry trekkers being stranded there for several days because low cloud effectively prevented aircraft from getting in.

If you plan to fly, and have sufficient time, Phaplu below Junbesi offers an alternative to Lukla, with better opportunities to acclimatise as you walk in towards the high mountains of Khumbu.

NEPAL AND THE MAOISTS

Democracy came late to Nepal, and it was only in 1957 that the country's first elections were held, giving power to the conservative Nepal Congress Party. But bribery and corruption played a part, and two years later King Mahendra took control and had the whole cabinet arrested. He then introduced the *panchayat* system, which supposedly gave power to locally elected village leaders to nominate candidates for higher positions. This did little, however, to prevent widespread corruption, and eventually led to a rare outbreak of protest and violence on the streets of Kathmandu in April 1990. The king (by now Mahendra's son Birendra) was forced to lift the ban on political parties, and in 1991 elections were held that returned the Nepal Congress Party to power. The king remained the constitutional head of state, but political infighting and continued corruption and mismanagement did little to enhance the democratic cause. In 1996 a grass roots Maoist rebellion broke out with the proclomation of a 'People's War' whose aim was the overthrow of the monarchy and establishment of a communist republic. A 40-point charter of demands was presented to the prime minister, but when the government made no response within 10 days, the Maoists began to attack remote police posts. In the decade since, numerous Nepalis (police, soldiers, officials and rebels) have been killed, enforced strikes have shut down businesses, and the rebels claim to control large districts of the hill country.

To date there is no record of foreign visitors being attacked. Indeed, the Maoist rebels claim to appreciate the need for trekkers to continue to come to Nepal; after all, they provide employment for many of their background constituency of support.

But at the time of writing practically every trekking route in the country passes through Maoist-controlled regions, and many trekkers have been 'invited to give donations' to the cause. Invariably the response is a receipt being given which effectively affords the trekker (or trekking party) immunity from further demands (or invitations) for donations elsewhere. A number of reports suggest that commercial trekking companies now include a sum within their budget to take care of such 'donations'. As I write, there is no suggestion that you should cancel plans to go trekking in Nepal while the insurgency continues; just be aware. But let's hope that, for the sake of the deserving Nepali people, peace and justice for all will come to the country soon.

For up-to-date official advice on the situation, check out the foreign office website: **www.fco.gov.uk/travel**. See also **www.nepalnews.net**.

By road to Jiri Public buses make the journey of 188km (117 miles) between Kathmandu and Jiri in something like 9–12 hours, including a *daal bhat* stop at Lamosangu. Buses for Jiri depart from the 'old' bus terminal in Kathmandu near Ratna Park, the first departure being at 6.00am.

Public buses provide an 'interesting' and very cheap way to travel in Nepal. Invariably overcrowded, discomfort is guaranteed as the seats are designed with Nepalis in mind, who as a race are generally several inches shorter than Europeans. Occasionally seats may have a bit of padding; often they don't. On a long journey it is virtually certain that several passengers will be overcome by travel sickness and watch the miles pass by throwing up out of the windows. Although against the law to do so, it is often more comfortable to spend the journey on the rooftop with piles of baggage.

As an alternative way of reaching Jiri, it may be worth hiring a car or minibus with a driver. Several agents in Kathmandu can provide this service – but be prepared to haggle for a reasonable price. Expect to pay between Rps5000–6000 for the journey. It may help to shop around, but you should insist on seeing the vehicle before making a firm commitment. Travel by private car allows you to stop whenever you choose, and is especially useful in this respect for keen photographers. You'll also arrive in Jiri several hours earlier than you would by bus, feeling much less exhausted too.

For travel in and around Kathmandu taxis are both cheap and ideal for sightseeing purposes. It can often be worth hiring a taxi for a whole day (agree a price first), especially if you plan to visit a number of different sites.

PERMITS AND VISAS

And the end of the fight is a tombstone white with the name of the late deceased, And the epitaph drear: A fool lies here who tried to hustle the East.

Rudyard Kipling

All foreigners, except Indian nationals, require a valid passport and tourist visa to enter Nepal. Single entry, 60-day visas are available on arrival at Kathmandu's Tribhuvan International Airport, or at a land border. You will need one passport-sized photograph, and the current fee payable is US$30, which must be paid for in foreign currency.

Visas can also be obtained in advance from Nepalese embassies abroad (see Appendix D). Application should be made to the Nepalese Embassy or Consulate in your home country. This is a straightforward process that involves minimal form filling, the provision of two passport photographs and payment of the appropriate fee. Postal applications should be made at least one month before the date of departure. Postal applications ought to be made by registered post or

A trail linking Kyangjuma and Khumjung gives striking views of Ama Dablam

recorded delivery, and the envelope clearly marked 'Visa application' (don't forget to include a stamped addressed envelope for its return). If you apply in person at the Embassy, be warned that you will not normally be able to collect it until next day. Visas are valid for a period of three months after the date of issue, and have a duration of 60 days.

From January 2008 all trekkers must obtain a TIMS Registration Card, available either through a registered local agent (for group treks), or from the Kathmandu office of the Trekking Agencies Association of Nepal (TAAN). You will need a copy of your passport information page, plus two passport-sized photos.

In addition visitors to the Sagarmatha National Park will need an entry permit. This currently costs

Rps1000 and is payable at the park entrance at Mondzo. You will need your passport for this.

Other formalities

Note that a departure tax must be paid (in Nepalese rupees) at Kathmandu airport prior to leaving the country. Currently this costs Rps770 for flights to SAARC (South Asian) countries, but Rps1100 to other destinations.

PRE-TREK HEALTH MATTERS

Since the War expeditions have had the advantages of antibiotics, and have tended to neglect the rules of hygiene.
John Hunt *The Ascent of Everest*

For a normal active person in good physical condition, trekking in Nepal should not present any undue health risk. Yet first-time visitors to the Himalaya often become obsessed by their health, and on occasion the trails become hypochondriacs' highways. Conversations in teahouses and lodges alike zone in on topics related to bowel and bladder movement, on concerns related to the digestive tract, headaches, chest infections and the fear of altitude sickness. Obviously the farther you wander from 'civilisation' the more important it is to look after your health, but don't allow these concerns to become obsessive.

Before leaving home it would be wise for anyone with a particular worry to undergo a thorough medical examination, and it is important to have those inoculations deemed necessary by the health authorities before you go. Take a first aid kit with you, adopt a sensible attitude towards food and hygiene – and trust to luck. On the whole, trekking is a healthy pursuit. Things will not be as they are at home, but if you expect no risk at all when wandering in a developing country, save your money or book a holiday elsewhere.

Pre-trek health

The following information has been gathered from a variety of sources, but for up-to-date health advice in the UK, call the Department of Health Helpline (tel: 0800 555777). Alternatively contact MASTA (Medical Advisory Service for Travellers Abroad) on 01276 685 040, or visit their website:

www.masta.org. Another useful source of information in advance of a trip is the Nomad Travellers Store & Medical Centre, STA Travel, 40 Bernard Street, London WC1N 1LJ. See also the World Health Organisation (WHO) website: **www.who.ch**, and that of the CIWEC Clinic in Kathmandu: **www.bena.com/ciwec** which provides advice on the most recent health concerns.

It is important to start planning your immunisation programme at least three months in advance of your trip, to ensure any 'new' vaccination required is in date and effective before you travel.

At the time of writing Nepal does not require visitors to show proof of immunisation, except for travellers coming by way of Africa or South America, in which case a certificate of vaccination against yellow fever will be needed. However, it would be sensible to be 'in-date' or seek specialist advice in regard to the following:

- **BCG (tuberculosis)** – Most adults in the UK will have been immunised already, but a skin test is available should you be in doubt.
- **Diptheria** – The risk is moderate, but consequences could be serious if precautions are not taken. Immunisation is good for ten years.
- **Polio** – Immunisation lasts for ten years.
- **Tetanus** – Make sure you're 'in-date'; immunisation is good for ten years.

- **Typhoid** – Injectable and oral vaccines are available.
- **Hepatitis A** – This is endemic across Asia, and caused by poor sanitation and lack of hygiene. One shot of Havrix Hep A two to four weeks before departure should protect.
- **Hepatitis B** – Potentially more serious than 'A', this is transmitted through unprotected sex and transfusions of contaminated blood, or by means of contaminated needles and syringes. It may be possible to have a combined vaccination for both Hepatitis A and B.
- **Japanese Encephalitis** – This viral infection is transmitted by mosquitoes passing through rice paddies. There is significant risk during the monsoon and through to November. Immunisation gives three-year cover. If you plan to visit the Terai or trek in from Jiri during the risk period, you're advised to arrange immunisation.
- **Meningococcal Meningitis** – Seasonal outbreaks occur. If travelling between November and May, consider immunisation.
- **Rabies** – The risk of being bitten by an infected animal may be small (1 in 6000 visitors to Nepal receives a potentially fatal bite) but the Rabies immunoglobulin is only available at the CIWEC clinic in Kathmandu, so you should consider pre-exposure immunisation in advance. An expensive multi-jab course at set intervals is required.

Malaria – Current advice suggests there is no risk of **malaria** in the Kathmandu valley or the main trekking areas of Nepal, and the risk in the Terai is low except in the east, and close to the Indian border. However, precautions should be taken against mosquito bites; cover exposed skin at dusk and use repellent spray.

Anyone with a record of **lung or heart disease** should avoid treks that go to high altitudes, and should consult their GP before committing themselves to a trip to Nepal. It is in any case sensible to have a medical check before setting off on a lengthy Himalayan trek.

Once you leave Kathmandu prospects of **dental care** on trek are virtually non-existent. It would be wise, therefore, to make sure you have no loose fillings or even the first hint of tooth decay before leaving home. Arrange a dental check-up in advance of your trip, for there's nothing quite like high altitude, low temperatures and the knowledge that the nearest dentist is many days' walk away, to set your teeth aching!

ON-TREK HEALTHCARE

You have to use your judgement as to how much you get involved in some shaman's kill-or-cure schemes.
Rob Ryan *Stay Healthy Abroad*

On an organised group trek the Western leader usually has some experience of first aid and basic medical care in remote places, and can make a reasonable judgement about the physical condition of an ailing client, while the independent trekker needs to be almost completely self-reliant. In the Khumbu a few health posts have been set up whose services may be called upon in emergencies, but the prevention of health problems is something to which all who go trekking need give serious consideration.

Try to avoid the almost inevitable last-minute rush and stress that builds up just before taking a holiday. This will make you vulnerable to the germ-laden atmosphere of a long-haul flight which, coupled with a touch of jet lag on arrival, will have you worn out instead of bursting with energy and enthusiasm for the trek.

Although trekking should be beneficial to health by increasing vitality and a sense of well-being, the art of maintaining good health in a comparatively remote area can be seen by some as a bit of a challenge. It need not be, for with a little care and forethought you should have no undue problems. Use common sense with regard to personal hygiene, for this can be the key to staying healthy. On trek staying healthy is all about minimising risk. Carry a copy of a little book entitled *Pocket First Aid and Wilderness Medicine* by Dr Jim Duff and Dr Peter Gormly (TREK-SAFE, 2005), available from the KEEP office and several bookshops in Kathmandu. Full of useful information and sound advice, this 'portable doctor' should form part of your first aid kit – see list below.

Water

Trekking is thirsty work; so is living at altitude where it's essential to drink copious amounts of liquid to combat the effects of AMS (Acute Mountain Sickness), of which more later. Yet the most frequent cause of health problems in Nepal is via contaminated water. With poor sanitation, a variety of organisms live in the country's streams and rivers. All water (including that in hotels and restaurants in Kathmandu) should be considered suspect unless it has been vigorously boiled, treated with iodine (neutralise the taste with vitamin C tablets or powdered fruit drink), or comes in a bottle with an unbroken seal. Certain advanced water filtration systems, such as the portable Katadyn filter, claim to be effective even in removing *giardia* cysts, and could be worth carrying by independent trekkers. On a group trek, the cook should be well-versed in the need to boil water for drinking, and trekkers need not worry too much on this score, while tea, coffee and lemon drinks bought in teahouses and lodges along the trail should likewise be safe.

Remember, though, it is not only by drinking contaminated water that you might catch something nasty, but also when cleaning your teeth. If you cannot be certain about the quality of available water, do not even rinse your teeth with it.

Personal hygiene

Maintaining a high standard of personal hygiene on trek should be second nature, if only to avoid gastro-intestinal problems. So whether using lodges or tents, try to be scrupulous in keeping hands and fingers clean, not only before you eat and after going to the toilet, but throughout the day. Wash your hands thoroughly whenever you can. A supply of antibacterial handwash gel, or a pack of baby wipes, can be useful for those frequent occasions when soap and water are not available.

The Khumbu quickstep

Most trekkers suffer a mild dose of diarrhoea at some time or other during their stay in Nepal, although often this is simply reaction to a change of diet. There's no need to be unduly alarmed unless blood is passed in the stools (a sign of possible dysentery), for it usually remedies itself in a few days. Simply take plenty of liquids to prevent dehydration, reduce solid food intake and avoid dairy products and alcohol. If it persists after a few days take a rehydration solution, such as Dioralyte or Jeevan Jal (the Nepalese brand obtained in Kathmandu), which is quickly absorbed into the system and will help speed recovery. If the bug that caused the diarrhoea is not flushed out of your system and the problem persists while on trek, break open the first aid kit and take Immodium.

Be as circumspect when choosing food and drink in Kathmandu as

you would be on trek. Avoid uncooked fruit (unless you can peel it yourself), salads, raw vegetables and ice cream. Eat food you can be sure has only just been cooked and is still hot. The time to relax your guard is when you arrive home. That being said, do keep your concerns in perspective and don't allow them to dominate your time in Nepal. With a little forethought, and detail to personal hygiene, you should remain perfectly fit and healthy.

Chest problems

Coughs, colds and chest infections are exacerbated by smokey lodges, trail dust and the dry cold air of high altitude. The sound of locals emptying their lungs with a serenade of coughing and spitting is a Himalayan dawn chorus, to which most trekkers add voice at some time or other. Soluble lozenges will soothe inflamed throats, catarrh pastilles are worth taking, as are antibiotics (Ampicillin or as recommended) to combat chest infections. For sore, inflamed throats, try gargling soluble aspirin dissolved in warm (previously boiled) water – repeat at six-hour intervals.

Chest infections are usually marked by uncontrollable bouts of coughing, and the release of a lot of green-yellow sputum; the latter especially first thing in the morning. If there's difficulty in swallowing or talking, take a full course of antibiotics: 500mg Ampicillin at eight-hourly intervals.

Mountain sickness (AMS)

Perhaps the number one concern of first-time trekkers in Nepal is altitude, or mountain, sickness. Acute Mountain Sickness (AMS) is potentially a very serious condition that can affect anyone, but by being aware of the symptoms and abiding by the rules of acclimatisation, **AMS need not affect you**. Nowhere along the trails of Solu-Khumbu is it too high for a normal healthy body to acclimatise, given time, but some take much longer than others to do so. Some experience headaches at 2500m (8200ft) while others can happily climb to twice that altitude without discomfort other than shortness of breath. And it is not possible to predict in advance who among first-time trekkers will suffer from it, or when. Physical fitness is of no apparent benefit, neither is youthfulness; in fact it would appear that young people may be more prone to AMS than older trekkers.

A failure to allow sufficient time for acclimatisation is almost guaranteed to bring on AMS. The best way to avoid it is to ascend gradually to about 3000m (10,000ft), then ascend no more than about 400m (1300ft) per day after that. On some sections of the Everest trail it is not easy to follow the golden rule of 'climb high, sleep low' so it is important to make gradual height gain, with planned rest days, in order to allow the body to adapt to the reduced oxygen levels.

Another important consideration is the intake of fluids. At altitude it is necessary to drink at least 4 litres (7 pints) a day in order to avoid

Chorten above Dingboche

dehydration, and to urinate a minimum of half a litre per day – a great deal of fluid is lost at altitude simply through breathing. Yellow-coloured urine is a sign that liquid intake needs to be increased.

AMS can be detected in several ways. Signs to look for are: extreme fatigue, headache and loss of appetite. Some trekkers also find that they become breathless with only minimal exercise and suffer disturbed sleep. If these symptoms develop do not go any higher until they've gone away. If they show no sign of leaving after a day or two, but instead become worse, it is important to descend to lower levels. Do not take strong painkillers or sleeping tablets as these can mask the symptoms.

A worsening condition is indicated by vomiting, severe headache, lack of co-ordination, wet, bubbly breathing, increased tiredness and breathlessness, even at rest. Such symptoms warn of the onset of a very serious condition (fluid on the lungs or brain – pulmonary or cerebral oedema) which, if ignored, can result in lack of consciousness and death within 12 hours. The only cure, if acted upon in time, is to descend at once – in the middle of the night if necessary – until symptoms decrease and finally disappear completely. An improvement is often experienced after just 300m (1000ft) or so of descent. But it is imperative that the patient should not be left to descend alone.

As with all health concerns it is important to be aware of potential dangers, but keep them in perspective and do not allow unnecessary fears to devalue the pleasures of the trek. Be aware of symptoms, act upon them if they occur and, time and energy willing, continue with your trek when signs of improvement indicate it is safe to do so.

Remember: do not go too high too fast, and descend promptly if ill.

If you've been to altitude before and found it difficult to acclimatise, speak to your medical practitioner before going on trek, and he may prescribe Diamox (*acetazolamide*) as a way to combat mild AMS. Diamox does not mask the symptoms of AMS, so if you still experience them it's essential to act accordingly. Many patients taking the drug experience mild tingling in the hands and feet – these are not signs of developing AMS. You will probably notice increased urine output, though, as Diamox is used to reduce fluid retention.

Medical care and emergency evacuation

A **medical post** run by the Himalayan Rescue Association (HRA) is situated in Pheriche. During the main trekking seasons it is manned by volunteer doctors who specialise in altitude-related problems and attempt to educate trekkers on the dangers of going too high too fast. They give lectures each afternoon on the subject of mountain sickness, which are well worth attending, and are usually available for medical consultations. Consultations and treatment must be paid for, and those who attend lectures should make a donation towards the cost of running the health post.

It is also worth making a visit to the HRA office, located in the Tilicho Hotel in Kathmandu, prior to going on trek (open daily except Saturday, 11am– 5pm). Not only will you receive good advice on AMS and other health matters, forms are also available to enable you to register with your Embassy – very useful in the case of emergency.

There are **small hospitals or health posts** at Jiri, Phaplu, Junbesi, Manidingma, Kharikhola, Lukla, Choplung, Namche, Khunde, Machhermo, Deboche and upper Pangboche in addition to the HRA post at Pheriche mentioned above. Please be aware that not all these health posts are permanently manned. Namche Bazaar has a **dental clinic**.

Emergency evacuation depends on the weather, and may take several days to be effectively carried out. Evacuation from the more remote areas of Khumbu is difficult to organise and extremely expensive. Rescue by helicopter will only be attempted when a guarantee of payment has been made. If you're trekking with a reputable adventure travel company and something goes wrong it may be possible to arrange emergency evacuation by air. If you're travelling independently, you'll need to be able to guarantee payment by quoting your credit card number – so long as you have sufficient funds in the bank to back it. (In 2004 the cost to summon a rescue helicopter to Pheriche was $3150.) Make sure you've registered with your country's embassy in Kathmandu.

Should you need to consult a Western doctor on return to Kathmandu, the best known clinic is that of the Canadian-run CIWEC Travel Medicine Centre situated near the Russian Embassy in Baluwatar (tel: 228531). It is expensive, but facilities are said to be very good.

More detailed medical advice and preparation may be gleaned from reading James A. Wilkerson's *Medicine for Mountaineering* (The Mountaineers), or Peter Steele's *Medical Handbook for Mountaineers* (Constable).

THE FIRST AID KIT

You should be able to repair yourself in the event of an injury or accident, at least enough to survive until help arrives.
Chris Townsend *The Backpacker's Handbook*

All trekkers, whether travelling independently or with an organised group, should carry a personal first aid kit, the very minimum contents of which should be: ▶

- Elastoplast or similar dressing strips
- Blister prevention & treatment
- Bandages (cotton gauze & elastic)
- Aspirin and/or Paracetamol
- Throat lozenges (& cough pastilles)
- Thermometer
- Iodine tablets (for water purification – chlorine tablets may also be used, but be aware that not all germs are eliminated by this treatment)
- Immodium (or similar for diarrhoea relief)
- Scissors
- Cotton buds
- Rehydration solution (Dioralyte or Jeevan Jal)
- Antiseptic cream
- Antibiotics (Ampicillin, Ciprofloxacillin, Tinidazole and so on, and/or as prescribed)
- Emergency dental kit
- Safety pins
- Knee supports
- Tweezers
- Surgical gloves
- Vaseline
- *Pocket First Aid and Wilderness Medicine* (see On-Trek Healthcare)

Also recommended is a pack of sterile needles for use in emergencies where injections are necessary, in order to reduce the risk of accidental transmission of HIV (AIDS) and Hepatitis B viruses through contaminated equipment. MASTA (see Pre-Trek Health Matters section) produce a sterile medical equipment pack that contains syringes, sutures and dressings as well as needles.

Most medicines, including antibiotics, are readily available without prescription in Kathmandu (general pharmacies are located on New Road and in various parts of Thamel). Do not rely on the diagnostic advice of untrained pharmacists; where doubts occur seek medical assistance. Make sure you have all you might be expected to require in the way of medical aid before setting out on trek.

EQUIPMENT CHECKLIST

Having only brought one coat, which was wet, spent the evening in a sweater. Luckily I had two.
G. H. Bullock, writing from 20,000ft on Mount Everest

Bullock took part in the first Everest reconnaissance expedition of 1921, when clothing and equipment used by the climbers was unbelievably basic –

he even carried some of his gear in an old suitcase! When we compare that with some of the state-of-the-art gear worn by a few once-only trekkers on the Khumbu trail today we can see just how far equipment design and manufacture has advanced. This is not the place to discuss the merits of one product against another, but to provide a list of items likely to be needed by trekkers using this book.

Clothing
- boots and spare laces
- light shoes/trainers
- down jacket
- fleece or sweater
- shirts x 3
- socks x 3
- trekking trousers (or long skirt for women)
- waterproof jacket/poncho
- overtrousers
- underwear (include thermals)
- gloves
- woollen hat/balaclava
- sunhat
- money belt

Optional
- camera, films, batteries and lens tissues
- insulation mat (Karrimat or similar)
- plastic bags*
- binoculars*
- umbrella
- notebook and pens
- altimeter

Other essential items
- rucksack (day-sack only for members of an organised group trek)
- kitbag (group trekkers only)
- trekking poles
- sleeping bag (4 seasons +)
- sleeping-bag liner
- water bottle (min 1 litre capacity)
- headtorch, spare batteries and bulbs
- mending kit*
- first aid kit
- penknife
- sunglasses
- suncream (factor 25+) and lip salve
- towel and washing kit
- money belt
- map*
- whistle
- toilet paper and lighter
- passport ▸

- small padlock (to secure kitbag for group trekkers or lodge bedrooms for teahouse trekkers)
- guidebook

Note i Items marked with an asterix (*) can be shared between members of a group.

Note ii A collapsible umbrella that fits easily into a small rucksack can be extremely useful on rainy days; especially in the lower hills when humid conditions may deter you from wearing waterproofs.

Note that a kitbag (holdall) and not a full-sized rucksack is used on group treks where porters carry the loads. Most porters will carry more than one trekker's gear, bound together with string or rope, and held with a *namlo* or tumpline round the forehead. Several adventure travel companies supply kitbags for their clients, but they can also be bought from outdoor retailers. Make sure you buy one made from tough material and with a robust zip, for they take a lot of battering on trek. The day-sack included in the list for group trek members is to contain daily essentials.

It's useful to have a complete change of clothes waiting for your

Village scene, Namche Bazaar

return from trek, and most Kathmandu hotels have a storage facility. Contained in a small holdall, make sure your left luggage is secure and clearly marked with your name and expected date of return.

There is a tendency by some group trekkers to take far too much clothing and equipment with them, knowing that porters or yaks will shoulder the burden. As Baedeker once wrote, 'To be provided with enough and no more may be considered the second golden rule of the traveller.' Don't be tempted to pack too much. Remember that most airlines have a free baggage allowance of only 20kg (44lb), and there's no need to go to the limit.

MAPS

In third world countries, mapping is at best erratic and imprecise.
The Adventure Travel Handbook

That quotation could be true of many regions of Nepal, but as the area covered by this guidebook contains the highest mountain on earth, it is certainly not apt here. As Ed Hillary once said of the Khumbu, it is 'the most surveyed, examined, blood-taken, anthropologically dissected area in the world'. The map-makers have been busy.

The best coverage, beautifully drawn and produced on 'trek-proof' paper to a scale of 1:50,000, is the four-colour series published by Freytag-Berndt in Vienna, generally known as the Schneider maps after cartographer Erwin Schneider who undertook the initial fieldwork. Their quality is outstanding, a quality that is reflected in their price. They are stocked by Stanfords in London and The Map Shop, Upton-upon Severn, and are sometimes available in Kathmandu.

Three sheets deal with the Jiri to Everest route:
• *Tamba Kosi* includes the trail from Jiri to Junbesi
• *Shorong/Hinku* deals with Junbesi to Namche
• *Khumbu Himal* covers all the country north of Namche included in this guide.

The same publisher also produces a more detailed sheet at a scale of 1:25,000 which concentrates on Mount Everest and its immediate environs.

In 1988 the National Geographic Society in Washington DC published their own high-quality map of Mount Everest at a scale of 1:50,000. Although it may have little practical trekking value (it concentrates as much on the Tibetan side of the mountain as it does the Nepalese, and spreads as far south only as Pangboche and Ama Dablam), it is one of the most accurate sheets ever produced of the Everest region and serves well as a souvenir of the trek to it. This map is generally on sale in Kathmandu bookshops.

Also published by National Geographic/Trails Illustrated is a 1:50,000 scale trekking map, *Everest*

Base Camp, for the Khumbu region between Lukla and Base Camp, with part of the Gokyo valley included. Trails and groups of lodges are shown, and on the reverse there's a street map of Kathmandu and Patan. (**www.trailsillustrated.com www.nationalgeographic.com**)

Perhaps the most readily available of all maps in Kathmandu are those published by The Himalayan Maphouse. Under the name of Nepa Maps, they have produced a series of sheets aimed specifically at the needs of trekkers. One sheet at a scale of 1:100,000 covers the whole route from Jiri to Everest and includes the Gokyo side valley (*Khumbu: Sagarmatha National Park*), while two alternative sheets at 1:50,000 concentrate on the respective Gokyo and Everest Base Camp treks: *Trekking from Lukla to Gokyo the Sacred Lakes*, and *Trekking from Lukla to Everest Base Camp*. The second of these maps also includes the Gokyo route. Each of these three sheets contains additional trekking information in a side panel, but detail on the maps themselves is not entirely accurate, and there are some glaring omissions. However, for practical trekking purposes they are certainly worth having.

Himalayan Maphouse also publishes a sheet under the name of the Himalayan Kartographisches Institut, which covers the route from Jiri to Kala Pattar and Everest Base Camp and includes both the Gokyo and Imja Khola valleys. *Khumbu* is produced at a scale of 1:125,000. Contours are marked at 100m intervals, and as with the Nepa Maps mentioned above, a side panel provides additional trekking information. Some of the routes depicted on the map, however, are misleading and, as with the Nepa Maps, there are several omissions. (maphouse@wlink.com.np)

It is worth noting that the spelling of village names, mountains and features vary widely from map to map, as do altitude measurements.

Under the Nepa Maps imprint, an astronomical sheet (*Deep Sky of Nepal*) has been produced which you may wish to take with you on trek. The Himalayan night sky is as magically clear as you'll find anywhere outside the desert regions, and this sheet will aid identification of much that is on show.

MINIMUM IMPACT TREKKING

Take nothing but photos, leave nothing but footprints, kill nothing but time.

The wilderness mantra, and motto of the Sierra Club

The first officially sanctioned trek to the Everest region took place in 1964, and following the construction of the airstrip at Lukla the following year, there has been a massive increase in the number of visitors to Khumbu – not only trekkers, but anthropologists, aid workers and mountaineers whose forerunners first opened the eyes of the developed world to the scenic and cultural riches of the area. The resulting people-pressure has imposed great demands on the environment and had a profound effect upon the economy and lifestyle of local people.

Much has been written about deforestation caused by an expanding population and the requirements of large numbers of trekkers. Much publicity (some quite justified, but some ill-informed) has been given to problems of litter and the disposal of human waste; others complain about inappropriate or badly planned forms of development.

Yet the passage of time has not been entirely negative, for the natural beauty of the mountains, as seen from the trekking trails, remains untainted. As for the Sherpas, in the main they are every bit as hospitable, warm-hearted and friendly as their reputation suggests. They are not, of course, simple mountain peasants, for education is widely available (thanks in no small degree to Sir Edmund Hillary's Himalayan Trust), and the comparative wealth brought by mountaineering expeditions and thousands of trekkers has helped improve the lot of a number of lodge and teahouse owners, some of whom may have travelled as widely as the trekkers who use their facilities.

Creation of the Sagarmatha National Park, and its elevation to World Heritage Site status, has helped focus attention on some of the environmental problems and begun seriously to address them. Small hydro schemes have been set up in selected areas (in Khumbu and in the Middle Hills),

Throughout the trek porters will be seen preparing their meals beside the trail

bringing partial relief from demands for firewood, and the Himalayan Trust is tackling the question of deforestation through the development of local tree nurseries. But although the Park authorities have banned the cutting of trees, firewood and construction timber is regularly brought in from outside the Park, so a local problem has merely been transferred elsewhere. Awareness and responsibility by all visitors to the Everest region are essential to the future success of trekking there.

Litter The most obvious visible sign of negative impact, and the easiest to control, is litter. A large amount of the rubbish found on the trails leading to Everest – from toilet paper to cigarette butts and sweet wrappers – can almost entirely be blamed on Western visitors. It's incomprehensible why anyone drawn to the Himalaya by its stark beauty would consider spoiling those scenes by discarding litter – yet, in the words of Oscar Wilde, 'Each man kills the thing he loves.' Carry out what you carry in. Rules of the National Park state that all rubbish generated by trekking groups must be taken out, but this is rarely attended to, and food packaging is usually burnt, bashed and buried. Most lodges have a policy of burning their rubbish, while many villages have garbage pits. Toilet paper? Carry a lighter with you, and if you get caught out during the day, carefully burn soiled paper.

Don't pollute water sources Use the toilets provided at lodges and teahouses, but if defecation is

60

unavoidable in the wild, stay at least 50m (160ft) away from water sources, and bury your faeces in a hole dug with a small trowel or penknife. Failing that, cover with stones.

Don't buy bottled water Abandoned plastic 'mineral water' bottles have been a problem in the major trekking areas of Nepal for decades. In the year 2000 it was estimated that tourists discarded more than 200,000 non-biodegradable bottles in the Annapurna region alone. With so many lodges and teahouses providing drinks, there's no need to buy bottled water in the Khumbu. Visitors on a group trek can get safe, boiled water from their cook. If independent trekkers need water, purification tablets are easily available in Kathmandu. Or carry a filter system.

Firewood The huge consumption of firewood on heavily trekked routes has added to Nepal's problems of deforestation. On group camping treks meals should be prepared using kerosene stoves rather than wood fires, and campfires banned in order to reduce the demand for cut timber. When using lodges limit your demand for a hot shower to those establishments using back boilers or solar panels for heating water. Be considerate when ordering meals. If you make your order for an evening meal on arrival, and keep it simple, the lodge owner can prepare a number of dishes at the same time, thus minimising the amount of fuel consumed. Better still, coordinate meal times where possible.

Stay on the trail On the trek from Jiri, take care not to damage crops, irrigation ditches and terrace retaining walls when passing through agricultural land. In the higher country where topsoil is meagre and plants struggle to survive in a harsh environment, limit erosion by not taking short cuts.

CULTURAL INTERACTION

Rupert Murdoch beaming down Sky TV onto the heads of communities ... in the Khumbu was going to have a far greater influence on the expectations and attitudes of the Sherpas than trekkers ever would.

Ed Douglas
Chomolungma Sings the Blues

I'm sure Ed Douglas is right. Sherpas are no more immune to cultural change than most societies, but in the Khumbu, as in the rest of Nepal, there are traditions, beliefs, mores and conventions that deserve the respect of all who visit their homeland.

Interaction with local people can be one of the major highlights of a trek, for enrichment is bred by rising above the cultural divide and becoming sensitive to the ways of those whose land you wander through. But when it comes to cross-cultural interaction, most of us are innocents abroad. Our Western society is no preparation for the kaleidoscopic cultures of the East, and it is arrogant to assume that our ways are superior to those of the Nepali hillfolk whose culture has developed separately from ours. Observation of its intricacies is an important ingredient in successful trekking, and through it we may

Buddhist decoration beside the trail through Thamo

discover our hosts have more to teach us with regard to living in contentment than we can possibly teach them. In the unfussed ways of simple villagers we learn that patience, kindness and tolerance for all are virtues worth striving for. In turn it is necessary to observe certain rules of behaviour in order to avoid giving offence to our hosts. The following guidelines are therefore offered as a form of cultural code, which may help when preparing for a trek in the Khumbu. But for an in-depth and highly readable introduction to the cultural interface of the country, read Stephen Bezruchka's excellent *Trekking in Nepal*, in which he says: 'Nepal is not only a place on the map, but an experience, a way of life from which we all can learn.'

Affection Avoid public displays of affection, for these can cause embarrassment and are frowned upon.

Begging Discourage children who ask for school pens, balloons, money or candy, for responding to children begging will erode their self-respect. On the other hand, making donations to schools, health centres or other worthwhile community projects will help Nepalis help themselves.

Dress Be modestly clad, for a state of undress is unacceptable in both sexes. Women should not wear revealing blouses or shorts. Choose instead a long skirt or trousers. Men should always wear a shirt and preferably long trousers.

Food Avoid touching food or utensils that Nepalis will use, and never give or take food with the left hand which is considered unclean, as it's used for washing after defecating. If cutlery is unavailable, use only your right hand for eating.

Giving Use both hands when giving donations or gifts; receive with either your left hand or both hands.

Haggling Whilst haggling is part of the trade culture of Kathmandu, do not haggle over prices in teahouses or lodges on trek. Don't condone over-charging, but pay the going rate, for prices are often set by the local community.

The hearth If invited into a Nepalese house, be aware that to many hillfolk the hearth is considered to be sacred. You should not discard rubbish into your host's fire, no matter how small and insignificant it may seem. Nor should you sit next to it unless specifically invited to do so, as this is a place of honour.

Legs and feet As feet are considered less clean than other parts of the body, the soles should not be pointed at a Nepali, nor should legs be so outstretched that they need to be stepped over by others.

Monasteries When visiting monasteries (*gompas*) remove boots or shoes before entering, and make a donation before leaving. In respect of local culture and beliefs, please refrain from smoking or noisy behaviour in or near a sacred site.

Photography Be discreet when taking photographs of local people. Try to imagine how you would react if

Teahouse didi on the way to Phortse

a stranger pointed a camera lens directly at your grandmother. Make time to build a relationship with your potential subject, ask permission before taking their photograph – and respect their right to refuse.

Prayer walls Always pass to the left of prayer walls (*mani* walls), *chortens* and other Buddhist symbols, and turn prayer wheels in a clockwise direction.

Shaking hands If someone shakes your hand using both of theirs, do likewise.

Smile Retain a sense of humour, act with patience and friendliness towards local people – and smile. The Nepali people smile a lot. That warmth should be reflected back.

Touching Avoid touching Nepalis on the head.

Wealth Be discreet when handling money; do not tempt locals into envy

by making an obvious display of the contents of your wallet. Keep a few small denomination rupee notes handy for paying bills along the way. Don't leave valuable items unattended.

Finally, the word *Namaste*, spoken with palms pressed together, is the universal greeting of Nepal; it means 'I salute the God within you.' Use it with a smile – and mean it. From such simple beginnings may grow a flower of understanding.

NEPAL – FACTS AND FIGURES

The whole of Nepal is like a pretty woman, with a blush ever ready to erupt.

The Times of India

Rectangular in shape and measuring roughly 800km by 240km (500 miles

63

by 150), Nepal is bordered in the north by Tibet (China) and elsewhere by India. Although it contains the world's largest number of 8000m (26,000ft) peaks, mountains form only the northern part of this beautiful country. In the south lies the tropical belt of the Terai – a low-lying extension of the Gangetic plain – while the broad central region is one of fertile hills rising from 600m to 2000m (2000–6500ft) in altitude. The sub-tropical Kathmandu valley is included in this central strip, as are neighbouring valley basins.

It is the world's only Hindu monarchy. Officially some 89.5% of the population of about 24 million are said to be Hindu, while just 5.3% practise Buddhism. Yet **Hindu** and **Buddhist** coexist in remarkable harmony, and their faiths appear to merge compatibly in so many different ways that it is not always easy to separate them here. When trekking in Solu-Khumbu one sees more evidence of Buddhism than any other faith, and it is partly due to the spirituality of the local people that the area is so appealing. Since Buddhists are more tolerant of outsiders than are Hindus, the trekker has several opportunities to visit monasteries and other religious structures along the way.

The official **language**, Nepali, is derived from Pahori which comes from northern India and is spoken by some 58% of the population. But with more than 60 ethnic groups and 70 languages, and a reputation for having almost as many dialects as there are villages, the sheer diversity of the spoken word makes Nepal a rich vein of oral tradition while at the same time paving the way for confusion. In the

Autumn fields near Choplung

Kathmandu valley the original Newari language uses no less than three different alphabets. Fortunately for the Western trekker English is widely understood, not only in Kathmandu and in most lodges along the popular trails; most Sherpas who generally make up the crew of organised treks speak a modicum of English – while the more educated among them often learn smatterings of other European languages too. But an attempt to speak a few words or phrases of Nepali will reap dividends for the visitor.

Although Nepal counts among the world's **poorest nations** in terms of per capita income, the sense of hopeless poverty that is so prevalent in a number of other Eastern countries is not apparent here. Over 80% of the population depends for its livelihood on **agriculture**, much of which is subsistence farming on the intricate terraced fields of the foothills. This subsistence farming, of course, falls outside the cash economy, so although statistics show an average annual income of around $210, and more than half the children are thought to be undernourished, the reality is partly masked as far as the hill country visited by the trekker is concerned. Some 17% of land is under cultivation, and about 30% covered by forest, but due to improved health care and a fast-growing population, Nepal's self-sufficiency in food production 50 years ago has deteriorated into a situation of grain deficiency and a serious reduction in forests. As a result Nepal faces dire economic and environmental problems which only radical government policies and considered development can arrest.

Foreign development aid projects continue to pour money into Nepal, although a number of these have been of questionable value. In his 1988 book *Travels in Nepal*, Charlie Pye-Smith provides an interesting commentary on the question of foreign aid in the late 1980s. This is a theme taken up by other writers with a concern for the way some donor countries have influenced development along lines that are not entirely appropriate for either Nepal's geography or culture.

Tourism is a major source of income (only 5% of labour is employed in industry), and accounts for about 30% of Nepal's essential foreign exchange earnings, yet a large proportion of that income leaves the country again to pay for foreign goods. **International telecommunications** are good. Kathmandu has plenty of public communications centres from which you can make direct calls to almost every country in the world. Not only Lukla and Namche Bazaar, but several other villages in the areas covered by this guide also have telephone links of variable quality. **Cyber cafés** can be found in the tourist areas of Kathmandu, and also in Namche, where you can send and receive emails at a very modest rate.

Nepalese currency is the Rupee (Rps), which is made up of 100 Paisa.

Banknotes are available in the following denominations: Rps1, 2, 5, 10, 20, 25, 50, 100, 500 and 1000. Being a 'soft' currency the Rupee has no value outside Nepal. Travellers cheques and 'hard' currency can be exchanged at Kathmandu's Tribhuvan International Airport on arrival, and at a number of banks which open daily (not Saturdays) from 10am until about 2pm. Numerous hotels in Kathmandu have **money-changing** facilities, and in tourist areas you will find plenty of 'no-commission' money-changing kiosks.

Namche also has several exchange facilities. Always collect your exchange receipts as these will be needed should you wish to change any remaining Nepalese cash into 'hard' currency at the end of your trip. A few 'hole in the wall' ATMs are found in the Thamel district of Kathmandu. Major **credit cards** are accepted at many hotels in the city, as well as in some shops and banks.

Nepalese time is GMT +5¾hours (15min ahead of Indian Standard Time), 10¾ hours ahead of New York,

ONLINE INFORMATION

There's no shortage of information available about Nepal on the internet, and the following sites may be worth consulting in advance of a trip.

- **www.nepalnews.net** for up-to-date news.
- **www.nepalnow.com** is another news site worth checking.
- **www.info-nepal.com** not only gives information in regard to latest news and travel, but contains many other features including development issues, politics, culture and so on.
- **www.visitnepal.com** contains a number of features of interest to the first-time visitor.
- **www.welcomenepal.com** is the website of the Nepal Tourist Board.
- **www.kmtnc.org.np** gives details about the King Mahendra Trust for Nature Conservation.
- **www.bena.com/ciwec** for advice on altitude sickness and other medical problems associated with Nepal. This is the website for the CIWEC Clinic in Kathmandu.
- **www.fco.gov.uk/travel** is the official site of the UK Foreign and Commonwealth Office, with regularly updated information and advice for travellers.
- **www.mnteverest.net/trek.html** has an index of Nepalese trekking companies.
- **www.taan.org.np** for up-to-date trekking regulations and information.

WHAT'S A NEPALESE RUPEE WORTH?

Since currency exchange rates fluctuate daily, it might seem fool-hardy to publish rates as of April 2008 in a guide that's likely to remain in print for some years. However, the following list may give an indication of the Rupee's value against major currencies. For up-to-date exchange rates see **www.nepalnews.com/forex**

1 US$	Rps61
1 £	Rps124
1 euro	Rps92

4¼ hours *behind* Sydney. Nepal has no daylight saving.

Postal services are best dealt with in Kathmandu at the General Post Office located at the junction of Kantipath and Kicha-Pokhari Road. The office is open daily (except Saturdays and public holidays) from 10.00am to 5.00pm (4.00pm November to February). Always ensure that stamps on postcards, letters or parcels are franked by the counter clerk. There is invariably a queue at the special counter reserved for this. Several villages along the trail to Everest have Post Offices of some description. Postcards and letters may be sent from these, and mostly they get delivered – often long after you've returned home from trek.

The **Poste Restante** service at the GPO in Kathmandu is reasonably efficient, but being largely self-service it would be prudent to have nothing of obvious value sent there. Mail is usually kept for two months. Be prepared to show your passport in order to collect mail.

TIME IN KATHMANDU

And the wildest dreams of Kew are the facts of Kathmandu.

Rudyard Kipling

First-time visitors to the East sometimes experience a form of culture shock on the short journey from the airport to their hotel in the heart of Kathmandu. And no wonder, for there's nothing in the West that will prepare you for the extraordinary kaleidoscopic mix of colour, noise, bustle; the sites both of exquisite beauty and of squalor; the anarchic traffic chaos and pollution of the senses. Yet when that shock subsides you may come to see, as many have done before you, that Kathmandu is one of the world's most magical cities. It's not just a springboard for Himalayan adventures, but a brimming complex of sites and cultures that would take a lifetime to unravel and several generations properly to understand.

After weeks among the mountains it is a great place to sample a change

Kathmandu

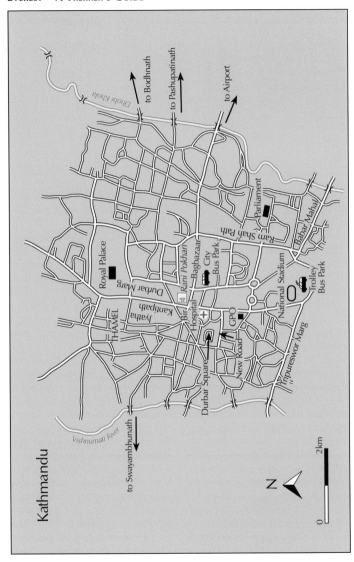

Vegetable market, Kathmandu

of menu, too, for there are dozens of restaurants to satisfy all appetites at a price easy to afford. There are hotels and guesthouses of varying standards of comfort, and enough shops and street traders offering a thousand and one 'bargains' to drain the last of your money before heading for home. Hotels range from the extravagent one-time Rana palaces and multi-star establishments on Durbar Marg, with 24-hour room service, satellite TV, sauna and swimming pool, to the host of unpretentious lodgings that would suit the budget-conscious world traveller, tucked away in Thamel back streets or the former hippy hideout of

Freak Street on the south side of Durbar Square.

In truth, Kathmandu wears many different faces. It's an enigma; a chaotic enigma that somehow works, for through all the apparent chaos a bewildering sense of order prevails. In the 1870s David Wright, a surgeon at the British Residency, produced a report which cynics might consider apt today. It read: 'The streets of Kathmandu are very narrow, mere lanes in fact; and the whole town is very dirty ... to clean the drains would be impossible without knocking down the entire city ... In short, from a sanitary point of view, Kathmandu may be

Hair ribbons for sale in the streets of Kathmandu

said to be built on a dunghill in the middle of latrines.'

That is but one view. Kathmandu is a cornucopia of colour, of smells, of noise. It *is* dirty, but it's also exciting, vibrant. A dull cloud of pollution hangs over the city, but below it there's unbridled gaiety, and in countless streets medieval buildings are adorned with carvings of delicate beauty. There are people everywhere, the narrow alleyways and broad modern roads acrush with activity. Traffic streams in an endless honking procession through the daylight hours along its main highways. Bicycle rickshaws and taxis bounce and weave through the

teeming streets, and somehow manage to avoid collision with crowds of traders, the bustle of porters, tourists and beggars, and the occasional cow.

Thamel, the ever-popular tourist district in the northwest of the city, is the quarter seen by most visitors. But Thamel is not typical of Kathmandu; it is representative only of itself. In it will be found a plentiful supply of budget accommodation in small hotels and guesthouses, a selection of cafés, restaurants and bookshops, mapshops, specialist trekkers' foodstores, suppliers of climbing and trekking equipment, and outfitters of all kinds. Should you arrive in Kathmandu to discover that

KATHMANDU'S WORLD HERITAGE SITES

The three neighbouring cities of Kathmandu, Patan and Bhaktapur contain a wealth of historic monuments, old palaces, shrines and temples, but outlying villages and small towns also have much of cultural interest to discover. Within a radius of 20km the Kathmandu valley boasts no less than seven World Cultural Heritage Sites, and a modest entrance fee is charged to all foreign visitors for conservation and restoration work.

- **Swayambhunath** – The so-called Monkey Temple on a hilltop overlooking the valley.
- **Bodhnath** – The largest Buddhist *stupa* in Nepal, and centre of Tibetan culture.
- **Pashupatinath** – Nepal's largest Hindu shrine beside the Bagmati river.
- **Durbar Square, Kathmandu** – More than 50 monuments, shrines and temples crowd the Square.
- **Durbar Square, Patan** – Beautifully restored buildings make this a justifiably popular site.
- **Durbar Square, Bhaktapur** – 16km east of Kathmandu, it boasts many architectural splendours as does the rest of the city.
- **Changu Narayan** – An exotic temple complex built on a hilltop 7km north of Bhaktapur.

your airline has sent your baggage to Khartoum, don't despair, for in Thamel you can buy or rent every item of equipment you'll need on trek.

Its wealth of religious and cultural sites makes Kathmandu extraordinarily appealing. 'There are nearly as many temples as houses, and as many idols as inhabitants' wrote W. Kirkpatrick in 1811, and while there are certainly more houses and inhabitants today, plus a great number of tourists, there is no shortage of places to visit. The following suggestions merely scratch the surface. For more detailed information, background history and a pointer to the full glories of the valley itself, the

Insight Guide: Nepal (APA Publications) is highly recommended, as is the more recent *Kathmandu: Valley of the Green-Eyed Yellow Idol* by Bob Gibbons and Siân Pritchard-Jones (Pilgrims Publishing).

Kathmandu

Durbar Square is a must. Containing more than 50 important monuments, shrines and temples, as well as the home of the Kumari (the living goddess), and a huge former royal palace, it offers a superb roofscape of exotic shapes. Intricate carvings adorn every building: erotic figures, faces, patterns and religious symbols etched by the metre on struts and beams, and around doorways and windows. Early morning is the best time to visit. Street vendors are setting out their wares, porters gather to await employment, the faithful scurry to various temples for their first devotions of the day, and the place comes alive with streams of light, colour and movement. By mid-morning the Square is crowded with foreign visitors and touts, while in the nearby Basantpur Square, between Kumari Chowk and Freak Street, rows of identical kukuri knives, carved Buddhas and bangles gather dust in what is surely the ultimate flea market.

Kumari Chowk is where the prebuscent living goddess spends most of the years of her reign until menstruation casts her back to mortality. Guarded by two stone lions, the building has a tiny accessible inner courtyard bounded by exquisitely carved pillars, doors and windows.

To the north of Durbar Square, midway between the Square and Thamel, and secluded from the busy street of Shakrupath, stands the biggest *stupa* in central Kathmandu. **Kathesimbhu** is a colourful gathering place for Buddhist monks, tourists and the children of a neighbouring school who use the surrounding space as a playground. A new and lavishly decorated *gompa* (Buddhist monastery) has been built to one side of the *stupa*, adding to the site's interest and attraction.

Just 2km from Thamel, on the western side of the Vishumati river, the 2000-year-old *stupa* of **Swayambhunath** looks down on Kathmandu

Durbar Square, Bhaktapur

Bodhnath's stupa is the largest in Nepal

from its lofty hilltop. Around the base of the hill hundreds of prayer wheels are interspersed with small 'shrines', while colourful prayer flags strung from trees and tall poles add to the scene. Large Buddhas guard the main entrances to the site on both east and west sides. On the Vishumati side a steep flight of 365 stone steps leads to the crowning *stupa* between trees in which monkeys play. Monkeys also scamper over and around the *stupa* itself, giving it the name of the Monkey Temple. More prayer wheels encircle the *stupa*, and to one side there's the *gompa* of Shree Karma Raj Mahavihar which visitors are free to enter. Inside hundreds of butter lamps cast an orange glow, while the sound of trumpets, gongs and drums accompanies the devotions. If you visit in the early morning to catch sunrise over the valley, you'll experience a full *puja* ceremony at the open-faced building beside the *gompa*, as Newari musicians and chanting devotees begin their day with prayer, procession and the singing of religious songs. As well as the *gompa* and large *stupa*, the crowded summit of the hill has a gilt-roofed temple built in honour of Harati, the smallpox goddess, and numerous shrines, statues and symbolic votive monuments.

Northeast of Kathmandu city centre, **Bodhnath**'s 40m- (130ft-) high dome makes it the largest Buddhist *stupa* in all Nepal. Seen from afar it marks the country's centre of Tibetan culture, and pilgrims are often found making a *kora* here – measuring their length upon the ground on a circuit of the *stupa*. *Gompas* and pilgrim rest-houses line the square, and at the start of the Tibetan New Year monks take part in colourful ceremonies. Masked dances are performed for the public in a nearby field, while other dances take place in a monastery courtyard. One of the best places from which to study the site is the rooftop restaurant, Stupa View – especially at dusk with the sound of monks chanting, when haunting music drifts from houses that ring the *stupa* and butter lamps glow in the gathering darkness.

The Bagmati river twists along Kathmandu's eastern boundary below **Pashupatinath**, the country's largest Hindu shrine. As a tributary of the Ganges the Bagmati is considered sacred by devotees who take part in ritual bathing in the fetid water. Overlooking it all stands a temple complex to which entry is forbidden to non-Hindus, but on the east bank a series of terraces lined with identical *chaityas* (in appearance like small *stupas*) provide viewpoints from which to study not only the gilded temple opposite, but also riverside activities below. In the river women do their laundry, while Hindus fast approaching death are carried from the nearby *dharmasalas* (resthouses) and lain on stone slabs with their feet in the water until all life has drained from them. Nearby *ghats* are used for cremation, the ceremonies carried out in full public view.

Patan

South of Kathmandu, and divided from it only by the Bagmati river, the once-

independent kingdom of Patan (Lalitpur – the 'City of Beauty') is said to have been founded in the 3rd century BC by the emperor Ashoka and his daughter Carumati. Primarily a Buddhist town it has around 150 former monasteries, but there are also many Hindu temples and shrines and scores of exotic secular buildings; so many in fact that it would take weeks of concentrated study to properly visit each one.

This 'town of a thousand golden roofs' has its own **Durbar Square** with the one-time royal palace facing a complex variety of Newari-crafted architectural splendours. The palace itself has three main courtyards open to the public, each displaying the skills of generations of woodcarvers. Nearby the beautiful **Hiranyavarna Mahavihara** (Kwa Bahal, or 'Golden Temple'), which dates from the 12th century, is guarded by gleaming lions, the buildings embellished with silver doors, gilded copper roofs and bronze Buddhas.

On the southwestern edge of Patan many Tibetan exiles have settled in the quarter known as **Jawalikhel** and established a thriving carpet factory there, visited by a number of tour groups.

Like Kathmandu, Patan is a bustling town but with a vibrancy all its own. But it is considerably less frenetic than the capital, and many Nepal 'old hands' prefer to stay there rather than in Kathmandu itself. It's a town of artisans, with metalwork a speciality, and the narrow alleyways and side streets ring to the sound of hammer on copper and tin. And when you've absorbed as much spiritual and architectural wonder as you can, it's worth strolling round the tiny workshops where craftsmen pick out ornamental filigree with hammer and punch, or spending an hour or two haggling for bargains with the street vendors in the bazaar.

Bungamati

Lying about 6km south of Patan, and surrounded by terraced rice fields, the settlement of Bungamati is almost completely untouched by tourism or new development, and as such is worth seeking out. In the heart of the village stands the impressive **Rato Machhedranath Temple**. The Red (or Rato) Machhedranath is the patron deity of the Kathmandu valley, and spends three months of the year in Bungamati, the rest of the time being kept in Patan. Once in every 12 years the huge Machhendranath chariot is manhandled all the way from Bungamati to Patan and back again, accompanied by rituals, prayers and offerings.

Bhaktapur

Also known by its former name of Bhadgaon, this handsome town of about 50,000 inhabitants lies 16km (10 miles) to the east of Kathmandu. Described by Percival Landon in 1928 as 'willingly remote from her neighbours, and one of the most picturesque towns in the East', Bhaktapur is reached by frequent trolley-bus service from Kathmandu. A taxi will give a less 'ethnic' and more expensive ride, but is likely to provide a much quicker and more comfortable journey.

Although badly damaged in 1934 by an earthquake that also devastated the capital, Bhaktapur nevertheless retains much of its medieval character and has some of the valley's finest buildings. Restoration work has been possible largely through a German–Nepalese development project that has so far helped to preserve some 200 buildings. The best is in **Durbar Square**, entered through a gateway. There you find an open approach to a magnificent collection of temples and monuments. At least two large temples were completely destroyed by the earthquake, but those that remain are set out with sufficient space to enable the visitor to study them from different angles without their being confused among other crowding buildings. It is this sense of spaciousness that makes such a contrast with the Durbar Squares of Kathmandu and Patan, and when you've managed to break free of the guides touting for business, it's worth studying at leisure the many appealing features. One of the most startling objects of attention is the brass-made **Golden Gate** through which access leads to the former royal palace, whose west wing houses the National Art Gallery.

FURTHER EXPLORATIONS

Once you've visited all the main sites – which will no doubt take several trips to Nepal to achieve – a random exploration is worth tackling. Avoid the known places and duck into mysterious back alleyways, for there you will discover the old Kathmandu, Patan or Bhaktapur, whose heart and soul belongs to the Nepal that is slow to change, where lives are played out beyond the camera lens. There you will find that urban, workaday Nepal has an appeal all its own. Then spread your exploration throughout the Kathmandu valley, hire a bicycle perhaps, or find a taxi driver willing to spend a day getting lost among lanes that disappear among fields of rice or millet. Go into the outlying settlements, or visit hilltop temples and *gompas*; or onto the rim of the valley where trails wind along ridge crests and give uplifting views across Helambu to the Ganesh, Langtang and Jugal Himals – part of the great Himalayan range, which is no doubt what brought you here in the first place.

Whilst Durbar Square is the main focus of attention, a short 100m stroll down a narrow side street leads to **Taumadhi Tole**, a smaller yet more lively square surrounded by fine old Newari houses and dominated by the pagoda-like **Nyatapola.** Bhaktapur's tallest temple dates from 1702 and stands on a five-stepped pedestal guarded by a succession of stone wrestlers, elephants, lions, griffins and goddesses. An excellent view of this, and the rest of the square, can be obtained from one of the balconies of Café Nayatapola, itself a splendid building.

Bhaktapur's oldest quarter is located east of Durbar Square where **Tachapol Tole** (or Dattatraya Square) has two old but not especially elaborate temples and a slender pillar-statue of Garud. Take particular note of the magnificent carvings that adorn so many buildings, especially around the windows and doorways. The art of woodcarving has reached the very height of perfection with the famed **Peacock Window**, hidden away down a side alley, being the single most celebrated piece of work in the Kathmandu valley.

ABOUT THIS GUIDE

He who knows not whither to go is in no hurry to move.

H. W. Tilman *Nepal Himalaya*

In common with other titles in the Cicerone series of guides to Nepal's major trekking regions, this volume has not been produced in order to encourage even more visitors to explore the trails of this Himalayan wonderland, but in the hope of adding something to the experience of those already committed to going there. Being forewarned about the nature of the routes and the seriousness of some of the trails is one way of reminding trekkers that in order to make the most of every step along the way, it is essential to be both physically and mentally prepared. 'Happiness is most often met by those who have learned to live in every moment of the present,' said Himalayan climber and explorer Tom Longstaff, 'none has such prodigal opportunities of attaining that art as the traveller.'

Although trekking in the Everest region can be pretty demanding at times, the majority of trails are so well travelled that it's almost impossible to get lost. But an idea of how long it's likely to take to trek from one village to another, and what to expect in the way of accommodation or services when they arrive, is something that many trekkers find essential when planning their journey. Times quoted, however, will not agree with every trekker's pace, but are offered anyway as a rough guide. After a day or two along the trail it should be evident just how much our times vary, and you can take

PRE-TREK CHECK

Reconfirm your homeward flight details before going on trek.
- Don't trek alone. If you have no companion, hire a guide.
- Register your personal details and route plan with your embassy in Kathmandu.
- Be adequately insured.
- Carry your passport with you to obtain an entry permit to the Sagarmatha National Park.
- Carry a first aid kit and know how to use it. Make sure you have any medication you are likely to need.
- Be aware of the dangers of mountain sickness, and watch for signs among those with you.
- Follow the Minimum Impact Code.
- Watch where you're walking, and remain alert.
- Respect local culture and customs.
- Don't wear revealing clothes, and avoid public demonstrations of affection.
- When staying in lodges, choose those that use alternatives to wood for cooking and heating.
- Discourage begging, and encourage fair dealing.
- Treat villagers, porters and guides with respect.

Kwandge, from above Syanboche

this differential into account when deciding how far to walk each day. Remember, **times quoted in this guide refer to walking time only**; they do not take account of rest stops, photographic interruptions or refreshment delays which can add another 50% or so to your overall day on the trail.

Altitudes quoted in the text do not always agree with other guides to the region, or some of the maps available, for different maps and publications give wildly varying measurements. Where published altitudes are undisputed I have used them, but in those instances where there seems to be no general accord, I have quoted readings from my own altimeter used during my latest trek. I make no claim for its accuracy.

In the following pages the main treks have been broken into groups of

several days, with each multi-day section divided into sub-sections, rather than manageable day-sized stages as in previous editions. This is to avoid concentrating attention on specific villages as overnight halts, to the detriment of others. There are now so many trekkers' lodges throughout the Everest region that it is invidious to single out any particular hotel or village in which to stay, for it is often in the quieter, less well-patronised places that the most rewarding experiences are gained.

Please bear in mind that lodge names sometimes change; groups of lodges become villages, villages grow in size and facilities generally improve. The mountains, however, remain unbelievably beautiful, and the smiles of those who live among them reflect that beauty.

THE TREKS – NEPAL

Everest has a magic which cannot be explained away.

Joe Tasker *Everest The Cruel Way*

The Trail to Everest

Prior to the outbreak of World War II all expeditions to Everest had to approach the mountain through Tibet as Nepal was firmly closed to foreigners. By the early 1950s the situation was reversed; Tibet was effectively closed by the Chinese invasion, but the doors to the once-forbidden kingdom of Nepal had slowly begun to open.

A party of Indian scientists gained permission to enter the Khumbu in 1948, and in 1950 the first Westerners were given leave to explore the southern approaches to Mount Everest. The Indian party climbed to the trading pass of the Nangpa La on the Tibetan border west of Cho Oyu, but it was the small, privately organised group (hardly an expedition) led by the Americans, Oscar and Charles Houston, who first reached the Khumbu glacier below Everest itself. With Houston was the legendary mountaineer-explorer Bill Tilman, who had already

Chaumrikharka, a short distance from Choplung, lies below Lukla

been on two pre-war Everest expeditions, and who was now eager for an opportunity to study the mountain from the unknown south and west.

Their route of approach began, not in Kathmandu, but way off to the south-east in Dharan. At first they followed the Arun river north towards Makalu before striking roughly westward across successive ridges that eventually brought them to the Dudh Kosi below Lukla. By the time they reached Chaumrikharka they had joined the main trail used by the majority of trekkers today, and followed it up-valley to Namche Bazaar and beyond, as far as the Khumbu glacier and the slopes of Kala Pattar.

Houston and Tilman's route is still used today, although it is much less frequented than either the direct flight to Lukla, or the long approach from the roadhead at Jiri.

Following Houston and Tilman's visit, and the 1951 reconnaissance led by Eric Shipton, a Swiss expedition made the first attempt to climb Everest from Nepal in 1952. Their route of approach began in the Kathmandu valley and took 23 days, including two rest days in Namche. Next, in the spring of 1953, came the successful British expedition under John Hunt's leadership, and they took basically the same route pioneered by the Swiss from Bhaktapur. In the wake of his team's success Hunt's book, *The Ascent of Everest*, proved enormously popular, as did the film made by Tom Stobart, which enjoyed a wide distribution. Together they made a huge impression on a generation of would-be mountaineers and fired the imagination of countless armchair adventurers who were excited not only by the success of Hillary and Tenzing in gaining the summit, but by the sheer beauty of the landscape leading to the mountain itself.

Gokyo Ri, one of the great trekking viewpoints

Trekking, as it is known today, was subsequently 'invented' by mountaineer and former Ghurka officer Jimmy Roberts, who rightly guessed that tourists would jump at the chance to follow in the footsteps of Hunt, Hillary, Tenzing and Co through those glorious valleys. Such people would not only enjoy but also pay for the privilege of sleeping in tents among such staggering scenery, and walk by day in the company of the fabled Sherpas with porters to carry their equipment and food. Not surprisingly, the first commercial trek ever organised in Nepal led across the foothills and along the valley of the Dudh Kosi towards Mount Everest.

Soon the country was sprouting roads like unruly tendrils of bindweed. By the time the Chinese-built highway that now goes to Tibet had reached Lamosangu in 1970, the approach walk to Everest had been reduced in length by several days. Then a spur, built under Swiss direction, reached Jiri from Lamosangu in 1984, thus making it possible to trek to Kala Pattar in less than a fortnight from the road-head. While the walk-in is maybe 10 days shorter than the Swiss took in 1952, once the road has been left behind the route is much the same, except the Swiss had to make a diversion over the Lumding La because the bridge over the Dudh Kosi below Manidingma had been washed away.

Today's route is full of variety and daily charm, but not without an awful lot of height gain and loss. Anyone expecting an easy but persistent incline from Jiri to Namche is in for a shock.

With the construction of an airstrip to Lukla, the long trek from the foothills has been overtaken in popularity by a much shorter approach. From Lukla, Namche is less than two days' walk away, and is therefore within the range of most people's holiday allocation. It is now possible to walk to the base of Everest and out again in less than two weeks, although no one who flies in to Lukla should consider making a rushed visit to Kala Pattar or Base Camp because they will need time to acclimatise.

CHOICE OF LODGES

A final word – there is a homing instinct among many trekkers who, seeing one particular lodge being patronised by Westerners, will automatically choose that one too, while the place next door, which may be identical in every other respect – or even better in some – remains empty. Unless there's a very good reason for doing otherwise, please spread the load, thus giving all the lodges an equal share of business. Teahouse trekking helps stimulate the local economy, and the few rupees you spend in a particular lodge or shop can have a positive effect.

Kusum Kangguru is seen to good effect when descending to the Dudh Kosi below Manidingma

TREK 1

JIRI TO NAMCHE BAZAAR
VIA LUKLA

There is much to be said for a simple mountain journey,
whose object ... is just to get from one place to another.
Eric Shipton *Mountains of Tartary*

Trek summary	
Distance	94km (58 miles)
Time	7–9 days
Max altitude	Lamjura La (3530m: 11,581ft)
Start	Jiri (1905m: 6250ft)
Finish	Namche Bazaar (3446m: 11,306ft)
Trekking style	Teahouse (lodge accommodation) or camping
Getting there	Public bus or taxi from Kathmandu to Jiri
Options	Flight from Kathmandu to Phaplu or Lukla

From the foothills to the foot of the high Himalaya, this first trek crosses a series of ridges separated by deep river valleys. It's a corrugated route, for the main ridges – long arthritic fingers of land – project southward, while the trail heads east across them. Between the ridges glacial rivers pour down to the valley of the Sun Kosi that flows at right angles through eastern Nepal. As Jiri lies west of the Dudh Kosi (the river that drains the Khumbu), it follows that in order to reach this valley there's no alternative but to head across the grain of the land. Only when the Dudh Kosi has been gained below Manidingma can the trek assume its longed-for direction – upvalley towards the north, towards Namche and Everest itself.

The first few days, then, are energetic days; climbing out of warm river valleys, up terraced hillsides, through forest and over high crests with far views to enjoy, then

As John Hunt wrote in *The Ascent of Everest*, this is 'big country, with long views across broad expanses of mountainside, vast, fertile and dotted with friendly cottages'.

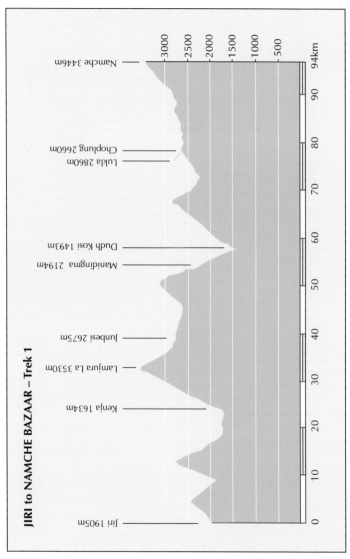

JIRI to NAMCHE BAZAAR – Trek 1

Jiri 1905m

Kenja 1634m

Lamjura La 3530m

Junbesi 2675m

Manidingma 2194m

Dudh Kosi 1493m

Lukla 2860m

Choplung 2660m

Namche 3446m

3000
2500
2000
1500
1000
500

0   10   20   30   40   50   60   70   80   90   94km

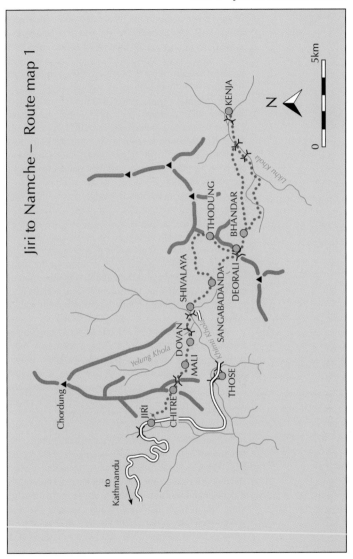

Jiri to Namche – Route map 1

to Kathmandu

Chordung

JIRI
CHITRE
MALI
DOVAN
Yelung Khola
Khimti Khola
SHIVALAYA
SANGABADANDA
THOSE
DEORALI
BHANDAR
THODUNG
Likhu Khola
KENJA

N

0   5km

steeply down again to the next river, milky-blue with glacier-melt. Despite much height gain after leaving Jiri, at the point of crossing the Dudh Kosi several days later you're more than 400m (1300ft) lower than when you started! Thereafter the trail heads upvalley, mostly along steep hillsides maintaining an up-and-down regime where mountain spurs intervene, though rather less severely than before. It's only when you leave Chaumrikharka to join the route from **Lukla** that suddenly the trail becomes busy. From Jiri the route is mostly used by individuals and local Nepalis; from Chaumrikharka to Namche it's trekking groups and their porters who make up most of the traffic.

Some fine, rarely crowded lodges are dotted along the trail, as well as interesting villages, the architecture of which steadily changes as you make progress through landscapes of great beauty. Hillsides are often clothed with a wide range of vegetation fed by the heavy rains of summer, for eastern Nepal receives more of the monsoon's annual downpour than almost any other part of the Himalaya, and in the foothills and middle hills terraces of agriculture provide a constant patchwork of delight.

As the majority of inhabitants of Solu-Khumbu are Buddhists you will pass an increasing number of *mani* walls, *chortens* and large, partially enclosed prayer wheels, each of which should be passed on its left-hand side. There are several *gompas* (monasteries) along the way too, but should you decide to visit any of these, please remove your footwear before entering.

Himalayan views will not feature very much in the early days of the trek, but shortly after leaving Junbesi the trail rounds a spur and a sudden panorama of big mountains opens up ahead; you catch a first, though only brief, sighting of Everest, Lhotse, Kusum Kagguru, Thamserku, Kangtega and Makalu. There's promise in that teasing view, but it's not until you reach Namche that the promise will be fulfilled. Yet the trail that leads to it provides plenty of inspiration, and helps you acclimatise for further treks in the high valleys of the Khumbu.

Route outline

Route	Distance	Height gain/loss	Time
Kathmandu–Jiri	188km		1 day
Section 1 24km/15 miles			
Jiri–Shivalaya	8km	495m (-600m)	3–3½ hr
Shivalaya–Bhandar	8km	905m (-511m)	4–4½ hr
Bhandar–Kenja	8km	(-651m)	3–3½ hr
Section 2 30km/19 miles			
Kenja–Sete	4km	1032m	2½–3hr
Sete–Junbesi	12km	955m (-855m)	6–6½ hr
Junbesi–Manidingma	14km	845m (-1326m)	6–7hr
Section 3 24km/15 miles			
Manidingma–Kharikhola	8km	579m (-701m)	4hr
Kharikhola–Chaumrikharka	14km	1191m (-550m)	8hr
Section 4 18km/11 miles			
Lukla–Choplung	3km	(-200m)	30min–1hr
Chaumrikharka–Mondzo	10km	410m (-314m)	4–4½ hr
Mondzo–Namche Bazaar	5km	611m	3–3½ hr

One of the two large prayer wheels at Ghat

PROLOGUE

Kathmandu to Jiri

Distance	188km (117 miles)
Time	10–12hr
Transport options	Public bus, or taxi

The journey by road from Kathmandu to Jiri is a scenic one. By public bus the 188km (117-mile) route will take a full day; a bone-numbing epic of anything up to 12 hours (or longer with breakdowns) that will have you yearning for the freedom of the trail long before the nightmare ends at the roadhead. As far as Lamosangu the road is in a poor condition and buses either crash over and through the potholes, or weave a slalom course around them. Once across the iron bridge over the Sun Kosi river, however, the surface improves to Swiss standards and those who are riding on the roof of the bus (illegal but popular) can begin to enjoy the views. As mentioned earlier, some may wish to forego the dubious pleasures of ethnic travel and hire a private vehicle for the journey.

Buses bound for Jiri depart from the old bus station east of Ratna Park in Kathmandu in the early morning (6am) and are invariably overcrowded. **Beware of theft and guard your baggage well.** Heading along the Chinese-built Kodari Highway the route makes for Bhaktapur, then climbs out of the valley to Dhulikhel. From the ridge crest in the cool of morning views of the Ganesh, Langtang and Jugal Himals can be stunning from here, with a long serrated horizon of big mountains showing as an extension of the clouds.

The road descends to the Indrawati, then follows it downstream to Dolalaghat where a bridge crosses the river. Beyond this the road climbs over another ridge before tracking the Sun Kosi ('Gold River') upstream to **LAMOSANGU** (78km: 49 miles) where buses often have

Lamosangu, where the road to Jiri leaves the Chinese-built highway

a scheduled stop with just enough time for a plate of *daal bhat* before setting off again on the next stage.

Lamosangu is a scruffy little township of shops, food-stalls and teahouses astride the Chinese road, about 40km (25 miles) south of the Tibetan border. Some of the houses stand perilously close to the water's edge, being built on the very bank of the Sun Kosi. Here the Jiri road breaks away to the right, crosses the river on a large iron bridge, and then begins a long, sinuous climb among a range of hills with another 110km (68 miles) to go before reaching the roadhead. From now on the road surface is much improved, thanks to a Swiss aid project that has made it the finest highway in all Nepal. It climbs to a watershed ridge, follows it north, then crosses at a 2440m pass.

THE SWISS ROAD

Planned, financed and engineered by the Swiss Association for Technical Assistance, the road from Lamosangu to Jiri was intended at the outset to be labour-intensive as a way of bringing direct financial benefit to the region. Instead of using machinery rocks were broken by labourers using hammers, and the wire netting that held the rocks in place beside or underneath the road was all hand-woven. At one time some 9000 Nepalese labourers were employed on the highway's construction. As a result of this reliance on man-ual labour instead of Western machinery, it took 11 years to build. But without question it's the finest road in Nepal, and a model which – sadly – has never been replicated.

Halfway between Lamosangu and Jiri the road comes to **CHARIKOT** (131km: 81 miles) where there are several lodges. Among a skyline of mountains seen from here the double-pronged Gaurishankar (7145m: 23,441ft) towers above its neighbours of the Rolwaling Himal. Charikot (or nearby Dolakha, 5km to the north by a side road) is often used as the starting point for treks into Rolwaling, thus providing an alternative route to Khumbu by way of the difficult and potentially dangerous pass of the Trashi Labtsa.

Below Charikot the road crosses the fertile Tamba Kosi valley just north of its confluence with the Charnawati Khola, then rises again over more foothills to top a ridge at the **HANUMANTE PASS** (about 2550m: 8366ft). Contouring along the hillside to a police post near **JIRI BAZAAR** where passports are checked, the bus then sweeps downhill, makes a left-hand bend, and the township of Jiri is seen just ahead, its cluster of lodges and houses set in a lush, fertile basin backed by wooded hills.

Jiri, the foothill bazaar town where the trek to Everest begins

JIRI (1905m: 6250ft) is more attractive, and a lot tidier, than some other roadhead townships in Nepal. On either side of the road a number of lodges and shops provide a service for trekkers, both at the start and end of their treks. On arrival a few touts gather round claiming, of course, that their's is the 'best lodge in town'. In truth there's probably not a lot between any of them. A camping area will be found near the entrance to the main street, on the left-hand side of the road. Over-sleeping is not an option here, for the first buses leave for Kathmandu at around 5am, and announce their departure long before that by loud blasts on their horns. Since few opportunities exist for buying more than a few basic items until the trek reaches Namche Bazaar, check Jiri's shops before setting out, should you have forgotten anything in Kathmandu. In the past the township received a lot of attention from the Swiss who centred a number of development projects here. Not only did they build the road from Lamosangu, but they also set up a cheese factory, and helped establish a technical school, hospital and an agricultural station as part of the Jiri Multi-purpose Development Project (JMDP). Charlie Pye-Smith's book *Travels in Nepal* discusses the successes and failures of these, and other, aid schemes, and makes interesting background reading. ▸

Note: The road is being extended to Shivalaya and Bhandar, but at the time of writing buses go no further than Jiri.

SECTION 1

Jiri to Kenja

Distance	24km (15 miles)
Time	1½–2 days
Start altitude	1905m (6250ft)
High point	Deorali (2705m: 8875ft)

The first few stages of any trek in Nepal have their own indefinable quality. Following a long road journey, such as that from Kathmandu to Jiri, one longs for the peace and tranquillity of the hills, becomes restless and eager for physical exercise after being cramped in an overcrowded bus for many numbing hours. Even if you've travelled in more comfort by taxi or minibus, the lure of the trail is a strong one. This, after all, is what you've come all this way for.

For those on a group trek the first day's walk will necessarily be a short one as porters have to be organised by the sirdar, and by the time that's accomplished the morning will be well advanced. Shivalaya has long been accepted as the limit of the first day's trek for groups, but even if you're on a teahouse trek don't plan to cover too much distance for a few days, until you've become used both to the terrain and the trekking routine. From the very start, try to establish an easy rhythm of walking; adopt a comfortable, unhurried pace and absorb the atmosphere of the countryside you're passing through. Don't think too far ahead, but accept each moment for itself.

With the extension of the road to Shivalaya you may prefer to follow that all the way, although you'll probably not save much time by doing so. But since road walking is not what you came to Nepal for, the traditional route is described here. A pleasant undemanding climb leads to a ridge-crest where the first view of distant snowpeaks may be seen across a succession of foothill ridges from the Patashe Danda, followed by descent to the valley of the Khimti Khola, a descent that is more tiring than the ascent on account of the steepness of the slope below Mali.

Although the basic linear distance between Shivalaya and Bhandar is not great, the trail makes additional demands on account of height gain. This is not excessive either, on paper, but the initial uphill section out of Shivalaya will be quite steep enough for trekkers not yet in Himalaya mode. There are two route options between Sangbadanda and Deorali above Bhandar, and more options to consider between Bhandar and Kenja. The alternative route to Deorali visits the Thodung cheese factory, while the descent from Bhandar to the valley of the Likhu Khola begins innocently enough, but soon develops into a sharp, knee-straining descent. In the late 1990s a new trail was opened (also described) which avoids the original very steep descent, and reduces the walk to Kenja by about 1 hour. It is still, however, a demanding trek.

Jiri to Shivalaya (3–3½hr)

At the end of the main paved road in Jiri, a stone-surfaced jeep track continues along the left-hand side of the valley on the way to Those and Shivalaya. In 10min cross a stream, and just beyond this take an unmarked trail which breaks off to the left and winds up the wooded hillside. About 15min later emerge onto a saddle with a few simple shacks and teahouses astride the trail. This is **BHARKUR**. Now out in the open the path continues high along the hillside on a charming belvedere above terraced fields, climbs a little and, 20min from Bharkur, comes to a school and the few houses of **RATOMATE**.

Continue climbing steadily through pastures and, about 1hr 15min from Jiri, the trail brings you to **CHITRE**, a small cluster of teahouses and a basic lodge perched on an open hillside. Beyond this the way leads across an area of shrubs, edges alongside pinewoods (fine foothill views to enjoy), and then tops the crest of a ridge. Off to the left the horizon is a jagged line of snowpeaks above Rolwaling.

In a little over 1½hr from Jiri you will come to a small pass on the **PATASHE DANDA** (2400m: 7874ft) marked with prayer flags and a couple of teahouses. Just below, 5min or so away, the first buildings of Mali can be seen, as can the big 6511m snowpeak of Karyolung whose southeast ridge forms a wall to the Dudh Kosi valley below Lukla. Descend on a trail that slopes down the left-hand side of the Danda, and come to a teahouse. The rest of **MALI**, a Sherpa settlement, is strung out below, with lodges, more teahouses and a school.

From here the trail continues to descend into the valley of the Yelung Khola, but quite steeply now, and care will be required after rain. Several primitive teahouses line the way. Some way below **DOVAN** cross to the left bank of the Yelung Khola by way of a bridge, and wander down towards the main valley which crosses at right angles ahead. Shivalaya is seen as you turn the hillside into the Khimti Khola's valley. Pass a solitary lodge, then cross a suspension bridge into the village, about 1½hr from Mali.

Shivalaya, in the valley of the Khimti Khola

SHIVALAYA (1800m: 5905ft) is a rapidly expanding bazaar village whose shops and lodges used to face one another across a single street. With the coming of the road all this has changed, as there's been a frantic spate of new building which has altered the character of the village. The road to Bhandar passes above the village, heading further upvalley before twisting back to climb the slope towards Deorali.

THOSE

Downstream from Shivalaya, and now visited by the road from Jiri, Those is a large bazaar village and one-time iron-ore mining centre, whose white-washed buildings stand alongside a cobbled street on the old expedition route from Kathmandu to Everest. When the 1953 expedition came this way Those had half a dozen smithies where chains for bridges were being forged. Though the industry has declined since then, a few iron products are still produced here.

Shivalaya to Bhandar (4–4½hr)

Leaving Shivalaya the path crosses a suspension bridge over the Chamja Khola where there are more houses with alpine views of mountains crowding the head of the Khimti Khola's valley. The trail now begins a steep climb up the hillside on a series of stone slab steps. Between here and Deorali several new lodges and teahouses are being built, so refreshment opportunities will be more numerous on the ascent. After about 15min you leave the shade of trees and come to a group of simple teashacks overlooking lush terraces on the opposite hills, and the broad, stony river bed below.

Note: From Sangbadanda there are two route options to consider on the way to Deorali; the standard direct route, and a higher, longer alternative, which visits Thodung. Both are described.

In a little over another hour you come to the small scattered village of **SANGBADANDA** (2240m: 7349ft, 1½hr) which has a school and a few lodges strung along the trail. Above this you come onto the Bhandar road, and shortly after reach a junction where a trail breaks away to Thodung. Both options eventually lead to the crest-top village of Deorali and are outlined below.

For the standard route, continue along the road for a short distance, then rejoin the original trail while the road makes its snaking progress uphill. At first the trail is less steep than below Sangbadanda. It passes a few houses, then climbs again in fits and starts, broken with more level sections and crossing a number of minor streams.

HIGH TRAIL TO DEORALI VIA THODUNG (3½hr)

The left-hand trail just beyond Sangbadanda climbs to the ridge at **THODUNG** (3091m: 10,141ft) by way of Buldanda. This is longer than the standard route, for it'll take about 2½hr or so to reach Thodung, and a further 1hr from there to Deorali where the trails converge. However, this alternative has its advocates, not least for the big mountain views. Thodung is the site of Nepal's first cheese factory, established by the Swiss in the 1950s but now run by the Nepalese Dairy Corporation, from whom it's usually possible to buy cheese and yoghurt. There's also a lodge here. From the ridge a fine panorama includes Gaurishankar looming on the northern horizon. From Thodung to Deorali the trail follows the ridge-crest southward, passing a *gompa* on the way.

Several teahouses are found along the way and about 30min from Sangbadanda you come to a lodge at **KHASRUBAS** (2300m: 7546ft). Much of the route leads through woodland, and the final climb to Deorali is among a forest of rhododendrons. By this route Deorali is reached in a little over 3hr from Shivalaya.

DEORALI (2705m: 8875ft, 3–3½hr by the main route) is a group of lodges clustered on the ridge that separates the valleys of the Khimti Khola and the Likhu Khola. Running between the lodges is a large *mani* wall. Meaning 'Pass', Deorali is aptly named, for the ridge dips to a saddle here. Wilfred Noyce, a member of the successful Everest expedition of 1953, commented (in *South Col*) that the *mani* wall has Tibetan rather than Nepali characters, and that the pass marks the beginning of Sherpa country. Tenzing led some of the party to an old *gompa* up the ridge towards Thodung. To Noyce, the *gompa* 'seemed to be a jumble of stone buildings, full of sheep-shearing and cloth-making, but not, apparently, of monastic life'. The caretaker showed them to a dark upper room which contained 'the usual erotic paintings ... two conch shells and a teapot [which] stood before the Buddha'. It would appear that they were the first foreign visitors.

THE SHERPAS OF SOLU-KHUMBU

It should come as no surprise to find that Sherpas speak a Tibetan dialect, since they originated in the province of Kham in eastern Tibet (*Sherpa* means 'people of the east') and migrated across the Himalaya more than 500 years ago. One of their migration routes crossed the Nangpa La which brought them into the Khumbu, known to be a *beyul*, a hidden valley of refuge made sacred by Guru Rimpoche, founder of their religious sect. But it was not only to the Khumbu that they came, however, for Sherpa clans spread throughout eastern Nepal and along the Indian border. Until the early 20th century they carried on a more-or-less nomadic or semi-nomadic way of life, influenced by a Buddhist theocracy that underpinned every aspect of their lives. Many carried on cross-border trade with Tibet, journeying over long-established passes with their laden yaks, while others settled in the high valleys to grow barley or potatoes and tend their herds.

In 1907 A.M. Kellas, a shy Scottish scientist with an interest in the effects on men of high altitude, made a visit to Sikkim, hiring a small group of Sherpas to carry loads. Perhaps as a result of his experience, Sherpas were recruited as porters for the Everest reconnaissance expedition of 1921. Kellas was a member of this reconnaissance, but died of a heart attack before reaching the mountain – and Sherpas have been associated with Mount Everest in particular, and Himalayan mountaineering in general, ever since. The advent of trekking in the mid-1960s brought new opportunities for those with influence and entrepreneurial skills. At first it was as guides and cooks that Sherpas accompanied trekking parties to the Khumbu and other high regions of the Nepal Himalaya. Then they began to open their homes to visitors, and soon established a reputation for hospitality, reliability and humour. Lodges grew from family houses, and the new-found income brought a taste of prosperity which has enabled some to travel the world, while others have stayed at home, adapting to change where change would bring benefits, and making the most of business opportunities as they occurred.

The second half of the 20th century was a period of rapid and sometimes bewildering change in the Khumbu region, but the main product of all this change was choice. At last Sherpas could choose whether to tend yaks, grow potatoes, climb mountains, accompany foreign trekkers or open their homes as hotels – or none of these things. Today there are some 3500 Sherpas living in the shadow of the mountains in Khumbu, and another 13,000 settled in the easier farming landscapes of Solu district. Despite adopting some of the outward trappings of Western society, Sherpa culture remains largely intact; the Buddhist faith and close family bonds are still important. Sensitive trekkers who choose Solu-Khumbu for their holiday of a lifetime will doubtless be enriched by their day-by-day meetings with these 'people of the east'.

Cross over the pass and descend steeply, and in 2min bear left where the trail forks. Bhandar can be seen below, nestling on a broad, sloping hillside shelf. The way to it is quite easy, and in places is paved with stone slabs. There are several *mani* walls, and as you come to Bhandar (1hr 15min from Deorali) you will notice two *chortens* and a *gompa* standing within the village, with the lodges nearby.

BHANDAR (2194m: 7198ft) has several good lodges, one of which (just below the *chortens*) has a pharmacy, which could be worth noting. There are also two or three possible campgrounds. This Sherpa village is located on a broad east-facing slope of meadowland, with views across the valley of the Likhu Khola to the hills of the Lamjura Danda onto which the next stage leads.

Bhandar to Kenja (3–3½hr)

Leaving Bhandar the trail slopes down the broad, fertile hillside, heading between a short avenue of trees and past a number of houses. Crossing and recrossing minor streams, about 20min from the upper village you will come to another group of lodges, houses and a covered wooden bridge at **DOKHARPA**. Cross the bridge and immediately bear left to follow the stream.

Below Bhandar the route crosses several streams

The way soon develops as a steep descending path that winds down a heavily vegetated hillside, passing a few simple teahouses. About 20min from the covered bridge you should reach a group of buildings where the

trail then drops very steeply to the left, making towards the bed of the narrow Surma Khola valley.

Soon after drawing level with the Surma Khola the path makes a long contour, the stream then falling far below once more. The trail is obvious, but when you come to a single house, make sure you take the path that descends left, steeply once more.

About 1½hr after leaving Bhandar cross the Surma Khola on a wooden bridge. On the left bank there are several buildings, a number of them teahouses. The trail continues down, then curves leftward into the broader valley of the Likhu Khola. Wandering between terraces you will come to a house near a suspension bridge (about 10min from the bridge over the Surma Khola). There is a

ALTERNATIVE ROUTE: BHANDAR TO KENJA (2½–2¾hr)

About 5min below Bhandar, a few paces after crossing a stream, the trail forks by a teahouse. Take the left branch through fields and beside a long *mani* wall. Just 13min beyond the teahouse branch right where the path cuts directly in front of a white-painted house, then turns left to slope downhill through more fields before the descent steepens to cross a major stream in a coombe. This is crossed on a wooden bridge about 30min from Bhandar. Two minutes later the path forks again and you take the upper branch to climb a flight of stone steps.

For some way the trail rises – frustratingly when you know that you'll eventually have to descend all the way to the river – and contours round rhododendron-clad hillsides, crosses numerous streams, and passes a number of simple teahouses.

After 1hr 15min the descent proper begins, and although there are one or two minor uphills, to all intents and purposes the way is down – steeply in places – to the valley of the Likhu Khola which crosses at right angles ahead. Once you reach the bed of the valley the path leads past a group of houses set among bananas and orange trees, then crosses a major tributary on a wooden bridge. The path then forks. Bear right to skirt alongside fields beside the Likhu Khola, and about 2½hr from Bhandar come to a suspension bridge, which you cross to the east bank of the river. Bear left and shortly after cross a second suspension bridge, this one spanning the Kenja Khola, to enter **KENJA** (1634m: 5361ft, 2½–2¾hr).

trail junction. Do not cross the river here, but bear left and continue along the valley path until reaching a second major suspension bridge. Cross to the eastern side where there are a few teahouses.

The trail maintains direction upvalley and soon becomes something of a switchback all the way to Kenja. The valley is very pleasant with several teahouses set beside the trail. Eventually you come to yet another suspension bridge. This one straddles a major tributary of the Likhu Khola, across which you enter the lodge settlement of **KENJA** (3–3½hr). Upvalley an attractive conical snowpeak towers over the river.

KENJA (1634m: 5361ft) has grown into a pleasant lodge village at the confluence of two rivers. Inhabited by a mixture of Sherpa, Magar and Newari hillfolk, the village has a school and a number of shops as well as several good lodges. A Japanese aid project brought electricity to Kenja in the late 1980s. On the south side of the Kenja Khola a trail heads off into the hills on the way to Pike Peak (4062m: 13,327ft), a popular twin-summited mountain (pronounced Peekay) and a noted viewpoint on the Toriphule Danda southwest of the Lamjura La.

SECTION 2

Kenja to Manidingma

Distance	30km (19 miles)
Time	2½–3 days
Start altitude	1634m (5362ft)
High points	Lamjura La (3530m: 11,581ft) and Tragsindho La (3071m: 10,075ft)

Rising to the east of the Likhu Khola the lofty crest of the Lamjura Danda is the highest obstacle to be crossed on the approach to Namche Bazaar and the Khumbu. This crossing is made at the Lamjura La, a pass 1896m (6220ft) above Kenja. Most trekkers who set out from Bhandar or Kenja choose to break the climb with an overnight at Sete, but beginning at Kenja, an early start might be sufficient for fit trekkers to cross the pass and descend to Junbesi in one fairly tough day's trek. A break at Sete is preferable, however. Although the climb is unrelentingly steep nearly all the way, there's plenty of scenic variety throughout, and unless you are affected by the altitude, it should be a route to enjoy.

Junbesi is usually chosen for a rest day. As the most interesting village on the Jiri to Namche trek, there's plenty to see, and it will not be difficult to fill a day there. As for the continuing route to Manidingma, the first highlight comes 1½hr after leaving Junbesi when (clouds permitting) Mount Everest is seen for the first time. Caught among a whole line of impressive mountains it is an exciting view, and one that is very much a tease since it does not last long. Later, after crossing the Tragsindho La on the approach to Manidingma, Kusum Kangguru looks especially impressive above the hinted cleft of the Dudh Kosi – the valley which then leads all the way to Everest.

But for the majority of this section of the trek, the big mountains are still remote and unattainable. Instead there are the middle hills to enjoy with their pinewoods, deep valleys and villages, Buddhist gompas, the orchards of Ringmo, and one of the most pleasant of all belvedere sections of path between Junbesi and Sallung.

Kenja to Junbesi (8½–9hr)

Almost immediately upon leaving Kenja the path begins its laborious climb to Sete. It can seem a brutal haul, but with another 3hr or more to go before reaching the lodges there, it's best to settle to a steady, comfortable rhythm and enjoy the ascent without being tempted to hurry. On occasion views towards the head of the Likhu Khola are very fine as more and more snowpeaks come on display. Then there's the pleasure of gazing steeply down on Kenja and, when that has disappeared from view, Bhandar may be seen way off to the west.

Plenty of teahouses line the trail, and you'll certainly get through a lot of liquids on this stage, especially if the

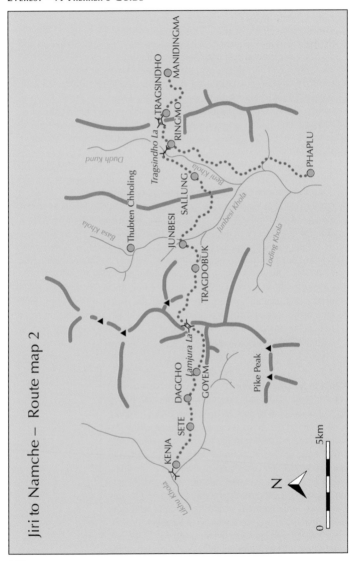

Jiri to Namche – Route map 2

weather is sunny and warm. About 2–2½hr above Kenja you reach a junction of trails at a place known as **CHIMBU** where there's a single lodge, *Top Himalayan Guest House*. Take the right fork, for this leads to Sete.

SETE (2575m: 8448ft) is little more than a few lodges and a small *gompa* set among a series of narrow terraced fields. After the harvest has been taken groups often camp on the terraces beside some of the lodges. In the late 1990s the *gompa* was partially destroyed by fire, but rebuilding work was in progress when I last came through.

Out of Sete the route resumes its persistent uphill course, perhaps not with the same degree of severity as that experienced out of Kenja, but still sufficient to get your lungs working well. About 1hr from Sete you will arrive at **DAGCHO** (2850m: 9350ft), a spartan settlement of teahouses and lodges built right on the ridge.

Continue straight up the ridge, soon among forests of rhododendron and pine, and about 45min or so from Dagcho you should reach the first part of another simple lodge settlement. This is **GOYEM** (3155m: 10,351ft, 2hr), a two-part village with 5min of trail between them. About a minute after leaving the last building you will come to a trail junction. Ignore the tempting contour path to the right, and instead continue up the ridge as before, steadily making height in easy windings through thinning forest. Views to the left show far-off snowpeaks again, while behind, Deorali (crossed on the way to Bhandar) is clearly seen. Foothills roll away to a blue distant haze.

Out of forest you come to yet another collection of primitive teahouses and a lodge, above which the trail has cut a groove between rhododendrons. In the post-monsoon trekking season the banks here are speckled with the lovely blue gentian *Gentiana depressa*, while rhododendrons come into their own in the spring.

When you reach a *mani* wall on the crest of the ridge, leave the ridge and slant left where the path contours through forest heading north. When it forks shortly after, take either option for they rejoin a little later. It's an easy trail now, for the most part fairly level with a few ups and downs, and it emerges from the forest to a large clearing in which there are several simple lodges. From here to the pass will take about 30min.

The trail maintains its contour along the hillside, much of the way having been paved with huge slabs of stone, and then suddenly swings to the right before twisting the last few paces to the **LAMJURA LA** (3530m: 11,581ft), a wide grassy saddle adorned with a litter of prayer flags, *mani* walls and great heaps of rock, reached about 3–3½hr from Sete. In clear snow-free conditions without a wind blowing, it's tempting to sit here for a while and enjoy the views. There are no big mountains in sight, but a great swelling of foothills wherever you look, and the valley ahead, into which the descent will go, appears to be utterly charming. And so it proves; it's the first valley of the Solu district, more properly known to the Sherpas as Shorong.

The descent trail is an obvious one, steep at first as it corkscrews through forest, and rough underfoot, too, as it has been cut by teams of packhorses that trade across the pass. There are a few basic teahouses, both in and out of the forest, but the only village, as such, is Tragdobuk (Taktor) which is situated some way farther downvalley after having wandered through open pastures and between stone-walled fields.

TRAGDOBUK (2860m: 9383ft, 5hr) has a lodge at its upper end. In the centre of the village the houses are grouped close together. There's a wind-powered prayer wheel and a small *gompa*, with another lodge nearby. On reaching this take the trail that slants left ahead – do not take the right-hand trail for this goes to Salleri, an important bazaar village and district headquarters way down the valley of the Junbesi Khola.

With about 45min to go before reaching Junbesi the trail makes a gentle rising traverse of the left-hand hillside, gaining a little height here, losing a little there. One

or two *mani* walls have been built along the trail; there
are also steps in places. Then you round a bluff and
suddenly a high and distant wall of snowpeaks ahead
blocks the valley of the Junbesi Khola – Karyolung,
Khatang and Numbur (also known as Shorong Yul Lha –
the 'god of the Solu'). Not far below lies Junbesi in its
own Shangri-La setting; a well laid-out village whose yel-
low-roofed *gompa* draws the eye. This first view is
appealing; the village looks idyllic, and a choice of trails
invite you down.

JUNBESI (2675m: 8776ft) is the most delightful of all
Sherpa villages on the trek to Namche. It has a number of
comfortable lodges with tempting menus. There are two
or three shops, a post office, **health clinic/hospital**, a
large school founded by Sir Edmund Hillary in 1964, an
interesting monastery, a library next to the post office, a
telephone office and a small hydro scheme that provides
basic lighting for the whole village. A number of houses
have their own gardens in which a wide variety of
vegetables are grown, and its setting is such that many
trekkers decide to take time off here.

*Junbesi, the largest
village on the way to
Namche, is a good
place in which to
spend a rest day*

TIME IN JUNBESI

Not only is Junbesi a comfortable village in which to spend a night or two, the valley in which it nestles has much to commend a few days' exploration, so treat yourself to at least one day without a rucksack in this early part of your schedule. From the village itself you cannot see the high peaks that were visible from the trail of approach, so you might consider wandering the path that heads north through the upper valley. It's enticing country, with pinewoods, pastures, small field systems and glacial streams draining out of the arc of mountains at its head. The red panda is thought to exist in some of the high forest areas nearby.

The **village monastery** is worth visiting, but there is another, a much smaller *gompa* perched on a crag just to the north of Junbesi. Partially destroyed by earthquake in 1989, it is being slowly rebuilt. Its position is dramatic, with a very fine view of the valley. To reach it a minor path breaks left from the main valley trail a short distance upstream of the health clinic.

Upvalley, about 1hr or so from Junbesi, but on the eastern side of the river, stands the important **Thubten Chholing Gompa** where a large number of Buddhist monks and nuns study under the leadership of Trulshik Rinpoche, the head lama, who had previously been at the Rongbuk monastery on the Tibetan side of Everest, from which he had been forced to flee in 1959.

Beyond Thubten Chholing, above the confluence of the Mampung and Basa Khola rivers, is the village of **Phungmuche**, site of a **Sherpa Arts Centre**. This is about 2hr walk from Junbesi.

Downvalley, perhaps 3hr away, are **Phaplu** and **Salleri**. Both

have trekkers' lodges; Phaplu has a STOL airstrip (scheduled flights to and from Kathmandu) and a hospital built by Hillary's Himalayan Trust, while nearby Salleri (45min from Phaplu) is the headquarters of Solu district. An alternative trail heads north from Phaplu to rejoin the main trail at Ringmo.

Teahouse below Thubten Chholing gompa, near Junbesi

Junbesi to Manidingma (6–7hr)

When at last you can tear yourself away from Junbesi, wander down through the village below the *chorten* to cross the Junbesi Khola by a wooden bridge. A few paces beyond this the path forks. The right-hand trail goes downvalley to Phaplu and Salleri, but we bear left and rise through a forest of rhododendron, blue pine and oak trees on a steady ascent. The trail again divides and once more you take the upper, left-hand option. Soon the forest is left behind and you're granted views overlooking the valley which drains towards Phaplu, the steep sides stepped with neat agricultural terraces. Looking back it's possible to see up to the Lamjura La.

The path develops a scenic belvedere course along the hillside, passing one or two farms on the way, and after about 1½hr from Junbesi it brings you to a lone teahouse. A few minutes later the trail curves round a hillside spur where a group of buildings, consisting of lodge, shop and cheese factory, hug the bend. This is the **Everest View Sherpa Lodge** (3048m: 10,000ft, 1½hr) – and what a view it has! If you're lucky a magnificent line of high, dramatic snowpeaks will draw your attention

Everest View, 1½hr beyond Junbesi, with its Himalayan panorama

towards the northeast. Mount Everest marks the left-hand end of this line, but seems dwarfed by some of the others. Also in view are Thamserku, Lhotse, Nuptse, Kusum Kangguru, Kangtega, Mera Peak and Makalu. It's a view to savour.

NAK CHEESE FOR SALE

Nak cheese (not *yak* cheese, since a yak is the male of the species!) is made by the owner of the Everest View Sherpa Lodge using methods introduced to Nepal in the 1950s by the Swiss, as at Thodung. The animals are grazed during the summer months on the ridge above the lodge which climbs to Numbur, and their milk is then processed into cheese which can be bought at the lodge.

The near-level, beaten-earth trail continues, now with those mountains ahead seen across a succession of intervening ridges, one of which will be crossed later at the Tragsindho La. The path follows an even contour before sloping down to the attractive village of **SALLUNG** (2953m: 9688ft), about 2hr from Junbesi, where views remain as magnificent as before. There are a few lodges here, and gardens full of produce.

Below Sallung the hillside is patched with pine

After leaving Sallung the route begins the long twisting descent to the Beni Khola (also known as the Dudh Kund or Ringmo Khola), with Ringmo seen on the opposite flank and the white *stupa* marking the Tragsindho La well above it. Although views of Everest and its neighbours are soon lost, at certain points on the trail it's possible to see the fine shape of Karyolung (6681m: 21,920ft) off to the left. On the way down to the Beni Khola, which drains Karyolung's glaciers, the trail crosses two tributary streams on wooden bridges. The Beni Khola is crossed on a suspension bridge at 2599m (8527ft), and from it a short, but fairly steep, climb heads up to a trail junction (the right-hand path is that which leads to Phaplu) by a *chorten*.

RINGMO (2805m: 9203ft, 3½–4hr) has several lodges linked by a stone-paved trail. Orchards of apple, apricot and peach line the path that takes you past the lodges and up towards the main part of the village. Locally produced cider, apple juice and brandy can be bought here, as well as apple pie and various other apple-based concoctions that grace lodge menus.

As you wander up the stone path to the village proper, you pass two *mani* walls, the second of which is nearly 50m long. Immediately on reaching the far end of this it is important to leave the main trail and head off to the right. Since you should have beeen walking along the left-hand side of the *mani* walls, the junction is not very clear, although it is sometimes signed. The path improves within a few paces of turning uphill among trees.

Soon come to a T-junction of trails where you take the left branch, shortly after which you cross a clearing with a simple teahouse in it. The trail climbs on and is badly eroded, then in less than 1hr from Ringmo you come to the **TRAGSINDHO LA** (3071m: 10,075ft), some 4½–5hr after leaving Junbesi. This untidy pass (also spelt as Trakshindo La) is marked by a large *stupa*, teahouse and a flotilla of prayer flags, and is the last ridge-crossing on the eastbound trek leading to the

Dudh Kosi. The descent on the eastern side of the pass to Tragsindho Gompa is a short but steep 15min trek. ◄

At the Tragsindho La you pass from Solu district to the region known as Pharak, which links the Sherpa country of Solu with that of Khumbu.

TRAGSINDHO (2930m: 9612ft, 5hr 15min) is an assorted cluster of buildings, mostly serving the large and impressive monastery that was founded in 1946. There is also a lodge and a school. If clouds allow, there's a superb view of Kusum Kangguru to the northeast. The trail swings left and then forks. Bear right to follow round the *gompa*'s lower boundary fence, passing one or two houses. About 5min below Tragsindho a second lodge stands beside the trail, formerly owned by the late Babu Chhiri Sherpa, one of the heroes of Everest.

BABU CHHIRI SHERPA (1965–2001) – FROM TRAGSINDHO TO EVEREST

Babu was born in Tragsindho in 1965. His father, Lhakpa, had worked as a porter carrying a load to Everest Base Camp for the successful 1953 expedition. Having missed out on a formal education, Babu started his own working life at the age of 13 by also carrying loads, this time for trekkers. Three years later he married Puti Sherpa. The young couple opened a small teahouse, which Babu financed when he was promoted to cook boy. With Puti running the teahouse, Babu earned extra money where he could by working for trekking and climbing groups, and gradually learned to speak English. Promotion to the role of climbing Sherpa brought added challenges and rewards. In 1989 he took part in the epic traverse of Kangchenjunga by a Soviet expedition, climbed Dhaulagiri the following year with a French team, and Everest by the South-East Ridge a few months later. He also climbed Shishapangma and Cho Oyu, and made another nine successful ascents of Everest. On one of these he achieved the incredible speed record of 16hr 56min from Base Camp to summit, and in May 1999 camped out on Everest's summit for 21 hours without use of supplementary oxygen. At home in Tragsindho, Babu was father of six daughters; he'd co-founded a trekking business, and was planning to build a school in his home village. But on 29 April 2001 he tragically died after falling into a crevasse in the Western Cwm of Everest whilst taking photographs. By then he had become a much-respected national and local hero.

Eventually the path becomes more obvious as it descends in a long sweep round the hillside. Part of the route goes through forest, some of it through agricultural land. The village of Manidingma is seen long before you reach it, and there's a lodge standing alone beside the trail a few minutes before entering.

MANIDINGMA (2194m: 7198ft) is also known as Nuntala, a village with several lodges and shops facing one another across a broad, paved main street. There's a post office, **health post** and a small generator that powers a flour mill by day, and provides electricity for the village after dark.

The finely terraced hillside below Manidingma

SECTION 3

Manidingma to Choplung

Distance	24km (15 miles)
Time	2–2½ days
Start altitude	2194m (7198ft)
High point	Khari La (2850m: 9350ft)

Below Manidingma the valley of the Dudh Kosi is joined at last. Here the trek loses its eastward trend and begins the northbound approach to Namche. A steady climb leads past Jubing and Kharikhola, then up steeply to Bupsa and on along a switchback trail to Chaumrikharka and Choplung. On the first section of the route there are good mountain views and some beautiful fertile countryside to pass through; later, views are mostly shielded by trees. Although this is Sherpa country, the first village on the trail up the Dudh Kosi is not inhabited by Sherpas, but by Rai hillfolk. Rai villages are found throughout eastern Nepal, but Solu-Khumbu is about as far west as they've settled, and Jubing is the only non-Sherpa village after Sete on the Everest trek. Rai houses and bridges are frequently decorated with garlands of marigolds.

Morning views from Manidingma are often much clearer than would no doubt have been experienced on arrival, so as you leave the village look northward where Karyolung may be seen, and northeast to Kusum Kangguru. The latter peak will be in view for much of the descent to the Dudh Kosi. The trail leading down to the river is clear and obvious, but it has some steep sections and after rain or heavy dew may be quite slippery.

The route between Kharikhola and Chaumrikharka is fairly long and demanding by contrast with the first section, much of it in forest and with a fair amount of height gain and loss; it's a roller-coaster trail where views are largely constrained by the valley's forested east flank. Yet despite the absence of views it will be evident that progress is being made towards Khumbu, and by the time you reach Chaumrikharka you'll know without doubt that big mountains are not far ahead. Choplung lies about 30min beyond Chaumrikharka, and this is where you join the much more heavily trekked route that begins in Lukla.

Manidingma to Kharikhola (4–4½hr)

Descent to the Dudh Kosi is steep but delightful, with an immaculately terraced hillside consisting of hundreds of narrow shelves stepping one after another down to the thin ribbon of silver seen far below where the Deku Khola drains the hills. It's a glorious landscape, growing more and more lush as you draw nearer to the river. Numerous houses dot the hillside, but there are few lodges or teahouses on the trail.

It takes about 1½hr or so to reach the confluence of the Deku Khola and Dudh Kosi rivers. Just before coming to the suspension bridge strung across the Dudh Kosi you pass a complex of teahouses overlooking the river. After this the next opportunity for refreshment is at Jubing, a little over 30min uphill walk away. Cross the suspension bridge to the east bank of the Dudh Kosi (Milk River), and wander along the trail that swings to the left, then rises up the lush hillside to the first village.

JUBING (1676m: 5499ft) is gained about 2½hr from Manidingma. This is a lovely Rai village set among fertile terraces; a bright and colourful place, clean and tidy and with flowers and vegetables growing beside the trail late into the autumn. Streams run through the village, one of which powers a small mill. There are several lodges; some of which appear especially inviting.

Passing through Jubing, in another 20min the trail makes a sharp right-hand bend, with another path cutting from it to contour among the terraces. Do not be tempted by this, but keep on the main trail that climbs to a group of three buildings standing about 10min walk away. This is **CHURKHA**. On reaching these the trail again divides. One climbs directly up the hillside above Churkha and

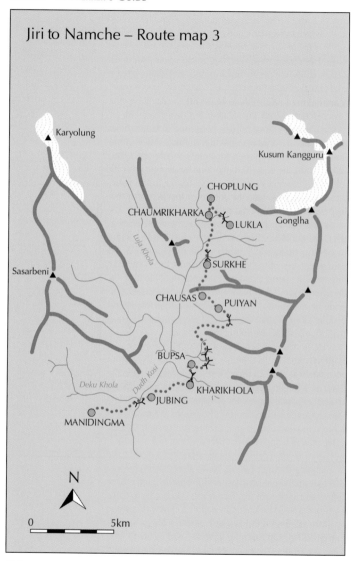

Jiri to Namche – Route map 3

Karyolung

Kusum Kangguru

CHOPLUNG

CHAUMRIKHARKA

LUKLA

Gonglha

Lula Khola

SURKHE

Sasarbeni

CHAUSAS

PUIYAN

BUPSA

Deku Khola

Dudh Kosi

KHARIKHOLA

JUBING

MANIDINGMA

N

0   5km

crosses a small pass before dropping to Kharikhola. The other, which is recommended, continues past the buildings to slant across the hillside, affording good views over massed terraces. After reaching a high point the trail rounds a corner, then looks across to the houses of Kharikhola scattered over the hillside ahead, on different levels of terracing. The way descends, then undulates a little, before entering the village.

KHARIKHOLA (2072m: 6798ft) is a clean and pleasant village, with friendly inhabitants, some comfortable accommodation and a couple of campgrounds. All the lodges here are set beside the main trail, as are several shops, teahouses and small tailoring businesses. After Junbesi, Kharikhola is one of the nicest places to stay, its shops supplying an amazing variety of goods. The village has a thriving school and its own electricity supply, and there's also a **health post**. The trek from Manidingma, although modest in length (4–4½hr), is a traditional porter stage, so most camping groups spend the night here. Make a point of setting out early in the morning, should it be your plan to go as far as Chaumrikharka next day.

Kharikhola to Choplung (8½hr) ▶

Out of Kharikhola the trail descends a little, crosses a suspension bridge near some watermills, then begins a steep, heart-pounding climb to Bupsa. The way is clear, yet uncompromising, but there's a teahouse providing an excuse to rest before making the final climb in zigzags above a landslip area.

BUPSA (2350m: 7710ft) is reached about 1hr 15min out of Kharikhola. Perched at the head of a precarious slope, it has a clutch of lodges and teahouses, a *chorten* and a small *gompa*.

Beyond the village the trek enters a jungly phase, the trail rising through damp forest with streams and small waterfalls cascading. Monkeys can often be seen

As the next stage to Chaumrikharka is about 8hr, independent teahouse trekkers might decide to continue beyond Kharikhola to Bupsa, seen on the ridge ahead, about 1–1½hr walk away.

swinging in the trees, or heard chattering among the foliage. There are a few simple teahouses, but nothing more substantial until you reach Puiyan. Continuing to gain height, about 2hr from Bupsa you should come to a high point at about 2850m (9350ft). This is below the true **Khari La**, a pass crossed on the original route from Kharikhola, but the present trail, created in the early 1980s, saves both time and effort by avoiding it. There are a few simple teahouses here.

This high point is not a true pass, but the turning of a spur of hillside marked by a *mani* wall and prayer flags. From it you may be able to see the mountain which rises above Namche, Khumbui Yul Lha (Khumbila). The Dudh Kosi has bored its way through the gorge-like valley hundreds of metres below the hillside, and in places you gain a sensational view into the depths of the gorge.

There is still a little more height to gain, and a return to forest where the way resumes its switchback course, cutting into the deep glen of the Puiyan Khola. Across the stream you soon come to the lodge settlement of **PUIYAN**.

PUIYAN (2796m: 9173ft) lies about 4–4½hr from Kharikhola, but there's another 3hr to go before you reach Chaumrikharka. Puiyan is growing rapidly, with several good-looking lodges and a campsite.

Beyond the village there's much less forest to wander through, and the trail enjoys a more open aspect. It continues as a switchback, and steadily increases altitude until the Dudh Kosi itself rushes 1000m or more below. In places the route is quite exposed. About 45min from Puiyan you reach the group of teahouses and lodges of **CHAUSAS**, and shortly after come to another high point on a spur with prayer flags strung above the path. Here you have a splendid view up the Dudh Kosi's valley. Lukla and its airstrip can also be seen. Far below lie the few buildings of Surkhe. The path winds through forest once more, then makes a long and seemingly endless descent on a flight of rough stone steps to reach those buildings, gained in about 2hr from Puiyan.

SURKHE (2300m: 7546ft) consists of a handful of farm-houses built amid fertile agricultural land in a basin just below the trail, with a number of trekkers' lodges built alongside the path. The Surkhe Khola runs through the basin, with one or two simple teashops near the bridge that are patronised by porters on their journeys to and from the Namche market.

After crossing the stream you begin to climb yet again, and about 15min later come to a *mani* wall where the trail forks. The right-hand option leads to Lukla; the continuing trail is the main path to Chaumrikharka. Continue rising beyond the *mani* wall and cross another stream which drains down from Lukla. Then there's a splendid waterfall pouring through a deep gorge. The way finally heads up among some boulders, goes along-side *mani* walls and reaches the first part of **CHAUMRIKHARKA**.

ROUTE TO LUKLA

At the trail junction by the *mani* wall, bear right and go up some steps. These lead to a clear path that climbs steeply, goes through rhododendron forest, then makes a contour to the left. Eventually come to a rough pas-tureland basin in which there are a couple of buildings. Cross a bridge on the left, then climb in loops up the hillside to reach another building at the entrance to a fairly level stretch of farmland. There's an insignificant-look-ing trail junction at this point. Find a narrow path climbing steeply to the right among shrubbery. It soon joins a more substantial trail that leads directly to **LUKLA** (2860m: 9383ft), about 1hr 15min from the *mani* wall junction above Surkhe.

CHAUMRIKHARKA (2591m: 8501ft) is made up of two or three settlements or groups of buildings gained about 1–1½hr from Surkhe. This is one of the nicest villages between Jiri and Everest, and the last on this trek before

Chaumrikharka is one of the nicest villages on the trek to Namche

you join the busy Lukla trail. If you have time, it would be worth taking a rest-day here. In addition to some comfortable lodges, there's a small *gompa*, a **health post** and a Hillary school. With its airstrip located up the hillside (but out of sight) above Chaumrikharka, the frequency of flights in and out of Lukla can be charted from the village.

Leaving Chaumrikharka the trail passes through a rich agricultural landscape with fields on either side of the pathway, and in an easy 30min rises to **CHOPLUNG** where it meets the trail from Lukla.

CHOPLUNG (2660m: 8727ft), or Chablung, is a neat settlement of several lodges, a shop or two, and a *gompa* built against a rock wall above the village. There's also a **health post** run by the French Association Christophe Viard, and a Japanese 'apple project' behind it. On arrival at Choplung the character of the trek changes, for the trail from now on will be much busier, and for a while those who have trekked in from Jiri will be able to recognise new arrivals from Lukla by their clean clothes and the smell of soap! There will also be yaks and yak cross-breeds lumbering along the trail, often carrying loads for trekking parties. Thus far on the way from Jiri you will probably not have seen any yaks at all, but from now on they will become a familiar feature. Beware their large menacing horns, and when faced by a yak on a mountain path, always let it pass on the downhill side to avoid being nudged off the trail.

LUKLA

Meaning 'the place of many goats and sheep' Lukla (2860m: 9383ft) is no longer an insignificant village of a dozen houses, for it has developed into a thriving township of lodges, restaurants and shops in direct response to the construction of the airstrip by Ed Hillary in 1964. That development continues apace in a seemingly anarchic, uncoordinated manner; Bill O'Connor (in *The Trekking Peaks of Nepal*) calls it an 'urban disaster'. In 2001 the once-stony runway was surfaced with tarmac; there's now a control tower and an ugly concrete terminal building. Some of the lodges have en-suite facilities; there's a **health post**, kerosene depot, school, pool room, satellite dishes, airline offices, and a heavy police and army presence. And rubbish. Porters, guides and yak drivers wait for employment; local youths play *carom* with rock music blaring behind dusty windows. But away from the razor-wire fencing that surrounds the upper airstrip, the town manages to either absorb or disperse the crowds of porters, Sherpas and high-season trekking arrivals with surprising efficiency.

For many trekkers, Lukla is their introduction to mountain Nepal. But (perhaps fortunately) it is in no way representative of a Sherpa village. It's no wonder there's an eagerness to get out of town and along the trail ...

Daily, when the weather permits, plane-loads of trekkers and mountaineers fly into, and out of, this rather unattractive hilltop perch. But when the weather does not permit – ah, then Lukla has an atmosphere all its own!

When clouds hang low for several days at a time – which is not at all uncommon – literally hundreds of people crowd the lodges in a mass of seething frustration. Never mind recent days of calm splendour, of patient hours spent gazing at mountains, of learning the art of contentment. Suddenly you're plunged back into the world of third-party schedules, and that's when the blood pressure rises. In spells of bad weather Lukla is a hotbed of rumour. 'There's a plane on the way ... there won't be any ▶

Lukla, starting place for most treks into the Khumbu

◄ flights for three days … you've lost your place on the waiting list … there is no waiting list!'

Happily the problem is not quite as bad as it used to be, now that RNAC has lost its monopoly and a number of private airlines using Twin Otters, Dorniers and helicopters operate flights between Kathmandu and Lukla. Helicopters in particular have made a difference, for they will often fly when fixed-wing aircraft are grounded by clouds that hide mountains.

The Lukla experience is not always a painful or frustrating one, of course, and if you've been walking in from Jiri you may decide that you'd rather fly out at the end of the trek than walk all the way back to the roadhead. So you didn't buy a ticket in advance in Kathmandu? Don't worry, there's still a chance to get one organised, for each of the airlines has an office in town and you stand a better than even chance of buying a ticket. But make sure you have dollars with you. (**Note:** If you have a ticket for a flight out you must reconfirm on the day *before* the flight is due. Airline offices in Lukla are usually open for business between 3–4pm or a little later.)

SECTION 4

Lukla (Choplung) to Namche

Distance	18km (11 miles)
Time	1½–2 days
Start altitude	Lukla: 2860m (9283ft); Choplung: 2660m (8727ft)
High point	Namche Bazaar (3446m: 11,306ft)

Having arrived in Lukla, either on foot from Jiri, or by plane from Kathmandu, you'll be anxious to leave and head upvalley towards Namche Bazaar and the mountains of Khumbu. Apart from the initial easy downhill walk to Choplung, the route is the same as that taken by trekkers coming from Chaumrikharka.

As it takes time to get porter- or yak-loads organised, group trekkers will probably have a short day's walk ending at Phakding or, at the most, Mondzo on the edge of the Sagarmatha National Park. Independent trekkers may be tempted to push on further towards Namche. But if you've just flown in to Lukla this would be unwise. Namche is an easy 1½ day's walk away, but the advanced altitude is enough to cause problems for anyone who rushes it. Prepare yourself for a steady walk and you'll enjoy the rest of your trek in Khumbu. Don't spoil it with impatience that could so easily lead to mountain sickness.

Read the section on Mountain Sickness under the heading On-Trek Healthcare in the Introduction.

Lukla (Choplung) to Phakding (2–3hr)

From Lukla the Namche trail is broad, clear and obvious. It heads north away from the airstrip along a lodge-lined street, passes through a *kani* (an entrance archway with a row of prayer wheels) then slopes downhill, soon to reach a low region of agricultural land which it skirts along its right-hand edge. In little more than 30min from

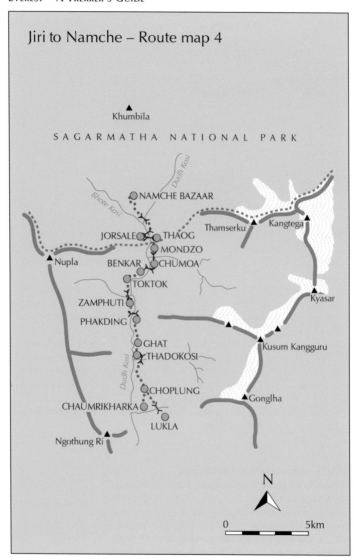

Jiri to Namche – Route map 4

Khumbila

SAGARMATHA NATIONAL PARK

Dudh Kosi

Bhote Kosi

NAMCHE BAZAAR

JORSALE — THAOG

Thamserku — Kangtega

MONDZO

Nupla

BENKAR — CHUMOA

TOKTOK

ZAMPHUTI

Kyasar

PHAKDING

GHAT

Kusum Kangguru

THADOKOSI

Dudh Kosi

CHOPLUNG

CHAUMRIKHARKA

Gonglha

LUKLA

Ngothung Ri

N

0   5km

The kani *through which you leave Lukla*

Lukla you'll come to a junction of trails in **CHOPLUNG** (2660m: 8727ft), and bear right on the main route to Namche. The way continues easily without any severe uphill stretches for a while, but then drops suddenly to the Kusum Khola with a suspension bridge in the mouth of a narrow gorge.

THADOKOSI (or Tharo Kosi) is a string of lodges that exploit a splendid view through the gorge to the graceful Kusum Kangguru, an impressive but very difficult 'trekking peak'. It's tempting to stop at one of these lodges for a drink or a meal, and to sit outside in the sunshine absorbing that view at leisure.

KUSUM KANGGURU

Thadokosi, with Kusum Kangguru as a backdrop

Seen from a number of vantage points on the trail to and beyond Namche, one glance is sufficient to know that this mountain is a very serious climbing proposition.

Located south of Kangtega on the ridge of the Kyashar Himal which separates the valleys of the Dudh Kosi and that of the Hinku, this savage-looking rock and ice peak has three summits: the main peak at 6367m (20,889ft); the East Summit (6356m: 20,853ft), and the West Summit (5579m: 18,304ft). Kusum Kangguru, whose name means 'mountain house of three snow peaks', has a reputation for being the most difficult of the so-called 'trekking peaks'. It's a complex mountain with five major ridges and as many faces (the West and South-West Faces are seen from Thadokosi). The climbing is said to be technically difficult, and it repelled four attempts by experienced parties before the first ascent was achieved by a Japanese team via the South-East Face in 1979.

Across the bridge the trail climbs a stone stairway past the lodges, contours round a corner and soon after slopes down again to the village of **GHAT**.

At Ghat the trail is divided by a large mani-inscribed boulder

GHAT (2591m: 8501ft) is a strung-out village with several lodges and teahouses. At its upper end you pass two large prayer wheels, and immediately beyond these some huge boulders that have been brightly decorated with the Buddhist mantra: *Om Mani Padme Hum*. Nearby there's a tree nursery and an information office for the Sagarmatha National Park's Buffer Zone. Within the village itself there's a small *gompa*, while a veritable forest of prayer flags adorns the hillside above.

Now the way heads through a rough, rock-strewn area, but it soon improves and with a small amount of up and down brings you to the larger settlement of Phakding. Just before coming to the village proper, a fancy new lodge complex stands below the trail. The **Yeti Mountain Resort** has 20 twin-bedded rooms in architect-designed buildings of stone construction (built 2004). Far and away the most upmarket accommodation on the trek to Namche, it will come as a shock to teahouse trekkers who have used lodges all the way from Jiri. Those who have just begun their trek from Lukla may need reminding that the Farakpa Village Resort is not a 'standard' trekker's hotel. In 2004, the cost of a double room with meals was $150.

PHAKDING (2652m: 8701ft, 2–3hr) is a village in two parts, separated by about 10min of trail and a suspension bridge over the Dudh Kosi. Both sections have lodges, but groups often choose to camp on the west bank of the river in flat meadows directly in front of two of the lodges. Phakding is often used as a first night's stop by groups who arrive in Lukla by one of the later flights from Kathmandu.

Phakding to Mondzo (2–2½hr)

Cross the long suspension bridge over the river. After passing between two lodges the path curves to the right, rises along the hillside and in another 10–15min comes to the few teahouses and lodges of **ZAMPHUTI** at the mouth of a tributary glen. Over the wooden bridge the eroded path climbs a short steep slope, then eases along the hillside above the Dudh Kosi, passing solitary farmsteads and the simple lodges and campground of **TOKTOK**, about 30min from Phakding. In another 20min you come to a waterfall just before reaching **BENKAR**.

BENKAR (2790m: 9154ft) has a lodge just above the waterfall. This boasts hot springs contained in a shed in the garden. Descending from the ridge on which this first lodge is located, the main village has two or three other lodges.

A short distance beyond Benkar the trail crosses back to the east bank of the Dudh Kosi on a Swiss-built suspension bridge, undulates along the valley, then rises to Chumoa, about 1½hr from Phakding. **CHUMOA** has several lodges and campgrounds set among graceful conifers and rhododendrons. From it the way descends steeply to

cross the Kyashar Khola, which drains a glacial system between Kusum Kangguru and Thamserku. There are simple watermills on the upstream side of the bridge. A flight of rough stone steps then takes you steeply uphill, and shortly after you enter Mondzo on the edge of the Sagarmatha National Park.

Shortly before entering Benkar the trail passes a slender waterfall

MONDZO (2835m: 9301ft), or Monjo, is a long paved village of shingle-roofed houses, lodges, a few basic shops, and a small *gompa* (the Utche Chholing monastery) nearby. It will have taken about 2–2½hr to get here from Phakding, and the onward trek to Namche Bazaar will need another 3–3½hr, initially through the narrow cleft of the Dudh Kosi gorge, a stark defile whose bed has been ravaged several times by natural calamities. One of these occurred in 1977 when a landslip on the lower slopes of Ama Dablam blocked a stream. When the lake that had built up behind it burst its banks, a wall of water rushed down through the valley, tearing away bridges, as well as part of the village of Jorsale, killing three people. A similar catastrophe happened in 1985 when a glacial lake above Thame also broke free,

127

destroyed a 2-million-dollar dam and wrought havoc all
the way down the Bhote Kosi and Dudh Kosi valleys.

Mondzo to Namche Bazaar (3–3½hr)

Minutes after leaving Mondzo you come to the entrance
of the **Sagarmatha National Park** where an entry permit
must be obtained. Keep it safe for it will have to be
shown on the way out. You'll need to provide details
from your passport, while porters and other crew members must also register and have their loads checked. Be
warned: all this can lead to bottleneck delays. ◄

*In 2008 entry permit
to the Sagarmatha
National Park cost
Rps1000.*

THE SAGARMATHA NATIONAL PARK

Enclosing an area of 1148 sq km, the vast majority of which is above 3000m,
the Sagarmatha National Park was established in July 1976 with assistance
from the New Zealand government, and declared a World Heritage Site
three years later. Managed by the Department of National Parks and Wildlife
Conservation from a headquarters sited above Namche, it is surrounded by
lofty ridges that nowhere fall below 5700m. It is the recognised habitat of the
endangered musk deer, various other mammals including the snow leopard,
the Himalayan tahr, at least 118 species of bird and around 25 species of
summer-visiting butterfly. In the 30-odd years since the park was created,
the amount of wildlife has increased, and tree nurseries established by The
Himalayan Trust have gone some way to address the problems of deforestation, not just within the park, but outside its boundaries where trees were
ruthlessly felled when park regulations forbade the cutting of timber inside
its territory. Current rules prohibit visitors from cutting firewood, so kerosene
stoves must be used not only by trekking groups but their porters too. During
2004 a ban was imposed on bringing pressure cookers into the park,
because Maoist rebels had made bombs from them. As a result of this ban
considerably more kerosene was needed for cooking. Needless to say, litter-
ing is forbidden; what you carry in should also be carried out.

Once through the kani the trail descends to river
level where the houses of **THAOG** are set among fields of
huge cabbages. Here you cross the Dudh Kosi on a long
suspension bridge, and on the west bank of the river soon
pass a few teahouses and simple lodges in **JORSALE**

(2775m: 9104ft), the last accommodation before Namche. Beyond this settlement the trail returns to the east bank by another suspension bridge.

Now the trail picks a way along the stony bed of the valley, winding among rocks towards the point where the Bhote Kosi and Dudh Kosi come together below a mountain wall upon which unseen Namche Bazaar is perched. The Bhote Kosi rushes through a gorge on the left, the Dudh Kosi from a gorge on the right. To reach Namche involves crossing the Dudh Kosi's gorge on a suspension bridge slung high above the river not far upstream of its confluence with the Bhote Kosi. The path leaves the valley bed and climbs steeply with the occasional aid of steps to gain the bridge.

Across the bridge you descend a few concrete steps, then begin the last long uphill to Namche, a climb of around 700m (2300ft) that will take anywhere between 1–2½hr, depending on fitness and how well acclimatised you are. Steep in places, the broad trail snakes its way up the slope. About halfway up at a bend, with the remains of a teahouse wall on the right, there's a brief view of Everest, Nuptse and Lhotse to be had from the ridge a few paces off the trail. Continuing mostly among trees, you will eventually come to a group of buildings, just beyond which a broad flight of stone steps rise above a water supply. The main trail continues ahead to enter Namche just below the Tibetan market, while the steps above the water supply climb steeply, then the trail turns a corner and brings you directly into one of the lower streets of **NAMCHE BAZAAR**.

NAMCHE BAZAAR (3446m: 11,306ft) is the Sherpa 'capital' and administrative centre for Khumbu district. The headquarters of the Sagarmatha National Park and a military post are both situated above the town, just off the trail to Thyangboche. The National Park HQ has an information centre worth visiting, while just below its entrance there's a Sherpa Cultural Centre and Museum at the excellent Hotel Sherwi Khangba. Namche has a *gompa* and several *chortens* overlooking the amphitheatre in

*Namche Bazaar is
built in a steep
amphitheatre of hills*

which the town is set. There are a great many lodges, restaurants and camping grounds, and thanks to a predictable power supply a number of the lodges have evening video entertainment. The town has a post office, bank, money exchange facilities, a **health post** and a **dental clinic**. It also boasts several **cyber cafés**, **telephones** and **fax facilities**. Numerous shops line its narrow streets with a vast range of goods displayed, including postcards, films, medical supplies, food, clothing, paperbacks, souvenirs and all sorts of second-hand expedition equipment. Boots, down jackets and sleeping bags can be rented here.

Saturday is market day. Then the place is crowded with porters and traders, many of whom will have trekked for several days from the foothills carrying *dokos* of fruit or vegetables that are impossible to grow in Khumbu. It's a bright, bustling affair that is often over by midday, followed by Sherpas celebrating with friends from afar in a local *chang* house.

There's also a semi-permanent Tibetan market, manned by Bhotias who bring a variety of often brightly-coloured Chinese-made goods over the Nangpa La at the head of Thame's valley.

As you stand amid the steep-walled horseshoe that curves round Namche, gazing across to the huge wall of Kwangde that soars out of the Bhote Kosi valley west of town, there's an understandable sense of relief that you've made it this far, and a buzz of anticipation for the continuing trek into the fabled country that lies just over the hill.

For most trekkers, especially those walking in from Jiri, Namche has a special appeal. To gain the town is almost a goal in itself. Yet Bill Tilman, one of the first Westerners to arrive here, was peculiarly dismissive: 'Namche Bazar,' he wrote in *Nepal Hiimalaya*, 'has never ranked as a "forbidden city". It is far from being a city, and it has remained unvisited not because of any very serious difficulties in the way, but because no one has thought it worth the trouble of overcoming them.' 'Nevertheless,' he confessed, 'it had for long been my humble Mecca.' Many a trekker would echo those last words.

TIME IN NAMCHE

Because of the altitude it will be necessary to spend at the very minimum two nights here to aid acclimatisation. That does not mean you have to sit around all day in a lodge or restaurant, although it may be tempting to do so. Trek 2 – which leads to Thame in the Bhote Kosi valley – is an excellent way of helping the acclimatisation process. But there are some interesting walks in the neighbourhood of Namche that will also be good for acclimatisation, and at the same time provide a scenic introduction to the high country of Khumbu. The following few paragraphs describe a recommended 3½–4hr circuit that visits two traditional Sherpa villages, provides stunning views, and reaches a high point of about 3870m (12,697ft) at the Japanese-built Everest View Hotel, where you can have lunch on the balcony with one of the world's great mountain panoramas spread before you.

This is a fine way to aid acclimatisation. Take the main Thyangboche trail, which leaves Namche's bowl over its eastern rim near the Sagarmatha National Park headquarters. This is a broad, well-trodden path that soon provides a heart-stopping view of Everest, Nuptse, Lhotse and Ama Dablam walling the Khumbu valley. In mid-distance it may be possible to see the Thyangboche monastery jutting above a wooded ridge. ▶

A memorable view of Everest peering over the Lhotse-Nuptse ridge is gained from the trail above Namche

◄   Continue along the trail for about 1¼hr to reach the lodges of **KYANGJUMA** (3600m: 11,811ft). Just beyond the second lodge take a narrow path climbing to the left. It skirts a number of walled fields, and winds up a scoop of hillside brightened with flame-coloured berberis in the autumn. With magnificent views back to Ama Dablam, you arrive at **KHUMJUNG** (3780m: 12,402ft), a large Sherpa village that appears remarkably unspoilt in its stony hidden valley. Note the *chorten* at the entrance to the village. To the left of this a trail heads up a ridge to the left to service the Everest View Hotel. Before ascending that trail, however, it would be worth exploring Khumjung and the neighbouring village of **KHUNDE** (3841m: 12,602ft) where there's a small **hospital** – another product of Hillary's Himalayan Trust, as is Khumjung's high school. Allow at least 1½hr to explore both these villages. The sacred mountain of the Khumbu, Khumbi Yul Lha (Khumbila for short), rises behind Khumjung, and is seen from almost every part of the Khumbu district.

The trail that links Khumjung and the Japanese hotel is a delight. The ridge is clothed with rhododendrons and stands of pine, and views are consistently dramatic. It leads directly to the 12-room **EVEREST VIEW HOTEL**, but you don't see the building until the very last moment as it has been cleverly designed to blend into the hilltop. ►

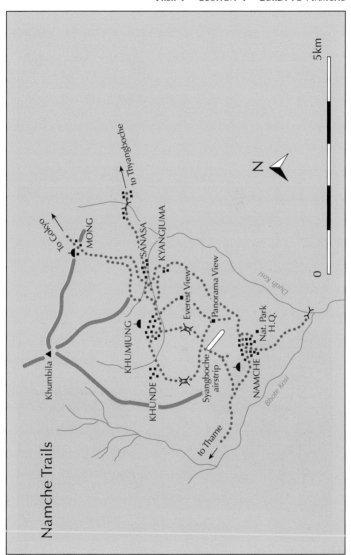

Namche Trails

◄ Typically Japanese in appearance, the main entrance is by a long and elegant flight of steps flanked by shrubs and trees. The surrounding pines seem to have been positioned in order to frame views of Thamserku, Kangtega and Ama Dablam.

Leave the hotel by its main entrance and follow the path leading from it. It reaches a lodge and continues a short distance to the large **SYANG-BOCHE PANORAMA HOTEL**, which has views to rival those of Everest View, but is less expensive for both food and lodging. Lunch in the garden is highly recommended. Just beyond the hotel the path slopes down through shrubbery to reach the end of Syangboche's airstrip. From there you can see Namche steeply below. A variety of trails lead down to it.

The Japanese-built Everest View Hotel enjoys a direct view of Ama Dablam

Note: More direct trails than the one via Kyangjuma lead to both **KHUNDE** and **KHUMJUNG** from Namche. One climbs a steeply-paved trail from a large rock near the top, eastern end of town, approached by way of the Thyangboche trail mentioned above. Leading to the Syangboche airstrip, this is the trail used on descent from the Everest View Hotel. Walk along the airstrip, then find a continuing trail that climbs northeast past a large *chorten* to a 'pass' with breathtaking views and strings of brightly-coloured prayer flags, then down through pinewoods into a glen where Khumjung high school is situated. Bear left for Khunde, right for the trail to Everest View Hotel.

Another route from Namche to Khunde leaves town by a trail above the *gompa*. This also climbs to Syangboche, and continues to gain height in order to cross a wooded ridge to Khunde. Allow about 1½hr from Namche.

KHUMJUNG (3780m: 12,402ft) is also worth considering as a base for one or two nights as an aid to acclimatisation. Less busy and more spacious than Namche it has some comfortable lodges, and also boasts the world's highest bakery, which serves mouth-watering cakes, pastries, gateaux and real coffee. Views from the village are impressive too, especially to Thamserku and Ama Dablam, and almost any walk from here will reward with magnificent panoramas. Several circuits and ridge walks are possible. Try, for example, taking the path which begins near the village high school and climbs by way of a long series of steps to a saddle in the southern pine-topped ridge, marked by a string of prayer flags, from which Everest appears over the Lhotse–Nuptse ridge to the northeast. Sloping gently down now, the path comes to a large *chorten* with Syangboche airstrip below. Either curve left to Syangboche Panorama Hotel and continue beyond on the trail which leads to the Japanese-built Everest View Hotel, and from there descend to the lower end of Khumjung; or bear right to regain the pine-topped ridge above Khunde. Almost everywhere you look mountain views are stunning. (For routes of approach to Khumjung from Namche, see 'Time in Namche' above.)

TREK 2

NAMCHE BAZAAR TO THAME

Thami was an amazing sight. Camped on the broad flat area below the village were thousands of Tibetan refugees who had escaped over the Nangpa La with all their yaks.

Sir Edmund Hillary *View from the Summit*

Trek summary	
Distance	10km (6 miles)
Time	3–4hr (2 days: 1 day there; 1 day back + time in Thame)
Max altitude	Thame (3820m: 12,533ft)
Start	Namche Bazaar (3446m: 11,306ft)
Finish	Thame
Trekking style	Teahouse (lodge accommodation) or camping

The trek to Thame in the valley of the Bhote Kosi north-west of Namche makes an excellent acclimatisation walk.

As Thame is some 370m (1225ft) higher than Namche, and takes from 3–4hr to reach, it is worth spending at least one night there before returning to Namche and then starting one of the higher treks, either to Gokyo or Lobuche for close views of Everest. Headed by the Nangpa La on the Nepal/Tibet border, the Bhote Kosi is a very fine valley, in the lower reaches of which lie a string of villages and several teahouses and lodges. North of Thame, on the way to the Nangpa La, there are as yet no facilities for trekkers, but Thame itself is a pleasant, unspoilt village with glorious views of Thamserku amd Kangtega. Above the village there's an important Buddhist *gompa* where the Mani Rimdu festival is celebrated during the May full moon, and at the head of the Thame Khola valley lies the Trashi Labtsa, a glacier pass that leads to Rolwaling.

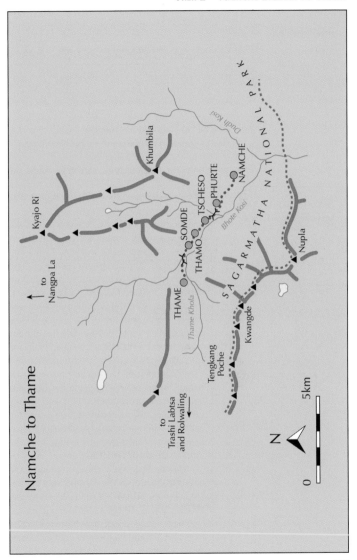

Namche to Thame

Route outline

Route	Distance	Height gain/loss	Time
Namche–Thamo	5km	+46m	1½hr
Thamo–Thame	5km	+327m	1½hr

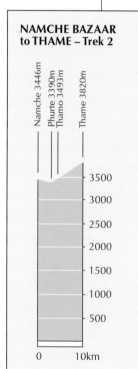

NAMCHE BAZAAR to THAME – Trek 2

Namche 3446m
Phurte 3390m
Thamo 3493m
Thame 3820m

- 3500
- 3000
- 2500
- 2000
- 1500
- 1000
- 500

0   10km

The trail to Thame leaves Namche Bazaar by way of the town's *gompa* on the western side of the horseshoe basin. It continues round the steep hillside and crosses its rim at a confusion of *mani* stones, carved boulders, and prayer flags. Beyond these the trail is reminiscent of an alpine path as it eases through pine and juniper woods with the Bhote Kosi seen as a green ribbon far below. On sunny days this gentle woodland walk makes a very pleasant, undemanding interlude, and after a while it is joined by another trail coming from Syangboche. The first village you reach is **PHURTE** (3390m: 11,122ft), where there's a forest nursery, a few simple teahouses and lodges, and a number of traditional Sherpa houses. *Mani* walls line the path through the village, above which there's a fine *chorten* and splendid views.

The trail loses height and turns several wooded spurs before coming to a narrow side valley whose stream drains the Kyajo glacier. Just before crossing the stream on a wooden cantilever bridge, you pass through a fairly new *kani* and then over the bridge enter the unspoilt village of **TSCHESO**.

Having lost height the continuing route now starts to rise. Turning another spur marked by a *chorten* **THAMO** (3493m: 11,460ft) can be seen ahead. This is a large, strung-out village with a school, lots of *mani* stones, prayer flags and a number of lodges and teahouses. Several houses have chimneys (a rarity in

Nepal); walled fields spread down towards the river, and the offices of the Khumbu Bijuli Company are located here. This is the company responsible for the Thame hydro-electric scheme that was largely funded by an Austrian aid project. Since late 1995 it has provided electricity not only for villages in the Bhote Kosi valley, but also for Namche, Khunde and Khumjung. ▸

Kangtega and Thamserku are both clearly seen from Thame

It's a fairly steep climb out of Thamo, and above the village the trail rises among fields before coming to the houses of **SOMDE** (Samde on some maps). Beyond the last of these a sudden uphill twist of the path takes you onto a high belvedere with slopes of scrub rising to one side, a long drop to the river on the other, and a fine view west that shows the trekking peak of Parchamo on the headwall of Thame's valley.

The name 'Tscheso' does not appear on the maps, but a local lodge owner assured me that Tscheso is how it is known by all who live there.

A short but steep descent leads to a sturdy bridge spanning the furious Bhote Kosi river as it explodes from the confines of a narrow gorge. Immediately before you cross this, the trail passes beneath a huge rockface decorated with three brightly painted Buddhas. Cross the bridge and follow the trail that rises in a few zigzags, then eases at a more comfortable gradient alongside the Thame Khola. Shortly after you come to the walled fields and typical Sherpa homes of **THAME.**

THAME (or Thami; 3820m: 12,533ft) is unlike any other village visited by the main Khumbu treks described in this guide. Although it has two or three lodges and plenty of space for campgrounds, there are practically no other facilities for the trekker, so you can more easily capture a flavour of how the district must have been before adventure tourism discovered it. Thame has a school built by Ed Hillary's Himalayan Trust. The village has long-standing trading links with Tibet, and the large open space in the centre is where Tibetan traders camp after (or before) crossing the Nangpa La, their yaks hobbled in the dust until preparations are made for moving on. There may well be yaks grazing the surrounding hillsides, but potatoes are grown in the walled fields. West of the village, and built in a spectacular position 150m above the fields, Thame's *gompa* enjoys a bird's-eye view over the valley. It is here that the Mani Rimdu festival is celebrated each year in May. The view downvalley from the village itself is truly stunning, with Kangtega, Thamserku and Kusum Kangguru backing the confluence of the Bhote Kosi and Dudh Kosi rivers, while the southern wall of Thame's valley is formed by the multi-peaked Lumding Himal. On this Kwangde Ri claims several summits, all over 6000m (19,685ft) high. Kwangde's western neighbour is Tengkang Poche (6500m: 21,325ft), whose awesome 1600m North-West Face was climbed in 2004. The valley's headwall is unseen from Thame village, but in that headwall lies the 5755m (18,881ft) Trashi Labtsa pass below the trekking peak of Parchamo. Big mountains, of course, form a physical presence and a dramatic backdrop to life in the Khumbu, and many Sherpas now earn their livelihood climbing them. Several villagers from

Thame have become Everest summiteers. Best known, of course, was Tenzing Norgay who made the first ascent with Ed Hillary in 1953. Although Tenzing was actually born in Tibet, he spent his childhood in Thame, and married a local girl, Dawa Phuti. More recently, Ang Rita, another Thame man, became the first person to climb Everest on more than 10 occasions.

Traders from Tibet bring goods by yak over the Nangpa La, and rest for a while at Thame

THE NANGPA LA

At the head of the Bhote Kosi valley in the shadow of Cho Oyu, the glacier pass of the Nangpa La (5716m: 18,753ft) is a long-established trade route between Tibet and Nepal, with Namche being the centre of Sherpa trade between the two countries. Tibetans know the pass as the Khumbu La, or Khumbu Kang La, which translates as the 'Snowy Pass into Khumbu', and it was by this pass that some of the first migrant Sherpa families came to Nepal over 500 years ago. More recently the Nangpa La has become a major conduit for Tibetans fleeing their country in the wake of the Chinese occupation. In 1959 some 5000 refugees fled across this pass, bringing with them their livestock and that much-needed commodity, salt. Other waves of refugees followed as the Chinese occupiers tried to destroy Tibet's culture and religion. Dodging armed guards, the pass was crossed by thousands of Buddhist monks and lay people, sometimes under cover of darkness, often inadequately clothed and risking frostbite, snowblindness and even death, their few possessions tied in bundles of cloth. They would breast the pass and stumble down the crevassed Nangpa glacier, and continue over rocks and moraine debris until a real path was traced that would bring them to the safety of Thame and the lower valley. Passing through Khumbu, the refugees would traipse down to Solu district where many would rest for a while in the Junbesi valley, then continue to Kathmandu and, eventually, to Dharamsala in India where the Dalai Lama's government in exile is centred.

YAKS, NAKS AND ZOPKYOS

Don't jump to conclusions – that 'yak' you see carrying a load for a trekking party is probably a crossbreed called a *zopkyo*. A true yak is a handsome, long-haired, wide-horned bull of the *Bos grunniens* species, and his female counterpart is a *nak*. Cross a yak or a *nak* with a Nepalese cow or bull and you'll have an infertile *zopkyo* (male) or a *dzum* if a female is produced. Not usually found below about 3500m (11,483ft), the true domesticated yak is a multi-purpose beast, used for load-carrying or pulling a plough; in summer its moulting hair is combed out and woven into blankets or ropes, and its dung is an important source of fuel. Milk from the *nak* and *dzum* is used to make butter or cheese (never ask for yak cheese!), while the comparatively docile *zopkyo* is mostly a beast of burden.

TREK 3

NAMCHE BAZAAR (OR KHUMJUNG) TO GOKYO

These peaks are nearer Heaven than earth below,
'Tis the blue floor of Heaven that they upbear,
And, like some old and wildly rugged stair,
They lift us to the land where all is fair,
The land of which I dream.

Horatius Bonar

Trek summary	
Distance	22km (13½ miles)
Time	3–4 days
Max altitude	Gokyo (4750m: 15,584ft)
Start	Namche Bazaar (3446m: 11,306ft) or Khumjung (3780m: 12,402ft)
Finish	Gokyo
Trekking style	Teahouse (lodge accommodation) or camping

With its enticing side glens, a string of turquoise lakes, Nepal's longest glacier and an arc of snow mountains, the Gokyo valley is arguably the most attractive in the Khumbu.

At its head, Cho Oyu and the lofty ice ridge that links the world's sixth-highest mountain with graceful Gyachung Kang, spawns the great Ngozumpa glacier. While Cho Oyu is a big snow massif casting out long ridge systems along the Nepal/Tibet border, the angular Gyachung Kang is built on steep walls, buttresses and clusters of ice. To the south of that is the glacial Nup La, first crossed in 1952 by Ed Hillary, George Lowe and three Sherpas. From it the international frontier continues in a long curve southeastwards to Pumori and Everest,

Gokyo, the upper valley of the Dudh Kosi, is a trekker's wonderland.

143

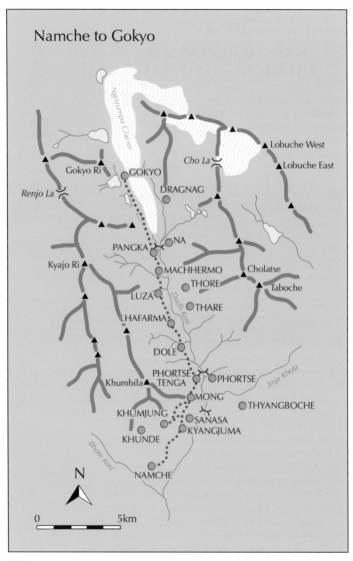

Namche to Gokyo

but a secondary ridge system breaks away to form the Gokyo valley's east wall; a wall punctuated by the singularly impressive Cholatse and Taboche.

The valley's west wall may not be as high as its counterpart to the east, but it's not without appeal. At its southern end rise rocky spires of Khumbila; viewed from some angles these are reminiscent of the Chamonix aiguilles in the French Alps. Of special beauty is the Machhermo glen with Kyajo Ri at its head, while north of this the 5417m (17,772ft) Renjo La provides a link with the Bhote Kosi valley.

Draining down the centre of the Gokyo valley the Ngozumpa glacier is covered with rubble and several coffee-colored lakes being carried slowly downvalley. The ablation trough running along its western edge is brightened by a series of beautiful tarns, and it is beside one of these that the Gokyo lodges are found. Overlooking this tarn (Dudh Pokhari) on its northern side, Gokyo Ri makes a strong claim to be the best accessible viewpoint in Nepal, for not only does it have

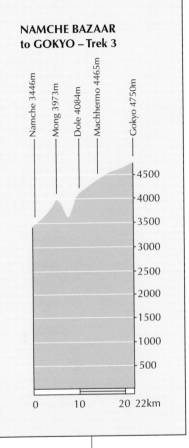

four 8000m peaks in its summit panorama, but seemingly dozens of 6000m peaks that crowd each horizon.

Beyond the glacier's snout the Dudh Kosi digs a deep and narrow trench as it works its way south before being swollen by the Imja Khola below Thyangboche's wooded spur. Hundreds of metres above the river, trails lead along terraces on both sides of the valley. Along the western flank there are lodges, teahouses and yak pastures. On the eastern side a handful of small villages are set in glorious isolation, at first glance untouched by tourism.

Careful acclimatisation is essential for safe trekking here. Elevation gain can be rapid, for the trekking stages are comparatively short and it's tempting to push on farther than would be good for you. It is all too easy to succumb to mountain sickness on this trek, and you would be wise to follow the advice of the Himalayan Rescue Association: do not set out from Namche or Khumjung until you've spent at least two nights there. If you flew in to Lukla it may well be necessary to spend a further day acclimatising.

Allow a minimum of three days to reach Gokyo, spending time perhaps in Phortse Tenga, Dole and Machhermo on the way. Inevitably you will arrive at your chosen lodge or campsite early in the day, but it is important that you resist the temptation to push on upvalley. Act with patience and prudence and you'll have enough energy to enjoy exploration of the upper valley when you get there.

While facilities are steadily improving, most lodges here are fairly primitive when compared with those in Namche, but they should be more than adequate for most trekkers' requirements. In the high season those lodges with a good reputation fill very quickly. Campsites are plentiful.

Route outline

Route	Distance	Height gain/loss	Time
Section 1 12km/7½miles			
Namche–Phortse Tenga	7km	527m (–330m)	3–3½hr
Phortse Tenga–Dole	4km	441m	2–2½hr
Section 2 12km/7½miles			
Dole–Machhermo	5km	381m	2–2½hr
Machhermo–Gokyo	7km	285m	3–3½hr

SECTION 1

Namche Bazaar to Dole

Distance	12km (7½ miles)
Time	1–2 days
Start altitude	3446m (11,306ft)
High point	Dole (4084m: 13,399ft)

This first stage of the Gokyo trek is a scenically extravagant one with views of Kangtega, Thamserku, Ama Dablam, Nuptse, Lhotse and Everest. From Namche to Kyangjuma the route is shared with the trail to Thyangboche, Pangboche and Lobuche, but shortly after passing the Kyangjuma lodges, you leave the main trail to begin a long climb to the Mong Danda, beyond which you enter the Gokyo valley. With Dole being more than 600m higher than Namche, it's essential to adhere to the rules of acclimatisation to enjoy continued safe trekking. Unless you are acclimatised before leaving Namche, consider breaking the route at Phortse Tenga. Take your time, enjoy the magnificent scenery, and remember to drink frequently along the way.

Namche Bazaar to Phortse Tenga (3–3½hr)

Leave Namche on the classic Everest trail, which climbs over the eastern rim of the township's bowl near the National Park headquarters. Having made that initial climb the trail now contours gently round the hillside and on turning a spur presents you with a magnificent view that will probably stop you in your tracks. Everest is seen peering over the ridge linking Nuptse and Lhotse, while Ama Dablam imposes its graceful personality on the whole valley.

The path curves into the hillside, then rounds another spur marked by a large white *chorten* and strings of coloured prayer flags. The *chorten* was erected to

Porters on the trail near Kyangjuma – Everest, Lhotse and Ama Dablam look on

commemorate the 50th anniversary of Everest's first ascent, and to honour Tenzing Norgay and the Everest Sherpas. Once again, this is a wonderful viewpoint; from it you continue high above the Dudh Kosi, and a little over 1hr from Namche come to a high point, after which the trail eases downhill among rhododendrons, trees and berberis shrubs. Pass the two lodges of **KYANGJUMA** (3600m: 11,811ft) that exploit a direct view of Ama Dablam, and keep ahead for a very short distance, still sloping downhill among rhododendrons, then cross a stream coming from Khumjung. A few paces beyond this the trail forks. One path cuts back to the left and is signed to Khumjung, but for Gokyo take the alternative left-hand path which slants off ahead – this is also signed. (The main trail continues to Sanasa, then descends to the river on the way to Thyangboche.)

The Gokyo path climbs steeply above the lodges of **SANASA**, and in another 10min brings you to a major crossing trail (the path from Khumjung). Bear right along it.

ROUTE FROM KHUMJUNG

Go down from the village to its eastern end where there is a large *chorten* near the last of the houses. The trail forks by a small house. Take the left-hand option which heads northeastwards along the slopes of Khumbila. The path forks again, although it may not be an obvious junction. Both trails lead to the Gokyo valley; the narrow upper route is less used than the alternative, for it mounts a very steep stairway of stone slabs (avoid if you have problems with vertigo) and eventually joins the main route some way before Mong. The main path at the junction very soon joins the Namche–Gokyo route described above.

Before long you climb a fairly steep flight of steps created up a band of rock, above which the path eases on a steady slanting ascent of open hillside with consistently fine views. Ama Dablam is a constant distraction; the village of Phortse can be seen on a sloping apron of

Mong marks the gateway to the Gokyo valley

land across the mouth of the Gokyo valley, while Thyangboche monastery is also visible on its wooded ridge to the east. Angling across the hillside the trail leads directly to a spur of Khumbila upon which there's a large white *chorten*, a few simple lodges, and yet more magnificent views of Ama Dablam, Kangtega and Thamserku, with Thyangboche below and directly across the valley. Reached in 2–2½hr from Namche, this small ridge-crest settlement is known as **MONG** (Mong Danda; 3973m: 13,035ft), the birthplace of the revered Lama Sange Dorje who, it is said, brought Buddhism to the Khumbu.

Crossing the spur here you enter the Gokyo valley with a steep descent by way of a series of zigzags that lose 300m or so of height before coming to a trail junction at **PHORTSE TENGA.**

PHORTSE TENGA (3643m: 11,952ft) consists of just two or three simple lodges. There used to be a National Park checkpost and an army post a little farther along the trail; these were both abandoned but remained intact on my last visit. Several metres below the lodges there are some good campsites on both banks of the river. Another very simple lodge on the east bank is backed by one of these sites. The bridge which spans the Dudh Kosi here carries a trail up to the lovely Sherpa village of Phortse on the east flank of the valley, which is visited on Trek 5.

Phortse Tenga to Dole (2–2½hr)
The continuing trail climbs away from the lodges of Phortse Tenga, passing through light rhododendron woods. About 15min later you come to the two remote outpost buildings, the first owned by the National Park, the second by the Nepalese army, from which you can see Cho Oyu for the first time at the head of the valley. From here to Dole will take another 1½–2hr.

The route makes some twisting ascents through woodland, and a steeper climb in the open. It crosses a number of streams, passes below long ribbon waterfalls, and often rewards with wonderful views back to

Trekkers contemplate the scene on the trail from Phortse Tenga to Dole

Thamserku and Kangtega. Not long after crossing a small yak pasture with a solitary herder's hut (**TONGBA**), the trail makes a hillside traverse, crosses a minor ridge, then enters the pastureland of **DOLE** with its handful of lodges and plenty of camping spaces.

DOLE (4084m: 13,399ft) is likely to be considerably colder than Namche or Phortse Tenga, especially when afternoon mists descend on the pastures. It's possible that you may also be feeling the altitude here. If you are suffering any of the symptoms of mild mountain sickness, do not proceed upvalley until they have gone. If symptoms persist, or increase in discomfort, return downvalley at least as far as Phortse Tenga where you will hopefully experience an improvement. Like other lodge settlements in the valley, Dole began as a *kharka*, or yak pasture with a few herders' huts, but once Gokyo was discovered as a trekking destination, lodges soon sprang up. Most of the lodges here stand high above the stream that drains through the scooped pastureland, but others are being built on the north bank as the valley grows in popularity. From Dole exciting views back to the south reveal the impressive shapes of Kangtega and Thamserku, while Cho Oyu spreads its white ridge across the valley to the north.

SECTION 2

Dole to Gokyo

Distance	12km (7½ miles)
Time	2 days
Start altitude	4084m (13,399ft)
High point	Gokyo (4750m: 15,584ft)

Between Dole and Gokyo the essence of the valley is revealed. It has a wild kind of beauty that gives it a sense of remoteness, despite the increasing number of lodges and trekkers on the trail. The avenue of peaks through which you make your way may not be familiar by name, but many have a stately, almost defiant appearance that adds to the valley's allure. Taboche and Cholatse are especially dramatic, while other highlights on this section include Machhermo's side glen, and the string of lakes in the ablation valley leading to Gokyo's lodge settlement.

Dole to Machhermo (2–2½hr)

Prospects of another short 2½hr day may not seem inspiring, but the demands of acclimatisation make this a necessity. The walk itself is a delight, and as there's such a brief distance to cover there's no need to scurry along the trail. If the weather's in your favour take your time, enjoy the views and let the day take care of itself. However, if you've the energy when you get to Machhermo, you may be tempted to spend some of the day exploring the magnificent tributary glen that projects behind it. It is one of the finest in all Khumbu.

Beyond the first of Dole's lodges the trail goes down the slope, crosses a stream, then swings right to climb round a shoulder of hillside, rising steadily with the great snowy block of Cho Oyu visible again at the head of the valley. The route crosses an undulating pastureland marked out with drystone walls and with several yak-herders' huts dotted around.

In a little under 1hr you will come to the Mountain View Top Hill Lodge, situated by a large boulder adorned with prayer flags. The trail continues past a few more stone-built huts, including the Holyday Inn at a place known as **LHAFARMA**, then contours along the hillside before descending into a small basin with yet more drystone walls, stone huts and lodges.

LUZA (4390m: 14,403ft) is reached about 1hr 45min from Dole. Another *kharka*, like Dole this has become the site for a possible overnight stay. Since the lodges at

Dole and Machhermo can be very busy in the autumn trekking season, Luza makes a tempting alternative.

The path rises out of the northern side of the basin to cross more high pastureland, the far side of which is marked by a *chorten* and prayer flags. There are splendid views: upvalley, across the valley, and back through the valley towards Kangtega. From the *chorten* you also look down into the tributary glen at whose entrance sit the lodges of Machhermo. At the head of the glen a spectacular rock peak soars above the moraines; on the eastern side of the Gokyo valley Taboche and Cholatse are majestic, while the Dudh Kosi is blocked at its head by Cho Oyu and Gyachung Kang. Sloping down into the glen the trail crosses a stream, then rises up a short slope to the yak pastures and lodges of **MACHHERMO**.

MACHHERMO (4465m: 14,649ft) enjoys an idyllic location, partially sheltered from the wind by steep hillside spurs to north and south, and with a tremendous view into the rocky amphitheatre that blocks the glen to the west. Campers can gain additional shelter by pitching

Machhermo, a yak pasture turned lodge settlement on the way to Gokyo

their tents beside the stone walls, while teahouse trekkers will find that most of the lodges here, though basic, are comfortable enough and run by friendly Sherpanis. There is now a large and more fanciful lodge which quickly fills with trekkers. Community Action Nepal, a charity founded by mountaineer Doug Scott, has built a porters' shelter and **health post** here. Tibetan snowcocks can sometimes be seen and heard here.

THE MACHHERMO YETI

Machhermo was the setting for one of Nepal's more believable yeti stories. In the summer of 1974 a Sherpa girl was tending her yaks there when a brown-haired yeti knocked her down the slope towards the stream. No doubt terrified, she watched as her attacker proceeded to break the necks of three yaks by twisting their horns, before loping back up the hillside. The Sherpani hastened to Khunde where she told her story to the police, who then investigated and found tracks similar to others photographed by Western mountaineers.

This story, which has been repeated in various books, was told to me by a sirdar whilst seated in a simple lodge kitchen not far from where the incident supposedly occurred. The dancing light of a yak-dung fire threw shadows around the room. Squatting by the fire preparing my meal the *didi* nodded agreement with every sentence of the tale being told. There was no doubting that both the sirdar and the lodge-keeping Sherpani believed in both the existence of the yeti, and this particular story. And when later I had to leave the warmth of my sleeping bag to attend a call of nature outside, I nervously shone my headtorch into the shadows with every sound that disturbed the frost-gripped night!

Machhermo to Gokyo (3–3½hr)
This is another short stage, during which the trek from Machhermo presents a constantly changing landscape. There are broad pastures, narrow clefts with steeply climbing trails, an icy stream to cross, stony wastes and the banks of tarns and lakes to wander by as you progress through an ablation valley beside the Ngozumpa glacier to reach Gokyo.

Immediately behind the northernmost Machhermo lodges the Gokyo trail climbs round the hillside spur to regain views of Cho Oyu. Now the route makes a steady contour and in about 30min or so reaches a *kharka* and three simple lodges which, following a tragic avalanche which killed more than 40 people (trekkers, crew and locals) here in November 1995, have been relocated to a safer site. This is **PANGKA** (4548m: 14,921ft). From it you gaze directly ahead at the terminal moraine that closes off the end of the Ngozumpa glacier.

Beyond the lodges the way slopes briefly downhill, then climbs through the ablation valley on the western side of the glacier on a much-improved trail. Staying close to the rock wall on the left, the way can be icy, so caution is advised.

Picking its way up stone steps, steeply in places, the trail then swings to the right to cross a stream on a short wooden bridge. Cairns guide the continuing route through a stony landscape with a small tarn (Longponga) on the left. The valley broadens and the trail meanders easily through, bringing you to a second tarn, much

The Gokyo valley is transformed after a three-day dump of snow

larger than the first. This is Taboche Tscho, or Taujun at 4740m (15,551ft).

Beyond this the way eases through a narrower section of the ablation valley where a spur of mountain projects from the left. As you emerge from it so you come to a third lake, known as the Dudh Pokhari, turquoise in colour and reflecting the white face of Cho Oyu seen ahead. On the eastern shore prayer flags add colour to the scene, and just beyond you'll come to the cluster of lodges of **GOKYO**, with the moraine wall rising behind them.

GOKYO (4750m: 15,584ft) is the valley's last lodge settlement, and it is invariably crowded during the main trekking seasons. Since groups trekking in the Khumbu often use lodges in preference to camping, some leaders will send a Sherpa ahead to block-book a particular lodge in Gokyo, which can be frustrating for individual

Prayer flags welcome trekkers to Gokyo

trekkers who arrive there to find beds at a premium. Accommodation facilities are increasing, however, as new lodges are built, and there's also a number of camping areas. Some of the lodges are reasonably warm but smoky; others are rather basic and very cold. My wife and I stayed in one lodge when the temperature fell overnight *inside* our room, to minus 16°C! Gokyo Resort has a greenhouse-style building attached to it that becomes very warm during the day when the sun has been on it; the annexe was built as a meteorology hut for Leo Dickinson's balloon flight over Everest in 1991. The same lodge has a small shop with a variety of goods for sale – everything from Cadbury's chocolate (made in India) to hot water bottles and batteries. Several other lodges also have modest shops with a few 'luxury items' for sale.

TIME IN GOKYO

The assumption is made that you'll spend at least two nights in Gokyo, but should you have sufficient time it would be worth staying longer, for there's plenty to do and to see here. The following suggestions merely hint at the possibilities.

Ngozumpa glacier moraine

The first suggestion is to go up onto the crest of the moraine wall immediately behind the lodges. It will only take a few minutes to reach the top, but once there you have an incredible view across the dirty grey, rubble-strewn Ngozumpa glacier to the great cocked-hat peak of Cholatse (6335m: 20,784ft) and its neighbour, Taboche (Taweche 6367m: 20,889ft). Views downvalley are equally impressive where Thamserku and Kangtega are once more in view. Upvalley it's Cho Oyu yet again that dominates the view.

A trail heads north along the very crest and brings you to a viewpoint overlooking a fourth lake, Tonak Tsho, at 4870m (15,978ft). From here you can descend into the ablation valley and walk back to Gokyo. This is an easy, short walk that is ideal to help acclimatise to the altitude, and it's worth tackling on the afternoon of arrival to help unravel some of the geography of the area.

Upper Lakes and Cho Oyu Base Camp

Beyond Gokyo several more lakes, of varying sizes, are found on the western side of the glacier. To explore them properly will take a full day at least. If you take a tent and supplies with you it's possible to spend time in the Cho Oyu Base Camp area where there is a cluster of six tarns and some tremendous wild mountain views. If you're fully acclimatised it would still be worth making a visit to them, even if you have to return to the Gokyo lodges the same day. But do carry food and plenty of liquid refreshment with you, plus a first aid kit and warm clothing.

The fourth lake in the valley has already been mentioned as being on view during a short walk along the moraine crest. A fifth lake known as Ngozumpa lies beyond that at about 4990m (16,371ft), about halfway between the fourth lake and Cho Oyu Base Camp. This is also worth a visit in its own right, for a viewpoint above it provides another surprise panorama with Everest drawing your attention. Some reckon it's even better than from either Gokyo Ri or Kala Pattar.

Between the fourth and fifth lakes a scramble up a slope of boulders promises even more extensive views, and will give a good day's exercise – but only if you're well acclimatised. ▸

The Ngozumpa glacier and turquoise lakes of the Gokyo ablation valley, spread below Gokyo Ri

Everest, viewed from Gokyo Ri

Ascent of Gokyo Ri (5340m: 17,520ft)

The ascent of Gokyo Ri (or Gokyo Kala Pattar as it's also sometimes known) cannot be recommended too highly. With some justification it is the highlight of most trekkers' visits to the valley, for the summit panorama is classed as one of the truly great Himalayan views, and one that rivals the better-known Kala Pattar above Gorak Shep.

Gokyo Ri is the obvious hill that rises directly above the lake's northern shore, and from the lodges you can clearly see the paths that snake up its southern flanks. There are no technical difficulties in the ascent, but there's a height gain of 549m (1801ft) to face. If you go early (say an hour or so before dawn) you stand a good chance of enjoying the summit in wind-free conditions. Afternoon clouds often clothe the mountain, but by sunset they've usually gone. Sunrise can be spectacular, while sunset views are supposedly very fine from the top; but if you plan to experience them, don't forget to take a torch with you to see your way down in the dark.

The path of ascent begins on the far side of the stream that feeds into the lake. At first there are numerous strands to this path, but inevitably they all converge towards the summit. This is marked by large cairns and streamers of prayer flags (1½–3hr from Gokyo).

A 360° panorama rewards those who get to the top on a clear day. Not only is Mount Everest clearly seen in the east, but also an outstanding galaxy of peaks: Lhotse, Makalu, Thamserku, Kangtega, Ama Dablam, Cho Oyu, Ngozumpa Kang, Gyachung Kang and many more fill every horizon. Far below Gokyo's lake is a turquoise jewel, while the grey glacier has a desolate appearance, the dirty tarns lying upon it making it seem even more so. But above the glacier Cholatse and Taboche make up for that.

Renjo La (5345m: 17,536ft)

To the west of Gokyo the spectacular Renjo La (Renjo Pass) provides a rarely used crossing to the Bhote Kosi valley above Thame (see Trek 2). By this way a return to Namche could be made in two very long and demanding days; thus creating a challenging circuit. Descent on the Bhote Kosi side is difficult and with danger from stonefall, and you'll need to camp out as Thame's lodges are too far for most trekkers to reach in one day. Alternatively, make the ascent to the pass (2½–3hr) as a day trip from Gokyo. There's not a path, as such, but cairns guide the way. Views are tremendous.

Notes on Gokyo's mountains

From Cho Oyu to Makalu the range is known as the Mahalungar Himal, and it includes four of the world's collection of 8000m (26,247ft) peaks: Cho Oyu, Mount Everest, Lhotse and Makalu.

At the head of Gokyo's valley **CHO OYU** (8153m: 26,749ft) is said to be the easiest 8000m peak, in climbing terms, and one that attracted attention almost as soon as Nepal became open to visitors from the West. Eric Shipton's party studied it in 1952 after their Everest reconnaissance, and made a half-hearted assault, which failed. The Swiss Raymond Lambert led an unsuccessful attempt in 1954. At the same time a small party consisting of the Austrians Herbert Tichy and Sepp Jochler, with Pasang Dawa Lama, reached the summit without supplementary oxygen after illegally crossing into Tibet by the Nangpa La (see *Cho Oyu By Favour of the Gods* by Herbert Tichy: Methuen, 1957). It has since received many ascents and now regularly appears on the list of big peaks being guided by commercial organisations.

Near-neighbour to Cho Oyu is the lovely **GYACHUNG KANG** (7922m: 25,991ft). Although it appears a formidable objective as it soars above the glaciers, its North-West Ridge provides a surprisingly straightforward route which was climbed by a Japanese expedition in 1964.

CHOLATSE (6335m: 20,784ft) is shown as Jobo Lhaptshan on the Schneider *Khumbu Himal* map, although it's hardly ever called by this name. Rising south of the Cho La it received its first ascent in 1982 by the Anglo-American rope of John Roskelly, Vernon Clevinger, Galen Rowell and Bill O'Connor. Its highly impressive North-East Face overlooks Dzonglha in the Chola valley.

TABOCHE (or Taweche) is a very distinctive mountain of 6367m (20,889ft), and a close neighbour of Cholatse. One glance is sufficient to appreciate that its routes are severely challenging. After Sir Edmund Hillary's American-New Zealand team made an

Cho Oyu, seen from the rubble-strewn Ngozumpa glacier

unsuccessful attempt in 1963, Taboche was put out of bounds to further climbing expeditions on religious grounds. However, in 1974 Yannick Seigneur and a group of Chamonix guides made a clandestine ascent of the South-East Face. When the Nepalese authorities found out, Seigneur fled the country and was subsequently fined and banned from Nepal for five years. The mountain was later 'reopened' and the second ascent was made (legally) by four Japanese climbers in 1985.

The trail to Dragnag descends the west bank moraine onto the Ngozumpa glacier

WAYS OUT

The route by which you leave Gokyo depends very much on your plans for the next few days. If your trekking is nearly over and you need to get back to Namche fairly soon, your best bet will be to head downvalley on the easy-to-follow **west bank** trail – reversing Trek 3. If you still have a few days left and wish to visit Thyangboche before leaving Khumbu, there's a fine alternative route down the Gokyo valley on its **eastern side** (Trek 5). Should you plan to visit Kala Pattar or the Everest Base Camp region, you have two options: the direct route over the 5420m (17,782ft) **Cho La** (Trek 4), or the longer but no less enjoyable valley route which is an extension of the east-flank route mentioned above (fully described as Trek 5).

TREK 4

GOKYO TO LOBUCHE
VIA CHO LA

The Nepalese mountains were a rich jumble of mouldings, chiselled and forged and welded strangely as far as the eye could reach.

Wilfred Noyce *South Col*

Trek summary	
Distance	20km (12½ miles)
Time	3 days
Max altitude	Cho La (5420m: 17,782ft)
Start	Gokyo (4750m: 15,584ft)
Finish	Lobuche (4930m: 16,175ft)
Trekking style	Teahouse (simple lodge accommodation) or camping

If trekking with porters, ensure they are adequately clothed and equipped, and take an ice axe and rope for security on this – at times – demanding route.

First reached, but not crossed, by Tom Bourdillon and Michael Ward in 1951, the glacier pass of the Cho La (Chhugyuma La) offers a direct route between Gokyo and the upper Khumbu valley. It's a fairly demanding route, with a very steep and rocky ascent from the west, a glacier at the col and on its eastern side, followed by a steep and possibly icy descent into the Chola (Tschola) valley which drains into the Khumbu. Under good settled conditions, experienced and well-acclimatised parties should encounter no great difficulties, but in low cloud route-finding could be problematic, while recent snowfall can make conditions treacherous. **If in doubt about conditions, do not attempt this crossing**. Lodge accommodation on both sides of the pass is somewhat basic, and it can be quite a tough day's trek from the Dragnag lodges on the Gokyo side, to those of Dzonglha. Teahouse trekkers should therefore be prepared to make

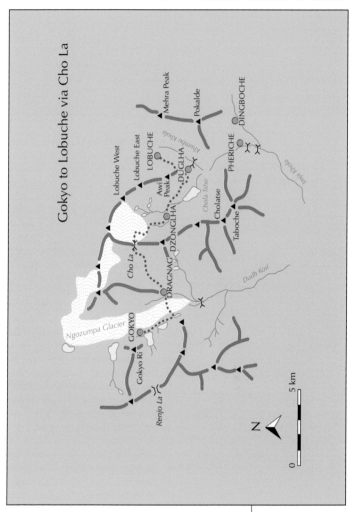

Gokyo to Lobuche via Cho La

Mehra Peak

Pokalde

DINGBOCHE

Lobuche West

Lobuche East

LOBUCHE

PHERICHE

Awi Peak

DUGLHA

Khumbu Khola

Imja Khola

Chola Tsho

Cholatse

DZONGNAG

Cho La

Taboche

DRAGNAG

Dudh Kosi

Ngozumpa Glacier

GOKYO

Gokyo Ri

Renjo La

N

5 km

0

an early start on the day of the actual crossing. Camping below the pass is in a boulder-strewn ablation valley, but you're spoilt for choice in the glorious Chola valley.

Route outline			
Route	Distance	Height gain/loss	Time
Gokyo–Dragnag–Phedi	7km	280m/–100m	3–4hr
Phedi–Cho La–Dzonglha	7km	490m/–590m	4–6hr
Dzonglha–Lobuche	6km	330m/–230	2–3hr

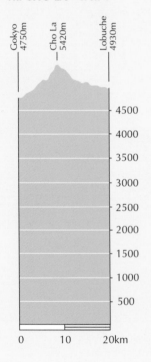

GOKYO to LOBUCHE via CHO LA – Trek 4

Gokyo 4750m — Cho La 5420m — Lobuche 4930m

Gokyo to Phedi (3–4hr)

Leaving Gokyo wander downvalley to the second lake, the Taboche Tsho, and continue beyond its southern end to where a cairn marks the point where the trail forks. Branch left ahead to make an easy rising slant across the slope, to crest the moraine wall at a little 'saddle' from where you have a splendid view along the length of the Ngozumpa glacier to Cho Oyu, and across to the southeast to Cholatse and Taboche. The way now curves a little to the right and descends onto the glacier, where an obvious path (clearly seen from the moraine crest) weaves a route around ice cliffs, over rocky lumps, skirts above small lakes and crosses flats of glacial sand. Views are impressive in every direction.

It takes about 30–45min to cross the glacier to the steep left bank lateral moraine, and once over this you descend into the broad ablation valley that opens below **DRAGNAG**. The low stone buildings and walled fields can be seen from the moraine, and it only takes a few minutes to reach them.

DRAGNAG (Tagnag; 4690m: 15,387ft) consists of three simple lodges and a couple of huts. The fields just below the buildings, apparently, are the highest in which potatoes are grown in the Khumbu. Behind the huts and lodges a narrow glen entices the route to the hidden valley which lies below the Cho La.

The continuing trail starts behind the uppermost lodge and rises steadily. Under normal snowfree conditions the way is obvious, and after 30min or so it swings slightly left to climb a projecting ridge of lateral moraine from whose crest, marked by a cairn, you gain a first view of the Cho La across a previously hidden ablation valley. A narrow cleft above a steep rock wall with a reddish band, it looks quite formidable from here, and it's worth making a note of the route to it. To the left (north), at the head of this valley, a snow-covered glacier can be seen which signals another pass to the right of the Kangchung peaks, while the valley itself drains gently to the right where, out of sight, it feeds into the Gokyo valley below Na.

At Dragnag, yak dung is piled high in readiness for use on the cooking fires

The view west from the Cho La

The trail now descends into that valley and crosses a few streams, then comes to a rough area of rocks and boulders directly below the pass. Sometimes known as Cho La Base Camp, it's also referred to as **PHEDI**, which means 'at the foot of the hill'. This is gained in about 1½–2hr from Dragnag.

PHEDI (c4930m: 16,175ft) has several places for tents among the boulders, but few of these are level. A water supply is found a short way below.

Phedi to Dzonglha (4–6hr)

The climb to the pass is very steep in places, and if the upper rocks are glazed with ice, extra caution will be called for. A trodden path begins the ascent by climbing a steep ramp of moraine debris, after which a line of cairns guides the route among boulders to the steep rock wall that guards the Cho La. There is some danger of stonefall, so keep alert. The trail tacks to and fro up the right-hand side of an open gully; sometimes on decent rock, at other times on scree, glacial sand or grit. Views

grow in extent back across the Gokyo valley as you gain
height – Khumbila above Namche is one of the most
attractive mountains in that view. It will take from 1–2hr
to reach the pass from Phedi, the final 50m or so being
the most draining.

The **CHO LA** (5420m: 17,782ft) is adorned with brightly
coloured prayer flags strung across the rocks of the pass.
The pass is known by Sherpas as the Chhugyuma La, but
most Western trekkers refer to it as the Cho La, or Cho La
Pass. Directly ahead there's a bergschrund to be crossed
to get onto the near-level glacier, but this should not be
problematic. On the far eastern side of this glacier rise
the majestic Lobuche peaks; beyond them can be seen
Everest, Nuptse and Lhotse and a brief glimpse of
Makalu. Back in the west Gokyo's walling peaks are
crowded by others of the Rolwaling Himal.

Cross the bergschrund onto the snow-covered
glacier, but keep to its southern (right-hand) side and
beware of any crevasses. There's usually an obvious
trench-like path where other trekkers have gone. The way
curves to the right and slopes downhill – take care when

*Chola Tsho and
Ama Dablam*

icy, and give assistance to porters where necessary. On coming to the rocks at the end of the glacier there are one or two steep and tricky sections to descend before reaching easier ground. Remain close to the right-hand rock wall where cairns and signs of a path lead down. Views ahead are now magnificent, as you gaze into the enticing Chola valley graced by the jade-green Chola Tscho lake. The valley is walled on the right by Cholatse and Taboche, and on the left by Loboche East, while in the distance ahead Ama Dablam presents a graceful pyramid shape above the Khumbu valley. The mountain is almost unrecognisable from this angle; its distinctive 'armchair' pose – when seen from near Namche – is completely lost in this view.

The steep descent continues in a series of rocky 'steps' consisting of boulders and glacier-smoothed slabs, until you come onto a crest of old moraine rib where the now-easy path takes you down to the valley bed. The rest of the day's trek to Dzonglha takes you through this lovely valley, and with all difficulties now behind you, you can amble along and enjoy the views which are truly stunning.

Towards the southern end of a long stretch of pasture, the path crosses the stream and makes a brief rise over an ancient mound of terminal moraine, across which you come to **DZONGLHA**.

DZONGLHA (4830m: 15,846ft) consists of two simple lodges and camping grounds in a walled enclosure. If you are camping it might be better to continue downhill to more yak pastures where there's a ready water supply. Otherwise members of the trek crew will have to descend some way to collect it. Dzonglha has a terrific close view of Cholatse's intimidating North-East Face, while ahead Ama Dablam continues to attract your attention. The Chola Tsho lake lies below to the southeast.

Dzonglha to Lobuche (2–3hr)

It's just a morning's walk to Lobuche, the penultimate group of lodges on the way to Everest Base Camp and

Trekkers' camp below Dzonglha, backed by Cholatse

Kala Pattar, but there's an alternative way down to the Khumbu valley for those who have no need to go to Lobuche, but plan instead to return to Namche. This option is noted below.

Departing the lodges at Dzonglha, a clear path descends southeastward to cross the stream, and continues down the left-hand side of the valley staying well above the Chola Tsho. There's a short stretch of rising traverse, followed by a steepish descent into a basin, then the way angles uphill again to turn a spur, around which the path forks. The right branch here is the one to take if you intend to return to Namche without going first to Lobuche. Down in the Khumbu valley the buildings and low stone walls of Pheriche are clearly seen backed by a large moraine; the path to Namche goes via that village.

For Lobuche remain on the upper path contouring to another spur which makes a wonderful vantage point. On turning this spur you enter the upper Khumbu valley and catch a first view of Pumori at its head, with the dark hill of Kalar Pattar below it. The Tibetan border runs along the ridge to the right of Pumori, but although Everest is along that ridge and only a comparatively short distance from Pumori, it cannot be seen from here. Nuptse can, and so can the awesome upper pyramid of Lhotse.

It's an undulating trail that now takes you high above the main route taken by most trekkers between Pheriche and Lobuche, but eventually it slopes downhill to join that route in the stony bed of the valley. Here the trail rises very gently, with the valley's headwall drawing you on. Then the way curves to the left, and suddenly just ahead you discover the lodges of **LOBUCHE**.

LOBUCHE (4930m: 16,175ft) is where most trekkers (independents as well as trekking groups) choose to stay before tackling Kala Pattar or Everest Base Camp, since the Gorak Shep alternative is notoriously cold. Because of this Lobuche is growing, and lodge standards slowly improving after years of poor sanitation and very basic amenities; the upmarket Eco Lodge is showing the way. There are a few reasonable sites for camping, but you'll need good sleeping bags to stand a chance of a comfortable night's sleep here.

The Italian Pyramid research station and lodge near Lobuche

For the continuing route to Gorak Shep, Kala Pattar and Everest Base Camp, please see Trek 6.

Lobuche

THE EVEREST MARATHON

A biennial Everest Marathon takes place on even-numbered years alternating between November and May. After allowing sufficient time to acclimatise, competitors race the 42km (26 miles) from Gorak Shep down past Lobuche and through the Khumbu valley via Pangboche and Thyangboche to Namche, then continue as far as Thamo in the valley of the Bhote Kosi before returning to cross the finishing line in the Sherpa 'capital'. The winner's time is usually around 4hr. On your return from Gorak Shep or Lobuche, that sort of timing will either inspire or appal you, depending on your point of view. With the large number of athletes and supporters who attend this event, the trail and the lodges alongside it can become overcrowded during the few days leading up to, and following, the race.

TREK 5

GOKYO TO LOBUCHE VIA PHORTSE, PANGBOCHE AND PHERICHE

A gentle but continuous bend tantalizes its admirers, draws them on impatiently to see beyond the next corner, maintaining for them the thrill of discovery almost to the end.

H. W. Tilman *Nepal Himalaya*

Trek summary

Distance	35km (22 miles)
Time	3–4 days
Max altitude	Lobuche (4930m: 16,175ft)
Start	Gokyo (4750m: 15,584ft)
Finish	Lobuche
Trekking style	Teahouse (lodge accommodation) or camping

This route to Lobuche and the head of the Khumbu valley is a terrific alternative to the more direct crossing of the Cho La.

The route takes an undulating trail along the sunny east bank of the Gokyo valley, during which you have very different views to those enjoyed on the trek to Gokyo from Namche. At the southern end of the valley Phortse is an unspoilt Sherpa village, from which it's possible to either return directly to Namche by way of Phortse Tenga, make a visit to Thyangboche across the other side of the Imja Khola, or take the high path that turns a spur and heads northeast along a partly exposed balcony route to upper Pangboche in the shadow of Ama Dablam. A short distance beyond Pangboche you join the main route to Pheriche and Lobuche.

Gokyo to Phortse (6–7hr)

Leaving Gokyo wander downvalley on the familiar trail by which you approached from Namche, but after

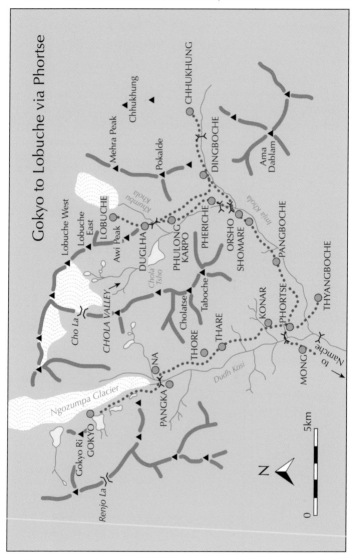

Gokyo to Lobuche via Phortse

Route outline

Route	Distance	Height gain/loss	Time
Gokyo–Phortse	15km	–950m	6–7hr
Phortse–Upper Pangboche	5km	200m	2hr
Upper Pangboche–Pheriche	7km	240m	2½–3hr
Pheriche–Lobuche	8km	690m	3–4hr

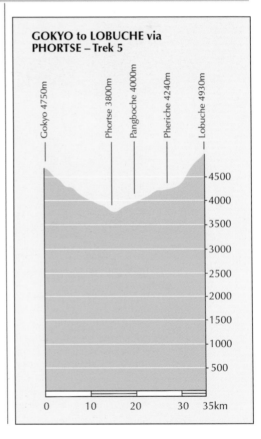

emerging from the steep descent from the ablation valley, instead of climbing up to Pangka, continue down to the river and cross to the left bank on a bridge. Shortly after this come to the tiny hamlet of **NA** (4400m: 14,436ft) where there are two small, very basic lodges. The trail goes through a walled enclosure to a junction of paths. Go straight ahead and descend to a second stream, also crossed by bridge. Over this bear right. The way now passes a *yersa*, descends to the Dudh Kosi, then winds among small streams and scrub before starting a long rising traverse of the left-hand hillside.

About 45min from Na you come to the scattered buildings of **THORE** (4343m: 14,249ft). This is unnamed

Seen from the trail to Phortse, Khumbila's satellite peaks are similar in appearance to some of the Mont Blanc aiguilles

on the Schneider map, and there is general confusion about whether this village is Thore or Thare. (Since most maps now call this first village Thore, we will join convention – but without conviction!) Thore has a basic lodge and a teahouse set just below the trail. Beyond it the way crosses a stream then continues an undulating course, coming to a spur with a magnificent view to the jagged aiguille-like peaks of Khumbila above the west side of the valley.

THARE (4400m: 14,436ft) is reached about 30min from Thore. This is a small settlement with one simple lodge. From it the trail continues as a splendid belvedere before dropping into a gully and climbing out again to a ridge topped by a solitary teahouse. Next comes a small pass adorned by a large *chorten* and lots of prayer flags, with a first view of Phortse way below. Thamserku and Kangtega make a very fine backdrop.

Descending steeply the trail crosses a tributary stream by the walled fields of **KONAR**. In a little under 1hr from there, having passed through juniper, birch and rhododendron forest, you come to **PHORTSE**.

Phortse, at the mouth of the Gokyo valley

PHORTSE (3800m: 12,467ft) is an attractive Sherpa village whose long houses are spread across a broad slope tilted to the south above the confluence of the Dudh Kosi and Imja Khola rivers. This is yak-grazing country, but buckwheat and potatoes are grown in the walled fields, and there's a variety of wildlife to be seen. The whole area in and around the village is full of charm, and with several fairly simple lodges it makes a great place to spend a night or two. A *gompa* graces the upper end of the village.

PHORTSE TO THYANGBOCHE AND NAMCHE

Although Trek 5 described here leads to Lobuche and the upper Khumbu valley, two alternatives are available. One crosses the Imja Khola to Thyangboche, where you can either join the standard Everest-bound route described as Trek 6, or head back to Namche and the way out to Kathmandu. The other option descends below Phortse to the Dudh Kosi at **PHORTSE TENGA**, then returns to Namche by reversing the Gokyo route described as Trek 3, crossing the Mong Danda to Kyangjuma and either taking the busy Everest trail to **NAMCHE**, or diverting via **KHUMJUNG**.

The Thyangboche trail begins east of the Khumbu Lodge, contours round the hillside and becomes rather narrow and exposed before making a steep descent to the Imja Khola. Across the river a steep trail climbs the forested ridge on which **THYANGBOCHE** monastery is found (about 2hr from Phortse). Here you join the main Namche–Everest trail.

Phortse to Upper Pangboche (2hr)

This trail begins at the upper part of the village by the *gompa* and leads round to where prayer flags mark the point at which the ridge-spur is crossed. Once over this it makes a high belvedere way above the river and is exposed in places. This trail is definitely not one for trekkers with a history of vertigo. That being said, it is a spectacular route with tremendous views. The way dips and rises, sometimes quite steeply, with a long drop to the Imja Khola – beware laden yaks on narrow sections. A little over 2hr from Phortse you enter the upper part of **PANGBOCHE** near the village *gompa*.

*Upper Pangboche
(gompa on right of
picture)*

PANGBOCHE (4000m: 13,123ft) is a two-part village, the upper (Te Lim) being set about 100m above the lower (Wa Lim). The lower village is usually visited by trekkers coming from Thyangboche, but this upper settlement is the more interesting. Dating from the 17th century, the ochre-walled *gompa* is the oldest in the Khumbu, and is worth visiting. It used to house what was claimed to be a yeti scalp, but this mysteriously disappeared in 1991. There are at least five lodges here, and a splendid grove of protected juniper trees. According to legend these appeared after the Buddhist saint, Lama Sange Dorje, tore

A WEEK OF SHERPA NAMES

While some are named to honour a religious devotion, or a Buddhist deity, Sherpas often name their children after the day of the week on which they were born: Nima: Sunday; Dawa: Monday; Mingma: Tuesday; Lhakpa: Wednesday; Phurba: Thursday; Pasang: Friday; Pemba: Saturday.

In the case of two generations in a family sharing the same name, to avoid confusion the prefix 'Ang' is used to denote the younger one; thus Ang Mingma means 'Young Mingma'.

out some of his hair which then took root when he cast it on the ground.

Pangboche to Pheriche (2½–3hr)

A short distance beyond the *gompa* square the path forks. Take the upper option (the alternative descends to the lower village), and rise steadily round the hillside to a large *chorten* from which Ama Dablam once again appears regal across the valley. The summit cone of Everest can also be seen peering over the Lhotse–Nuptse ridge. The trail now remains high for a while, then angles downhill to join the main trail from Lower Pangboche. Before reaching Shomare the way passes below a rock-face decorated with Buddhist paintings.

The trail passes through **SHOMARE**, which has several teahouses and simple lodges, and rising still goes through alpine scrub before crossing open yak pastures to **ORSHO** where there are two isolated lodges. After the second of these the way forks. The right-hand trail, which is the major one, goes to Dingboche, the left branch to Pheriche and the upper Khumbu. Although the Pheriche option is the more direct one to use for the onward trail to Lobuche and Gorak Shep, the Dingboche route gives an opportunity to take a higher trail round to Lobuche. Two nights in Dingboche are often advised to aid acclimatisation, and this route option is described in the box below.

For the route to Pheriche take the left branch, heading uphill to cross a ridge adorned with *mani* stones and prayer flags, over which you then descend to a wooden bridge spanning the Khumbu Khola. A short (10min) walk now brings you to **PHERICHE**.

PHERICHE (4240m: 13,911ft) is a notoriously cold and windy place consisting of stone walls, a few houses, several lodges, and a **health post** manned during the main trekking seasons by volunteer doctors on behalf of the Himalayan Rescue Association. The doctors are available for medical consultations (fee payable); they also give daily lectures on the effects of altitude. It is in the interests of all trekkers to attend one of these lectures

Ama Dablam from upper Pangboche

before going any higher. Please leave a donation to help with the running costs, as the service provided is a life-saver – not just for trekkers, but for porters, other trek staff and locals. In the yard outside the health post stands a highly polished stainless steel pyramid created by the British sculptor, Oliver Barratt, to commemorate Everest summiteers and those who have died on the mountain. Most of Pheriche's lodges have fairly well-stocked shops.

Before moving on, you are strongly recommended to spend at least two nights here to aid acclimatisation. On your 'rest day' either walk upvalley to the simple lodges at **DUGLHA** (1½hr), and return by the upper path which contours along the hillside above the valley; or cross the moraine ridge behind Pheriche to visit **DINGBOCHE**, then trek for a while through the valley of the Imja Khola which stretches to the east.

ORSHO TO DINGBOCHE

When the trail forks just beyond the second lodge at Orsho, take the right branch. Sloping down to a bridge over the Khumbu Khola, the trail then climbs above the western bank of the Imja Khola, and topping a rise gives a very fine view of the huge Lhotse–Nuptse wall, with **DINGBOCHE** spread out below.

DINGBOCHE (4350m: 14,272ft) is reached about 45min from the Orsho trail junction. It's a long village scattered among stone-walled fields; the lower part is in something of a frost-bowl and can be bitterly cold, while the upper part of Dingboche is marginally warmer. There are several lodges and plenty of camping grounds. At least two of the lodges advertise telephone facilities; others have shops of some description. Rising above the village to the southeast, Ama Dablam looks very different from the recognisable shape seen from the Namche trail, while the presence of Lhotse looms large.

For acclimatisation purposes you are strongly advised to spend at least two nights in Dingboche. Time could well be spent by trekking upvalley to **CHHUKHUNG**, a round-trip of about 9km, taking around 3–3½hr exclusive of halts. Chhukhung consists of several yak-herders' huts and simple lodges below the terminal moraine of the Lhotse glacier, at an altitude of 4730m (15,518ft). Views are wonderful. A brief description of the route to Chhukhung is given at the end of Section 1, Trek 6. ▶

Ama Dablam seen from the ridge above Dingboche

◄ **Note:** Should you experience any AMS symptoms at Dingboche, do not proceed towards Lobuche until they have gone. Lobuche is almost 600m higher, and you must acclimatise before trekking there.

Dingboche to Duglha

In order to rejoin the main route to Lobuche, it's not necessary to visit Pheriche. Instead, climb the moraine mound behind upper Dingboche to the large *chorten* seen on the ridge. From here take the trail that dips into a hollow, then rises along a moraine terrace heading northwest. It's a very fine trail that passes a few yak-herders' huts and rises gently with good views into the valley below, and up through the Chola valley ahead guarded by Taboche. About 1½hr from Dingboche the trail curves into the ablation valley sloping down the eastern side of the Khumbu glacier, to be joined by the main trail from Pheriche. Shortly after, the way crosses a bridge over the glacial river, then angles up to the simple lodges of **DUGLHA**. Please refer to the Pheriche to Lobuche description below for the continuing trek.

Pheriche to Lobuche (3–4hr)

Before leaving Pheriche for the upper Khumbu it is essential that you have no symptoms of AMS, so if you're suffering headaches or nausea, for example, either wait until you feel better, or descend. Do not go any higher.

The trail to Lobuche remains on the east side of the Khumbu Khola, rising at a steady gradient through the broad valley and crossing several small streams on the way to the stone-built hutments of **PHULONG KARPO**, a summer pasture with views back downvalley towards Ama Dablam. Shortly after this the trail climbs northward to the terminal moraine of the Khumbu glacier. In places this climb is quite steep, and about 1½hr from Pheriche you join the upper trail from Dingboche. At this point you bear left and descend a short way to the Khumbu Khola, which is crossed on a wooden bridge. The trail angles round the slope and brings you to the group of simple lodges at **DUGLHA**.

DUGLHA (4593m: 15,069ft) is also known as Thukla, and since there are no more lodges or teahouses until you reach Lobuche, this is the place to stop for lunch. Lobuche is another 330m (1000ft) or so higher than Duglha, so again it is essential not to continue if you have any AMS symptoms. If necessary, spend a night here.

The continuing trail rises steeply above Duglha, and can be exhausting work. It's a dusty trail cut by yaks and the boots of numerous trekkers, and it twists up a slope of old moraine to a ridge characterised by a large number of memorial cairns, *chortens*, prayer flags and *mani* stones that commemorate Sherpas and others who have lost their lives in the mountains. Among them is one to Scott Fischer who died in the 1996 Everest disaster immortalised in Jon Krakauer's book, *Into Thin Air*. From here the view downvalley is spectacular.

The gradient now eases, with the trail curving round a boulder slope to enter the more barren upper reaches of the valley headed by Pumori. Cross to the western side of the valley to gain a clear view of Nuptse ahead. The path

The bridge below Duglha

gently eases along the west bank of a stream, crosses a final rise and curving left comes to **LOBUCHE**.

LOBUCHE (4930m: 16,175ft) can be a cold collection of lodges when the sun goes down, and you will need a good down jacket and sleeping bag to ensure a comfortable night's sleep here. It's a busy place, for most trekkers use it as a two-night base whilst tackling Kala Pattar or going on to Everest Base Camp. There's plenty of space for camping, but sanitation is poor. However, sunset views of Nuptse can be breathtaking from here.

For a description of the route to Gorak Shep, Kala Pattar and Everest Base Camp, please see Section 3, Trek 6.

NUPTSE

Nuptse (7861m: 25,791ft) is the southwest guardian of the Everest massif, a long ridge system with abrupt plunging walls. At its most attractive, Nuptse is seen as a huge ice-gemmed spire from Kala Pattar, but this feature is just one of a number of 'tops', the main summit being located farther along the ridge towards Lhotse. It was first climbed by a route on the difficult South Face in 1961, by a British expedition led by Joe Walmsley. Dennis Davis and Tashi Sherpa spearheaded the ascent, and were followed to the top next day by Chris Bonington, Jim Swallow, Les Brown and Ang Pemba. It was the first Himalayan giant to be tackled by such a severe face route – alpine-type difficulties at advanced altitude.

TREK 6

NAMCHE BAZAAR (OR KHUMJUNG) TO LOBUCHE, GORAK SHEP, KALA PATTAR AND EVEREST BASE CAMP

Our journey up to the foot of Mount Everest was spectacular in the extreme.
Sir Edmund Hillary *View from the Summit*

Trek summary	
Distance	35km (22 miles)
Time	5–7 days
Max. altitude	Kala Pattar (5623m: 18,448ft)
Start	Namche Bazaar (3446m: 11,306ft) or Khumjung (3780m: 12,402ft)
Finish	Lobuche (4930ft: 16,175ft) or Gorak Shep (5160m: 16,929ft)
Trekking style	Teahouse (lodge accommodation) or camping

Beyond Namche the trail leads enticingly towards the heart of the highest mountain landscape on earth; a dramatic scene of ice-chiselled peaks and glacier-scoured valleys. In the shadow of these mountains, villages have a stark and solemn kind of beauty, looking out over an uncompromising land where agriculture is at its most basic, where husbandry of the soil appears at first to have progressed no further than the 16th century when the first Sherpas came over the mountains from Tibet. The humble potato, staple of their diet, was brought here in the 1830s, and its introduction is reckoned to have been one of the most significant events in Sherpa history – until, that is, Khumbu was opened to Western influence in the 1950s.

Before the trekking invasion Pangboche was the highest permanently settled village in the valley. But now

The mountain landscape of Khumbu is as scenically dramatic as anyone could wish: huge, soaring peaks, their summit snows either dazzling in the sunshine or teasing through a drift of wayward cloud.

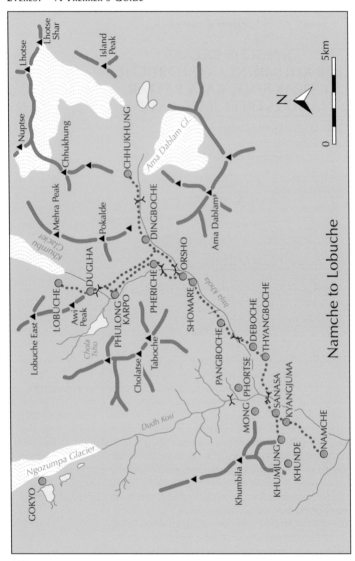

Namche to Lobuche

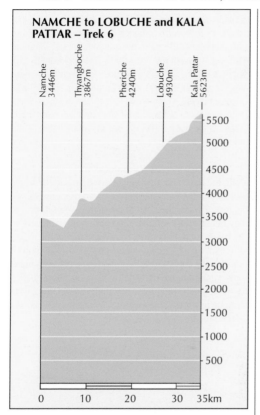

both Dingboche, formerly a summer-only community at 4350m (14,272ft), and Pheriche (4240m: 13,911ft), until recently a temporary yak-herder's settlement, have year-round occupation, and lodge-owners keep the yak-dung fires burning as high as Lobuche (4930m: 16,175ft) and Gorak Shep (5184m: 17,008ft) late into the post-monsoon trekking season.

Trekking beyond Namche is a very different experience to that of trekking from Jiri to Namche. In some ways it is less strenuous, for there are fewer corrugations to tackle; there are no trails crossing the grain of land that have to be followed – although options do exist for those who want them. But here the altitude plays a dominant part. Now above 3000m (10,000ft) it is important to gain height gradually to enable the body to adapt to the thinning air, so you should spend two nights in Pheriche or Dingboche before continuing to Lobuche or Gorak Shep. Drink plenty of liquids, even if you don't feel particularly thirsty, as the body can easily become dehydrated at altitude. Be aware of other signs of mountain sickness (see On-Trek Healthcare in the Introduction).

As before, there is no shortage of accommodation along the trail, and new lodges are being added to the route annually. Some of these are very fine, but as you progress towards the head of the high valley systems, so they become less sophisticated and more expensive to stock with food. Prices rise, standards fall, but the mountain experience grows more profound. Khumbu is probably the coldest trekking region in Nepal, with night-time temperatures demanding use of good-quality, four-season sleeping bags whether you're camping or sleeping in a lodge. Stay warm, stay healthy, and absorb all this fabulous region has to offer.

Route outline

Route	Distance	Height gain/loss	Time
Section 1 19km/12miles			
Namche–Thyangboche	9km	771m (–350m)	4–4½hr
Thyangboche–Pheriche	10km	502m (–87m)	4–4½hr
Thyangboche–Dingboche	10km	563m (–87m)	4–4½hr
Acclimatisation day in Pheriche or Dingboche			
Section 2 8km/5miles			
Pheriche–Lobuche	8km	678m	3–4hr
Section 3 7km/4½miles			
Dingboche–Lobuche	9.5km	587m	3–4hr
Lobuche–Kala Pattar	6km	693m	4–4½hr

SECTION 1

Namche Bazaar
to Pheriche (or Dingboche)

Distance	19km (12 miles)
Time	2 days
Start altitude	3446m (11,306ft)
High point	Pheriche (4240m: 13,911ft) or Dingboche (4350m: 14,272ft)

The first stage goes to Thyangboche, or Tengboche, one of those magical places of which dreams are made. Its situation, on a wooded ridge above acres of pine and rhododendron forest, is truly idyllic. Thamserku and Kangtega wall it to the south. Graceful Ama Dablam holds one's attention nearby, while the vast Nuptse–Lhotse wall blocks the valley ahead, with the crown of Mount Everest peering above it.

This part of the trek makes the best possible introduction to Khumbu. The trail is exposed in places, and as it makes a high belvedere way above the river, so the drama grows. It's a busy trail with much coming and going. There will undoubtedly be caravans of laden yaks lumbering along the path, and in dry conditions their hooves scuff the dust into small clouds. Again the warning is given to make sure you are uphill of them as they pass, for an inadvertent nudge from a horn, flank or load, could so easily result in your being sent crashing down to the river. End of trek. End of trekker.

As the trek proceeds beyond Thyangboche, so the landscape takes on a stark, raw kind of beauty, and by the time you've reached Pangboche vegetation will be sparse. At Pheriche both mountain and valley appear almost sterile by comparison with the luxuriant surroundings of Thyangboche.

Namche (or Khumjung) to Thyangboche (4–4½hr)

The Thyangboche trail climbs out of Namche's bowl up the eastern hillside. The upper part of the village, where the National Park headquarters and army post are situated, is known as Chorkang. A visit to the Park head-quarters is recommended. It houses an interesting exhibition, and views from the site are magnificent. The trail crosses the Namche rim at this point, then makes a fine, easy contour along the hillside with Thamserku and Kangtega gazing down as you approach a left-hand bend. Suddenly you're stopped in your tracks by a stunning view of Everest, Nuptse, Lhotse and Ama Dablam, and with Thyangboche's monastery seen as a speck on the crest of a dark ridge in mid-distance.

Now the trail makes a modest switchback along the steep hillside, and rounds another spur marked by a large white *chorten* built to commemorate the 50th anniversary of the first ascent of Everest, and to honour Tenzing Norgay and the Everest Sherpas. In a little over 1hr from Namche you cross a high point, then slope down among rhododendrons to the two lodges of **KYANGJUMA** (3600m: 11,811ft) that enjoy one of the great views of the area. It's pleasant to sit at a table here and relax with a drink before you and huge mountains all around.

From here the trail goes through a wooded area of pine, birch and rhododendron, and brings you to **SANASA** (3580m: 11,745ft), a small settlement with a group of lodges and teahouses. Both here and in Kyangjuma souvenirs, claimed to be from Tibet, are laid out beside the trail. If you're interested in buying, it's better to wait until your return rather than add any more weight to the rucksack.

Continue along the clear path that makes a long sloping curve round the hillside before descending

ROUTE FROM KHUMJUNG

From the village go down to its eastern end where there is a large *chorten* near the last of the houses. The trail forks. Descend slightly right ahead on a trail that breaks into several braidings, going down the slope among trees and scrub with Ama Dablam in view ahead. The path eventually goes alongside drystone walls and brings you onto the main crossing trail at the lodges of **KYANGJUMA**. Turn left and in 5min you'll reach **SANASA**.

among trees to the village of **TRASHINGO** (variously known as Teshinga, Tesing or Lawishasa) where there are a few more lodges and teahouses. Most of the village stands back from the trail, but just below it you pass a forest nursery financed by Ed Hillary's Himalayan Trust. The way then begins a steepish descent through mature forest to the Dudh Kosi. Just before reaching the bridge that crosses the river you will pass one more lodge and teahouse.

At 3247m (10,653ft) this bridge, with its tatters of prayer flags, is the lowest point on the trek since the approach to Namche Bazaar. A short distance upstream the Imja Khola and Dudh Kosi rivers converge. The main valley becomes that of the Imja Khola, while the Dudh Kosi's headwaters drain the glaciers of Gokyo's valley northwest of Thyangboche. From the bridge over the Dudh Kosi there's a long, steady, 2hr climb to Thyangboche, another 620m (2034ft) up the hill ahead. Don't rush it; get into a steady rhythm and enjoy the walk, keeping alert for signs of musk deer and Himalayan tahr (a form of wild goat) in the woods as you go.

Just beyond the bridge you enter the settlement of **PHUNKI TENGA** (3250m: 10,663ft), about 2–2½hr from

The former bridge at Phunki Tenga below Thyangboche

The trail below Thyangboche, with Kwangde in the background

Namche. A series of water-driven prayer wheels and lodges lines the trail. Now the climb begins in earnest. Steep at first, the trail is clear all the way, but while most of it is through forest, open stretches afford wonderful views towards the big wall of Kwangde rising above unseen Namche Bazaar.

Immediately before topping the ridge at Thyangboche the path leads through a *kani* (an entrance archway whose interior is covered with Buddhist paintings), and moments later you emerge by a *chorten* with the large *gompa*, or monastery, nearby. The view upvalley is a revelation. 'It would be difficult to imagine, much more find, a finer site for worship or for contemplation,' wrote Tilman. On his way to Everest in 1953 John Hunt was equally impressed: 'My senses were intoxicated by the fantastic surroundings,' he commented, 'Thyangboche must be one of the most beautiful places in the world.'

THYANGBOCHE (3867m: 12,687ft) is understandably popular. Groups of trekkers and mountaineers fill all available camping spaces, and the lodges are often full in the main trekking seasons. During the three-day Mani Rimdu festival, celebrated here at the full moon of October–November, every bed and every tent space will be taken. Should you find accommodation difficult, it would be worth continuing down the trail towards Pangboche for about 10min where you will find several more lodges.

All expeditions to attempt Everest from this side of the Himalayan divide pass through Thyangboche, many of which receive the blessings of the head lama before making a start on the mountain itself. Visitors are welcome. After passing through an enclosed courtyard, footwear should be removed before entering the richly decorated main hall, or *lha-khang*, where silk banners and ornamental scrolls hang from the ceiling. Sometimes visitors are presented to the head lama at the end of devotions. On such occasions you will be given a *katha*, a white ceremonial scarf, by another monk, and this

Thyangboche's gompa is an ornate building on a sublime site

should be offered to the Abbot with a donation concealed within it.

Although it's not the oldest in Khumbu (Pangboche and Thame are much older) the richly decorated monastery is the largest in mountain Nepal, and serves as the spiritual centre of the district, attracting novice monks from all over Khumbu who come here to study Buddhist teachings. Despite the valley having been settled for nearly 500 years the first Thyangboche monastery was not founded until 1916 under instruction from Dzatrul Rinpoche, the Abbot of Rongbuk on the north side of Everest. In 1934 it was almost completely destroyed by an earthquake that killed Lama Gulu, the *gompa's* founding father. A replacement monastery was built soon after to the same design as the original, but in January 1989, less than a year after it had been provided with its own small-scale electricity supply, it was destroyed by fire caused by a suspected electrical fault. The present monastery rose from the ashes of its predecessor, and was paid for by funds raised both locally and internationally.

IN RESPECT OF BUDDHISM

The origins of Buddhism go back some 2500 years when, after years of study and meditation, Siddhartha Gautama – who was born a prince in Lumbini in southern Nepal around 623BC – gained 'Enlightenment' and liberation from the cycle of birth, death and rebirth. He then became known as Buddha, which means 'Awakened One', and his teachings subsequently spread to many parts of Asia and beyond.

Buddhism is based on the four noble truths. Existence is suffering; longing and attachment create suffering; the reaching of nirvana brings an end to suffering; and the path to nirvana is by the eightfold way: right views; right resolve; right speech; right action; right livelihood; right effort; right mindfulness; and right concentration. Meditation and the recitation of the mantra *Om mani padme hum* are part of the journey of faith.

In the Himalayan regions of Nepal Buddhism is not only evident in the various *gompas* (monasteries), *chortens* (stone-built structures containing religious relics) and *mani* walls (stone slabs etched with the *Om mani* mantra), but in the countless prayer flags, prayer wheels and *kanis* (entrance archways) seen along the way. It is also clearly evident in the character of those who practise the faith, for many exhibit a remarkable cheerfulness, humour and a willingness to be of service.

As a show of respect to those whose faith adds much to the trekking experience in these high regions, please make sure you pass all Buddhist symbols on their left-hand side. Prayer wheels should be turned clockwise, and when entering a monastery you should be modestly dressed and leave your footwear outside. It is disrespectful to touch religious statues or paintings, and when you make your way around a place of worship, it should be in a clockwise direction, and on departing, back out, or bow slightly before turning to leave.

Thyangboche to Pheriche or Dingboche (4–4½hr)

The Everest trail slopes down the hill from Thyangboche *gompa* through a scoop of hillside among pine, birch and tall, elegant rhododendrons that are magnificent in springtime. In about 10min pass several large lodges, and a few minutes later come to **DEBOCHE** (3757m: 12,326ft). The main trail bypasses the few buildings of this settlement, which includes a Buddhist nunnery, and leads through lovely parkland-like scenery. In two places

Thyangboche's Everest view

the trail is divided by long *mani* walls. Then the valley narrows to a gorge and about 30–40min from Thyangboche you come to a suspension bridge over the narrows of the Imja Khola.

Over the bridge the way climbs upvalley, passes a variety of *chortens* and *mani* walls, then goes through a *kani* beyond which there's a narrow cleft in a rocky spur. A few paces after this cleft the trail divides. The left-hand path goes to upper Pangboche, the right-hand option (recommended here) passes more *mani* walls and *chortens*, then slopes down to lower **PANGBOCHE**, reached about 1½hr from Thyangboche.

PANGBOCHE (3901m: 12,799ft) is an important two-part village. Lower Pangboche, or Pangboche Wa Lim, is a comparatively large settlement with more than a dozen lodges set in a bewildering maze of drystone walls. Stray from the path at your own risk, for it's easy to get 'lost' among the walled-in fields! The upper village is more compact and is certainly worth a visit, so if you intend to return this way, you are recommended to take the trail that leads to it. It is in the upper village

The view downvalley to Kwangde, from Pangboche

(Pangboche Te Lim) that the oldest *gompa* in the Khumbu is located; it also has several reasonable lodges with wonderful views.

The trail winds through Pangboche, and on the far side crosses a stream with a water-driven prayer wheel just above the bridge. Beyond the stream the trail picks a route along the hillside now devoid of habitation for a while. Across the valley Ama Dablam begins to lose its familiar profile.

AMA DABLAM

Considered by many to be one of the world's most beautiful mountains, the 6856m (22,493ft) Ama Dablam is easily recognised by its characteristic shape when seen from the southwest, although it takes on a completely different appearance when viewed from the north. The name means 'Mother's Charm Box' which refers to the hanging glacial lump that appears high up on its southern face and resembles the turquoise or coral *dablam*, or charm box necklace, worn by Tibetan women. During an attempt to climb the mountain's North Ridge in 1959, two members of a British expedition disappeared on the final arête as the monsoon set in. The first successful ascent (by the South-West Ridge) was claimed in 1961 by Michael Ward, Mike Gill, Barry Bishop and Wally Romanes, who were members of a multinational scientific expedition organised by Ed Hillary. Ama Dablam has since become the most popular non-trekking peak in the Khumbu, and has been climbed by more than 15 different routes. In a busy year, the South-West Ridge receives more than 150 ascents.

Guru Rinpoche is commemorated on a rock near Pangboche

About 45min from Pangboche the left-hand rockface has been adorned with Buddhist paintings and some highly coloured *manis*. In another 10min you should reach **SHOMARE**, an expanding settlement with several

simple lodges. Wandering through alpine scrub, rising ever higher along the valley, the trail then enters a high, broad pastureland, about 3hr from Pangboche. This is **ORSHO**, a yak-grazing area with two isolated lodges, the last refreshment stop before either Pheriche or Dingboche. Ahead the valley forks. The left branch is that of the Khumbu Khola and the way to Everest, the right-hand valley that of the Imja Khola. Lhotse appears as a massive wall above the Imja valley.

The bridge over the Khumbu Khola below Orsho

LHOTSE

Lhotse (8501m: 27,890ft) dominates Dingboche and the whole of the Imja valley. It's the fourth highest mountain in the world, and while its name (meaning South Peak) seems to demote it to a mere appendage of the higher Mount Everest, it is an apt description, for it is indeed the southernmost peak of the Everest massif. The first attempt to climb Lhotse was made in the post-monsoon season of 1955 by a multi-national expedition led by the Swiss-American Norman Dyhrenfurth who, with Ernst Senn and the cartographer Erwin Schneider, spent nearly five months on a thorough reconnaissance of the area before launching their attack on the North-West Face. Although Dyhrenfurth's expedition failed to reach the summit, the first ascent was made the following year by Ernst Reiss and Fritz Luchsinger of a Swiss expedition led by Albert Eggler. To date it remains the least climbed of any 8000m peak.

Beyond the second lodge you come to a junction of trails marked by a small *mani* wall and a large rock on the left with the words Pheriche and Dingboche painted in red letters upon it, with accompanying arrows directing the respective routes. Whether you go to Pheriche or Dingboche will depend on your plans for the next couple of days. Pheriche is the most obvious, as it lies on the direct trail to Lobuche and Everest Base Camp, but to approach Everest via Dingboche will not add much to the overall trek in respect of time, while spending two nights there will give an opportunity to explore part of the Imja Khola's valley. Both villages are high enough to require careful acclimatisation by all who arrive there.

Route to Pheriche

The Pheriche trail is much less significant than the Dingboche route at this point, although it soon resumes its customary well-trodden appearance. It leaves the main path and climbs straight uphill, quite steeply in places, to reach a high point marked by cairns, *manis* and prayer flags. Beyond this the way eases round the hillside with continuing fine views of the vast Nuptse–Lhotse wall. Then the buildings of Pheriche can be seen in the broad Khumbu valley ahead. The trail slopes down to the river, crosses a wooden bridge and soon after enters **PHERICHE**.

Note: It is advisable to spend two nights at Pheriche or, perhaps more comfortably, at nearby Dingboche to aid acclimatisation. On the next stage of the trek to Lobuche you will be less likely to suffer altitude sickness if you do so.

◀ **PHERICHE** (4240m: 13,911ft) is a notoriously cold and windy place, but its outlook along the Khumbu valley is impressive. The village consists of an expanding group of lodges, houses, and an important **health post** manned in the main trekking seasons by Western volunteer doctors, and supported by the Himalayan Rescue Association. Lectures on how to avoid AMS are given each afternoon by one of the doctors, and all trekkers are strongly recommended to attend. Please be generous with donations, as the post's very existence depends on charitable giving, and every year the lives of trekkers, locals and trek crew are saved here. In the yard in front of the health post stands a highly polished stainless steel

TIME IN PHERICHE

To aid acclimatisation, a recommended outing from Pheriche leads up the hillside immediately behind the health post (there are several narrow trails) to gain the crest of a ridge which forms the divide between the Khumbu valley and that of the Imja Khola. A *chorten* crowns this ridge at about 4412m (14,475ft), with very fine views over both valleys. From here the continuing trail slopes down to **DINGBOCHE**. Either return to Pheriche by the same path, or descend on the main trail heading southwest on the right bank of the Imja Khola as far as its junction with the Pheriche, or Everest, trail at Orsho. Bear sharp right and follow the familiar route back to base. This circuit would make good use of half a day, or a full day if you spend time exploring Dingboche.

A full day's acclimatisation hike towards the upper Khumbu valley is possible by following the high trail that goes upvalley along the slopes of Pokalde to **DUGLHA**. Return downvalley from Duglha along the standard Pheriche–Lobuche route. To gain the high path take one of several narrow tracks slanting northwestwards up the hillside beyond the health post. Once you gain this upper trail bear left along a broad natural shelf with wonderful views of Taboche and Cholatse across the flat-bottomed Khumbu valley. The trail leads into the ablation valley below the Khumbu glacier where it joins the main route. Just beyond this junction cross a bridge over the Khumbu Khola, shortly after which the trekkers' lodges of **DUGLHA** (4593m: 15,069ft) provide an excuse to stop for lunch before returning downvalley on the main trail.

Yet another option is to climb again onto the dividing crest behind Pheriche, and head north along it, going up towards **NANGKARTSHANG GOMPA** (1½–2hr) on the slopes of Pokalde. Tilman and Houston went up this ridge in 1950 and enjoyed the spectacular mountain panorama, which embraces Makalu, Lhotse, Cho Oyu and Gyachung Kang. 'In this galaxy, which included a host of unnamed peaks,' wrote Tilman, 'neither the lesser nor the greater seemed designed for the use of climbers.'

Overlooking both Pheriche and Dingboche, Pokalde (5086m: 19,049ft) is one of the Khumbu's easier trekking peaks, first climbed from the Kongma La by Wilfrid Noyce, Tom Bourdillon and Michael Ward as part of the 1953 Everest expedition's acclimatisation programme.

---

pyramid created by the British sculptor, Oliver Barratt, to commemorate Everest summiteers and those who have lost their lives on the mountain.

Route from Orsho to Dingboche

From the trail junction just beyond the second of Orsho's lodges, continue along the main (right-hand) path which slopes down to cross the Khumbu Khola. Over the bridge the trail climbs up the western bank of the Imja Khola, through a wild landscape reminiscent of high moorland overlooked by the Nuptse–Lhotse wall. Cross a low ridge and, about 40min from the trail junction, **DINGBOCHE** will be seen ahead, dun-coloured and flat amongst a grid of drystone walls, and dwarfed by the immensity of the backing mountains.

DINGBOCHE (4350m: 14,272ft) has a number of lodges spread among its stone-walled fields. The lower part of the village is in something of a frost bowl and can be desperately cold, while the upper part warms in the sun much quicker than its counterpart. At least two of the lodges boast telephones, while several others have shops of some description. On the left-hand hillside, which divides the valley from that of the Khumbu Khola, two large *chortens* can be seen, while Ama Dablam rises in unfamiliar shapes to the southeast. The alpenglow on Lhotse can be magical from the village. As with Pheriche it will be necessary to spend at least two nights here to aid acclimatisation. The classic walk is up to Chhukhung and back, details of which are given below.

Trekking camp at Dingboche, with Lhotse behind

TIME IN DINGBOCHE

As it will be necessary to spend at least two nights in Dingboche for acclimatisation purposes, the following classic walk to the **CHHUKHUNG** *yersa*
is suggested as an ideal way to fill that time. It involves a round-trip of about
9km (5½ miles), a height gain of 380m (1247ft) and will take about 3–3½hr,
exclusive of rests.

The trail begins at the upper lodges of Dingboche and heads upvalley
on the northern side of the Imja Khola stream. The valley is broad and shal-
low, with Lhotse dominating on the left and Ama Dablam on the right. At the
head of the valley, beyond a wall of terminal moraine, can be seen Island
Peak (Imja Tse, 6189m: 20,305ft), one of the most popular trekking peaks in
the area.

About 20min before reaching Chhukhung you come to a solitary teahouse not far from the yak-herders' huts of **BIBRE**. Groups sometimes camp
near here, especially if they plan to climb Pokalde or cross the Kongma La
between Pokalde and Kongma Tse – the Kongma La being an optional high
route by which to reach Lobuche. Beyond the teahouse icy streams emanat-
ing from various glaciers have to be crossed. Usually plank footbridges are
placed across them to save jumping ice-sheathed rocks.

CHHUKHUNG (4730m: 15,518ft) consists of several yak-herders' huts,
drystone walls and some lodges set beneath the terminal moraine of the
Lhotse glacier. Views are stunning. The South Face of Lhotse soars an astonishing 3770m (12,369ft) above the lodges (its average angle is 53°), and the
great wall that binds it to Nuptse shows itself in a massive sweep of vertical
stone. Ama Dablam's North Face is seen full on across the valley, with an
ice-pleated wall seeming to extend from it. Below that ice wall the
Chhukhung glacier is born. Downvalley the shapely Taboche rises above
Dingboche, while southwestward, range upon range of snow-capped peaks
fill the horizon – Kwangde, already seen close-to from Namche, and
Karyolung, Numbur and Khatang north of Ringmo, are seen far off in
Solu district.

From the top of the moraine behind Chhukhung an interesting
overview of the valley may be gained, while Island Peak is seen to better
effect from this vantage point. Immediately above the lodges to the north is
a large bald hill, sometimes known as Chhukhung Ri and shown on the
Schneider map as Point 5043m. From its crown a tremendous view shows
Makalu to the east, and a clearer prospect of that amazing ice-pleated wall
to the south.

SECTION 2

Pheriche (or Dingboche) to Lobuche

Distance	8km (5 miles)
Time	3–4hr
Start altitude	4240m (13,911ft) or 4350m (14,272ft)
High point	Lobuche (4930m: 16,175ft)

The Khumbu valley sweeps toward Pheriche between the towering shape of Taboche and insignificant-looking Pokalde. It's a broad valley, gently tilted, with poor, stunted vegetation, but as you progress through it, so its character changes. Instead of continuing in a northwesterly direction, it's necessary to veer right and climb northeast towards the Khumbu glacier. The glacier is not properly seen, but the bulldozed moraines that line it become a prominent feature of the landscape. Some way above Duglha you enter a stony section with Pumori, Lingtren and Khumbutse blocking the valley-head. Along the crest that unites them runs the border with Tibet. All around huge mountains soar in a crescent of rock, snow and ice. Yet Mount Everest remains elusive despite its close proximity. Effectively hidden by Nuptse's South-West Face, it will not be seen until you climb above Gorak Shep to Kala Pattar.

It is essential that no one has any AMS symptoms before leaving Pheriche/ Dingboche. Should you be experiencing headaches or nausea wait until they disappear, or descend. **Do not go any higher**.

The trail to Lobuche remains on the east side of the Khumbu Khola, although there may well be several minor streams to cross as you approach the *kharka* (summer pasture) of **PHULONG KARPO**, with its stone-built hutments. Taboche and Cholatse both look very fine from here, and there's also an inspiring view downvalley towards Ama Dablam. Shortly after this the trail climbs northward to gain the terminal moraine of the Khumbu glacier. In places the gradient is quite steep, and although laden Sherpas may stride by chatting and laughing as

Taboche dominates the climb up to Duglha

they go, you'll no doubt be battling the altitude with no breath to spare for conversation.

About 1½hr from Pheriche the trail joins another coming from the right – this is the high route from Dingboche. At this point bear left and descend a short way to the Khumbu Khola where a wooden bridge spans the torrent. The continuing path then climbs to the opposite moraine where the few lodges of **DUGLHA** (4593m: 15,069ft) are situated.

Above Duglha the route heads up more steep moraine slopes. In the autumn trekking season this is a dusty trail, but it's easy to follow, and eventually you top a ridge characterised by a number of large cairns, *chortens*, prayer flags and *mani* stones placed there to commemorate Sherpas (and others) who have lost their lives in the mountains. One of the more recent of these memorials is to American guide Scott Fischer, who died in the Everest disaster of May 1996 immortalised by Jon Krakauer's book, *Into Thin Air*. From this ridge views downvalley are awe-inspiring.

DINGBOCHE TO DUGLHA

From the upper lodges of Dingboche a trail slants up to a *chorten* on the ridge dividing the Imja and Khumbu valleys. On the western side a variety of paths will be seen. Avoid those that descend to the Khumbu valley, but instead work around the hillslope heading northwest on a trail that follows a broad natural terrace. Views ahead to Taboche and Cholatse on the west flank of the Chola valley are very fine, and as you progress along the trail, so the panorama grows more impressive in all directions. Halfway along the trail you pass the yak-herders' huts of **DUSA**.

In about 1½hr from Dingboche the way enters the ablation valley which slopes down the eastern side of the Khumbu glacier, and there joins the normal route from Pheriche. Descend to the bridge spanning the glacial torrent and a few minutes later you'll come to the basic lodges of **DUGLHA**.

The high trail from Dingboche to Lobuche. A different view of Ama Dablam from this more northerly aspect.

The way now eases considerably, curves round a boulder slope and then enters the seemingly barren upper regions of the Khumbu valley headed by Pumori. Cross to the western side of the valley from where the trail provides clear views of the huge face of Nuptse. It's a pleasant stretch, being drawn as you are into the very heartland of the big mountains. Cross one last rise and round a bend, then come to the huddle of lodges at **LOBUCHE** backed by yet more moraines.

LOBUCHE (4930m: 16,175ft) is a busy place with groups camped on the far side of the stream and around the various lodges, of which there are at least half a dozen, as well as a porters' shelter. In the days leading up to the biennial Everest Marathon, lodge space is at a premium. It can be very cold here, and you'll need a good down jacket and sleeping bag to get through a night in comfort. Once the sun has left the valley temperatures plunge way below freezing. The lodges can be eye-wateringly warm though, especially when a yak-dung stove belches acrid smoke into the room you're sleeping in. The alpenglow on Nuptse can be thrilling when viewed from Lobuche, but for a wider panorama, try climbing onto the ridge immediately behind the lodges.

LOBOUCHE – A MOUNTAINEER'S HOLIDAY CAMP

Despite attempts to improve conditions here, Lobuche has a poor reputation for its dust, lack of hygiene and low standards of sanitation, and for some visitors it offers a miserable experience. But to members of the 1953 Everest expedition, it was their chosen 'holiday camp'. Hunt's book describes a wonderland of flowers and wildlife, and an atmosphere of peace and comfort. 'A spring of fresh, clear water bubbles out strongly from the turf just below the [yak-herders'] huts; weeds wave lazily in the current ... Bird and animal life were a delight after living for a time in a dead world' (*The Ascent of Everest*). Wilfrid Noyce wrote: 'At Lobuje everything called to idleness ... [and] after two days down here everybody felt enormously refreshed' (*South Col*). Perhaps, after all, a week or two should be spent at Everest Base Camp to put Lobuche in perspective.

SECTION 3

Lobuche to Kala Pattar
and Everest Base Camp

Distance	6km (4 miles) or 7km (4½ miles)
Time	4–5hr (plus return)
Start altitude	4930m (16,175ft)
High points	Kala Pattar (5623m: 18,448ft); Everest Base Camp (c5300m: 17,388ft)

The panorama of mountains and glaciers seen from the summit of Kala Pattar is justifiably famous, and includes the only close view of Mount Everest accessible to non-mountaineers on the Nepalese side. In itself, Kala Pattar has no great charisma, and from Gorak Shep appears to be little more than a big hill at the foot of Pumori. Only when you climb to its crown do you come to realise that this bare hill has a fine craggy ridge and summit of its own. Two summits, in fact.

Provided you are fit and well acclimatised the climb will be a highlight of the trek in more ways than one. But should you be affected by the altitude, sadly this could be a very hard day. It's a long day in any case, for unless you plan to spend a night at Gorak Shep, you'll have to return to Lobuche for accommodation.

Gorak Shep has three simple lodges, but the difference in elevation between it and Lobuche is noticeable, and the advanced altitude (5184m: 17,008ft) ensures a very cold and uncomfortable stay. Only if you intend to visit the Everest Base Camp site is it worth the experience. Base Camp does not have much to commend it by comparison with Kala Pattar. There are no views of Everest, just a bewildering prospect of the Khumbu Icefall. Not all expeditions in residence welcome the intrusion of trekkers, and the walk to and from it can be hard work over the rubble-strewn glacier, and difficult to find if there are no expeditions to keep the way open. If you're well acclimatised and have sufficient time at your disposal, by all means visit both Base Camp and Kala Pattar from Gorak Shep. But if it's a choice of one or the other, go for Kala Pattar – and don't forget your camera.

Departing the lodges at Lobuche cross the stream below and wander into the ablation valley curving leftwards. The path stays on the left-hand side of the valley, beside the unseen Khumbu glacier, then enters a higher, narrower step. On reaching a narrow side valley which cuts off to the left, a sign directs the route ahead: 'Way to Gorak Sep'. Should you stray left here, after about 200m you'll come to the 'Italian Pyramid' – a stone-built lodge and scientific research station which collects not only meteorological data, but seismic information too.

Continuing beyond the Pyramid's side valley, the trail comes to a more open area, at the far end of which you climb an old moraine – edelweiss grow on the slope here, but please do not pick. Views expand from the top of this, then the way cuts across a sandy area before weaving a course among heaps of moraine from the Changri glacier, crosses the glacial torrent and climbs again. Soon after this you round a curve and there below can be seen the buildings of **GORAK SHEP**. The path slopes directly down to them – about 1½–2hr from Lobuche, plus rests.

GORAK SHEP (5184m: 17,008ft) consists of three lodges perched on the rim of a level basin of glacial sand, with a small lake nearby. Tibetan snow cocks chase one another noisily across the sand, leaving their prints behind them. In 1952 the Swiss Everest expedition used this as their Base Camp site. The following year the successful British expedition called it their Lake Camp, choosing instead to have their main base on the Khumbu glacier within striking distance of the icefall.

Even though Everest is very close, it still cannot be seen from Gorak Shep. However, the majestic Nuptse soars above to the east, its great curtains and pelmets of

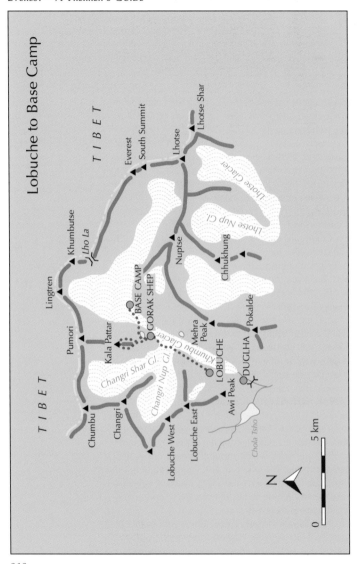

Lobuche to Base Camp

ice dazzling in the sunshine. Directly ahead, across the sand, rises Kala Pattar with Pumori (a Tibetan name given to it in 1921 by Mallory – 'Daughter Peak') forming a pyramid behind it. ▶

The small lake at Gorak Shep

Mallory was the first mountaineer to gaze into the Khumbu when, in July 1921, he reached a col between Pumori and Lingtren from the Tibetan side, hoping to find a way onto Everest from there.

Ascent of Kala Pattar

In Hindi, Kala Pattar means 'black rock'. This is the name given to the subsidiary spur of Pumori by Jimmy Roberts who is credited with making the first ascent with Dawa Tenzing. Kala Pattar has two summits and two ascent routes, both paths being clearly seen from Gorak Shep. The left-hand path of ascent wriggles its way to the sec-ondary summit at 5545m (18,192ft) in about 1–1½hr; the other trail slants up the eastern flank to gain the higher summit (5623m: 18,448ft) in about 1½–2hr or so. Neither route is bothered by technical difficulty, and the use of hands is barely necessary except to steady yourself as you pant for breath in the thin air.

Perhaps the best means of attack is to go up the left-hand trail (almost straight ahead as you look at the hill from Gorak Shep) to gain the lower summit, marked by a number of slender cairns. Continue along the ridge (take

213

care as it falls away steeply on the left), scrambling over rocks to reach the higher summit. As you progress from one to the other, more of Mount Everest becomes visible until at last, as you crouch on the spiky top of Kala Pattar amid a flutter of prayer flags, an incredible panorama is spread before you.

Should you choose the right-hand path, this climbs steeply at first whilst using zigzags, then eases into a long, gentle upward section before steepening again. After a while the main summit (black rocks and colourful prayer flags) is visible, and the trail continues upwards with more zigzags, eventually coming to a col between the first and second summits. Make your way across a boulder-field where there's some indication of a route, to emerge at the upper summit cairn.

Both summits provide spectacular views of Everest, its north and west ridges, its formidable South-West Face and, from the higher top, the South Col too. Trekkers well versed in Everest lore will recognise the various features on display and enjoy picking them out. A lightweight pair of binoculars will come into their own here as you scan the great black triangular face with an inevitable plume

Gorak Shep looks directly up at Kala Pattar, on whose slopes the two routes are clearly visible. Pumori looms above Kala Pattar.

of snow trailing from its summit (a short history of Mount Everest is given in Appendix B).

Everest, of course, is the main focus of attention, but of far greater beauty is the ice cone of Nuptse that, from this viewpoint, appears much higher than its more illustrious neighbour. At the head of the valley other peaks stutter from the frontier ridge: Pumori (immediately above Kala Pattar), Lingtren, Khumbutse, and to the south of that the difficult pass of the Lho La. West of Pumori a vast curving wall contains the Changri Shar glacier, while views downvalley extend far beyond the bulldozing, rubble-covered Khumbu glacier to a veritable sea of peaks filling every distant horizon. In that mountainous sea far-off Ama Dablam has adopted yet another guise. It is an unforgettable, awe-inspiring panorama.

We do not know precisely which point Tilman and Houston reached when they first surveyed the Khumbu side of Everest in November 1950 from their 'subsidiary feature of about 18,000ft to the south of Pumori'. It could not have been the higher summit of Kala Pattar, for they were unable to get a view of the South Col. However, they were probably the first men to go high

Mount Everest, with the South Col just showing, from the summit of Kala Pattar

on this spur, while the following year – during the Everest Reconnaissance expedition – Eric Shipton and Ed Hillary climbed quite a bit higher. This is Shipton's view: 'We found to our surprise that from the point we reached we could see right up to the head of the Western Cwm, the whole of the west face of Lhotse, and the South Col.'

Route to Everest Base Camp

Attempting to visit both Kala Pattar and Everest Base Camp in one day would be too much for most trekkers. If you plan to go to the Base Camp site it's advisable to make a day of it from Gorak Shep. The 7–8km (5-mile) round-trip will take about 4–6hr of rough going.

There's not one single location for the Base Camp, but most expeditions choose a site close to the Khumbu Icefall at about 5300m (17,388ft). If there's an expedition in residence, or a site being set up, the route to it should not be too difficult to follow. But at certain times of the year it may be somewhat tortuous to find. If there's been recent snowfall, forget it.

The trail begins just beyond the Gorak Shep lake where it traces along the moraine crest for some way, until indications suggest descending to the Khumbu glacier. Once in the centre of the glacier locate and follow whatever signs are there – sometimes little more than occasional 'cairns' of yak dung. If you're lucky there'll be porters or yaks moving up to the camp, in which case you can just tuck in and follow them. Note the upthrusting pinnacles of ice that adorn the glacier.

Everest Base Camp is not the place from which to gain a view of the highest mountain on earth. Everything is foreshortened from here, and Everest itself is well hidden. But the chaos of the Khumbu Icefall, spewing from the Western Cwm, makes an ominous choice as the key to the mountain's approach. With so much instability, ice cliffs the size of houses collapse with little advance warning, and bottomless chasms open at unpredictable points. Climbing this to reach the Western Cwm is mountaineering's ultimate game of Russian roulette.

Everest and the Khumbu headwall

In 1953 James (now Jan) Morris was the correspondent assigned by *The Times* to report on what turned out to be the first successful ascent of the mountain. What he wrote about Base Camp in his *Coronation Everest* is worth considering more than 50 years on: 'I would not say that Base Camp, Everest, was a lovely spot. It was too dead and aloof for beauty, rather as if some dread disease had passed this way, killing everything in sight, to be followed by some giant instrument of hygiene, so that the place seemed to have been effectively murdered, and then sterilised.'

Hunt (the leader of the '53 expedition) was himself brutally honest about this camp on the glacier: 'Base Camp,' he wrote, 'is not a beautiful place ... it was lifeless without the compensation of stark grandeur to impress the mind.' And 'an unpleasant odour permeated the close surroundings'. However, in an attempt to put a gloss on reality, he admitted that there were times when the Base Camp was 'enshrined in a certain beauty. At night the snow would often cease and the clouds disperse ... The moon was lighting the top of Pumori and Lingtren, making the slippery sides of the near ice pinnacles shine like polished silver ... At moments such as these it was possible to feel more kindly towards the camp on the Khumbu glacier.'

Returning from Lobuche to Namche by the same trail used on the approach is no bad thing. Seen from the opposite direction individual features of the valley, not to mention the mountains themselves, appear quite different. There'll be different light playing on the mountains too, so the scenery takes on a fresh appeal. You can vary your stopping places, visit other teahouses and lodges to those used on the upvalley route. You can also make slight variations in those places where the trail temporarily divides; instead of returning through lower Pangboche, for example, you could visit the upper part of the village to see the *gompa* there.

But there are also various options available by which to make an alternative way back to Namche, as outlined below. The first is a partial diversion, while for those who journeyed via Thyangboche and Pangboche the crossing of the Cho La gives a completely different route, going by way of the Gokyo (or upper Dudh Kosi) valley.

To Namche via Dingboche and the High Route (2–3 days)

Assuming you stayed in Pheriche on the way up and followed the standard valley route, it would be worth returning by way of the high trail that leads from Duglha to Dingboche. By this route allow at least two days to reach Namche Bazaar.

Descend to **DUGLHA** by the standard trail, cross the glacial stream below the lodges and go up and over the moraine crest on the eastern side. Once over this the trail divides. The standard route descends through the ablation valley, while the high trail pushes ahead, rounds a spur and follows a natural terrace southeastward. Passing the few herders' huts of **DUSA**, the Khumbu valley lies below, while views to Ama Dablam and Kangtega are soon extended to include dozens of peaks jostling for attention.

Above Pheriche the trail continues over the ridge that divides the valleys of the Imja Khola and Khumbu Khola, then descends to **DINGBOCHE**. Bear right and walk through the village heading downvalley. The trail remains on the right bank of the Imja Khola, crosses the Khumbu Khola and rejoins the main trail near the first lodge of **ORSHO**. Follow the now-familiar path downvalley to **PANGBOCHE, THYANGBOCHE** and **NAMCHE**.

To Namche via Cho La and Gokyo (4–5 days)

The crossing of the 5420m (17,782ft) Cho La from Gokyo to Lobuche was described as Trek 4, but the route has also become popular in the reverse direction as a link between the upper Khumbu and Dudh Kosi valleys. Perhaps tougher than the west-to-east crossing, this will take two to three days from Lobuche to Gokyo under good conditions by a fit party, and a further two days should be allowed for the route down to Namche from Gokyo.

It is a crossing that should only be attempted by experienced trekkers, and in good settled weather conditions. Following heavy snowfall, or in poor visibility, plans for the Cho La should be abandoned. In some seasons ice axe and crampons will be needed to tackle the bare ice of the glacier leading to the pass, although it is often snow-covered. Porters in particular must be looked after on the glacier.

The first day is a relatively short one. Leave the main trail where it crosses to the left bank of the Khumbu Khola below Lobuche, and follow a minor path rising ahead on a gentle hillside traverse. This turns a spur to enter the Chola glen with the Chola Tsho lake lying below. The trail now contours for a while along the valley's east flank, drops into a basin of pastureland, then climbs out again to continue heading roughly northwest. Crossing the stream that feeds into the lake, you then go up a final slope to reach the hutments of **DZONGLHA** (4830m: 15,846ft) where there are two simple lodges.

Day 2 begins by crossing the hill behind Dzonglha, continues through the beautiful near-level upper Chola valley, then picks a route along a moraine rib leading to a barrier of rocks. A vague line of cairns directs the way steeply up these rocks, keeping close to the left-hand wall until you come onto a glacier. Keep along the southern side, but beware of crevasses. When the glacier starts to level out, curve left to see the **CHO LA** ahead. There is a bergschrund to cross immediately before getting onto the pass, which may be bridged with snow.

Once over the pass the descent negotiates a steep slope, sometimes of snow, sometimes bare rock and loose stones. At the foot of this cross a narrow rock-strewn valley, then climb over a wall of lateral moraine on the far side. Over this the way is straightforward as you follow a path down through another valley, and about 3–4hr from the Cho La you reach the two simple lodges at **DRAGNAG** (4690m: 15,387ft). ▶

◄ If you need a quick return to Namche, you could turn left and walk down through an ablation valley to **NA**, then cross the stream coming from the Ngozumpa glacier and follow a clear path down the west bank of the Gokyo valley. The normal route from Dragnag, however, crosses the Ngozumpa glacier, and over the lateral moraine on the western side, you turn right and walk up the ablation valley to gain the lodges at **GOKYO** (for full details of this area, please refer to Trek 3).

Time and energy permitting, at least a day should be spent at Gokyo, if only to climb Gokyo Ri. When it's time to leave, simply follow the main trail downvalley on the right flank, in effect reversing Trek 3. There are plenty of lodges and teahouses evenly spaced along the path all the way to Namche.

The stainless steel sculpture adorns the yard in front of the Pheriche health post

MOUNT EVEREST
FROM TIBET

*On the north side, in Tibet, [Mount Everest] does indeed
stand up proudly and alone, a true monarch among
mountains. But it stands in a very sparsely inhabited part
of Tibet, and very few people ever go to Tibet.*

Sir Francis Younghusband

Trek summary	
Distance	65km (40 miles)
Time	3–4 days
Max altitude	Advance Base Camp (6200m: 20,341ft)
Start	Tingri (4500m: 14,764ft)
Finish	Advance Base Camp
Trekking style	Camping (some lodging possible)
Getting there	By private vehicle from Kathmandu or Lhasa
Options	By vehicle all the way from Tingri to Everest North Base Camp via Rongbuk

Before the forbidden kingdom of Nepal became accessible in the early 1950s all attempts to climb Mount
Everest had been conducted from the north. But following the invasion of Tibet by China in 1950, the country
was effectively sealed off from the outside world. Only
belatedly – and well after trekking had become well and
truly established in Nepal – did the closed-door policy
of Chinese-occupied Tibet, which was strengthened
during the Cultural Revolution, begin to ease. In the late
1970s the first commercial groups of tourists were
allowed to visit Lhasa; in 1981 American mountaineer-
photographer Galen Rowell led the first trek to Everest
Base Camp above the Rongbuk monastery. It has since

become an increasingly attractive goal for mountaineers, trekkers and travellers, making it the most popular trekking destination in Tibet. But this is a high-altitude land, where even the valleys are at an elevation of over 4000m (13,000ft), and mountain sickness can strike those unacclimatised whilst simply sitting on a bus. Adherence to the rules of acclimatisation (see On-Trek Healthcare in the Introduction) is essential to successful trekking in Tibet.

Given favourable weather conditions it is possible to trek to the Rongbuk site at any time of the year, but the best season is reckoned to be from May to October, although July to September can be wet.

The north side of Everest

Since 1989 all the Tibetan side of the mountain has been included within the Chomolungma Nature Reserve, a huge area that extends far beyond the immediate confines of Mount Everest itself. Under the terms of the agenda for the Nature Reserve programme, not only is wildlife and the natural environment due for protection, but so too is the important cultural heritage of the area. However, in view of the large-scale desecration of monasteries and other symbols of the Buddhist faith that has occurred under Chinese occupation, it will be interesting to see how this ambitious project is maintained.

The southern boundary of the Chomolungma Nature Reserve is the lofty frontier ridge which, in the immediate Everest area, butts directly against the Sagarmatha National Park of Nepal, thus providing complete protection for the world's highest mountain – on paper, at least.

While it is necessary to climb to the viewpoints of Kala Pattar or Gokyo Ri to see anything more than the summit tip of Everest from the Nepalese side, the mountain's northern aspect is clearly visible far off on the Tibetan plain. It was, of course, from the north that it was first properly explored – the first seven expeditions approaching through the windblown fastness of Tibet.

From the summit pyramid the West Ridge of

Chomolungma (Mount Everest) slopes down to the Lho La before rising again to Khumbutse, forming the border between Tibet and Nepal. On the Nepalese side the Khumbu valley stretches south of this ridge, while the great Rongbuk glacier flows northward from it. The North Ridge (Changzheng Ling) projects from the North-East Ridge and effectively separates the Rongbuk from the East Rongbuk (Rongphu and Dong Rongphu) glaciers.

The North-East Ridge terminates at the Rapiu La (Rabu La), a glacier pass of 6548m (21,483ft) which separates the East Rongbuk and Kangshung glaciers. At the head of the Kangshung Face is the South-East Ridge which plunges to the South Col, then rises again to Lhotse. This ridge also carries the Nepal–Tibet border.

Here on the northern side of the mountain glaciers are much longer than their southern counterparts. But it is by way of the rubble-strewn highway of the East Rongbuk glacier that trekkers in Tibet are able to gain a much broader perspective of the highest mountain on earth than is possible from Nepal. Pressing up to the site of Advance Base Camp at the foot of the North Col is, surely, one of the highest treks in the world.

Looking back towards Nylam from the Kathmandu–Lhasa highway (Joe Williams)

TREK 7

TINGRI TO EVEREST RONGBUK BASE CAMP

The Rongbuk valley is well constructed to show off the peak at its head ... At the end of the valley and above the glacier Everest rises not so much a peak as a prodigious mountain mass.

George Leigh Mallory

For this description of the trek to the Rongbuk Base Camp, I am indebted to Joe Williams.

◄ Northwest of Mount Everest, in a plain formed by the Bum-chu (Phung Chhu) river, Tingri (or Dingri) is the key to a trekker's approach to both Everest and Cho Oyu Base Camps. The town is on the Lhasa-to-Kathmandu

Kodari from the Chinese road up to Zangmu (Joe Williams)

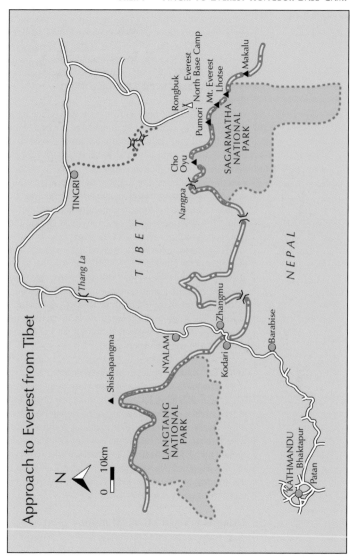

Approach to Everest from Tibet

highway, and – when coming by road – is less than a day's drive from the Nepalese border. For those travelling via Lhasa in Tibet, buses travel the 544km (338 miles) to Tingri by way of Shigatse, where a night is usually spent.

From Kathmandu to the Friendship Bridge
128km (80 miles)

Kodari, the Nepalese border town, is situated northeast of Kathmandu, by which it is linked by some 128km (80 miles) of road varying in quality from tarmac to a stony dirt track, but which nevertheless sees a lot of traffic. A scheduled bus service begins at the 'new' bus park at Gongabu, on the Kathmandu Ring Road, with stops in several townships along the way. The journey by private vehicle can take a minimum of 4hr, but 6hr or more are likely, depending on conditions. During the monsoon, landslides often block the road.

From Kathmandu the route as far as Lamosangu – in the valley of the Sun Kosi river – is the same as that to Jiri (Trek 1). But while the Jiri road crosses the river here, the road to Kodari and Tibet continues alongside the river, whose name changes to the Bhote Kosi as you near the border. The quality of the road diminishes, but the scenery is fantastic, with steep gorges and plunging waterfalls shaping the valleys.

KODARI (1640m: 5380ft) is a ramshackle township with shabby buildings perched perilously close to the edge of a gorge. A straggling bazaar with a few teahouses and lodges, Kodari – the lowest point on the Nepal–Tibet border – marks a long-established crossing point. A short walk through the informal Nepalese customs post leads to the **FRIENDSHIP BRIDGE**, the actual border between the two countries. Above here, 600m higher than Kodari, the Chinese buildings of **ZHANGMU** (Khasa) can be seen. The scenery is spectacular.

Zhangmu to Tingri 147km (81 miles)

After negotiating the first Chinese customs post, some 8km (5 miles) of winding dirt road brings you to the main customs and immigration facility in **ZHANGMU** (c2300m: 7546ft). All visa forms and passports must be in good order for a trouble-free passage through southern Tibet's most important land border with the outside world, where queues of lavishly decorated trucks are likely to be seen passing through. The town is pretty uninspiring, but it has a selection of hotels and restaurants.

The road continues upwards along the Matsang Tsangpo gorge, hugging the precipice and passing waterfalls on both sides of the valley, until **NYALAM** is reached after 31km (19 miles). For centuries this was one of the main trading posts between Tibet and Nepal; today there are roadside restaurants, a petrol station, a small hospital and three simple guesthouses. A good camping area can be found on a bend in the road about 4km south of the town. ▸

The road to Tingri heads north, and passes through the small villages of **PENGYELING** and **TSANGDONG**. For another 55km (34 miles) the road ascends steeply to gain the **TONG LA**, a 5200m (17,060ft) pass where pilgrims raise prayer flags, burn incense and build cairns. Once again Shishapangma can be seen to the west, and high mountains of the central Himalayan chain to the

Nyalam is ideal for **acclimatisation walks**. West of the road hills rise for a few thousand metres, with stunning views of Shishapangma (8012m). The peaks immediately south-west provide good mountaineering objectives.

The Shishapangma range from the Tong La pass (5200m) (Joe Williams)

south and east, while the Tibetan Plateau spreads away to the north.

Now descending eastward, the villages of **MENKHAB-TO** and **GURTSO** are passed by the side of the Men-chu river and, 61km (28 miles) from the Tong La, the road reaches **TINGRI**, one-time staging post on the Lhasa-to-Kathmandu caravan route.

TINGRI (4500m: 14,764ft) is a windy, two-part town lying in the centre of a vast plain; the old town is located on the far side of a small hill, with a Chinese army camp; the new town is crammed along the main road. There are several hotels, shops and restaurants in the new town, including the Sunshine Hotel; the owner can organise pack animals for local treks, and guides can also be hired. An ideal campsite can be found by continuing east along the road out of town, then turning right just before the large ridge is reached; a dirt track leads to a flat area beside the Rachu-Tsangpo river. About 12km away, in Tsamda, there's a hot spring bathing facility. From Tingri the first sighting of Everest is made, and Cho Oyu also graces the view south. This is a good place to do some walking; the ridgeline east of town provides opportunities to gain altitudes in excess of 5500m in an almost Martian landscape. The hills to the north also offer good walking, but the Bum-chu river has to be crossed. As well as the trek to Everest Base Camp (described below) it's also possible to trek for 1½–2 days from Tingri to Cho Oyu Base Camp.

Trekking to Everest Base Camp 65km (40 miles)

From Tingri there are several ways to reach the Rongbuk Base Camp. The road east can be continued for around 21km (13 miles), followed by a turn south to **PEDRUK** (Phadhruchi) via the 5150m (16,896ft) **PANG LA** to join the Rongbuk valley heading south to Everest (3–4 day trek).

Another option, providing a superb and remote 3–4 day trekking opportunity, heads south from Tingri, then curves east to cross the **LAMNA LA** into the Rongbuk valley, as described here.

Tingri to Rongbuk via the Lamna La (3–4 days)

Follow the motorable track heading south along the plain from Tingri on the east bank of the Rachu-Tsangpo (Ra Chhu) river. The track winds past several small villages, including **CHHOLLING** and **LUNGJHANG**, the latter being the last on this part of the Tingri plain; continues through a narrowing in the valley, then onto the east slope of moraine – where there are possible campsites in a few flat areas. The track hugs the side of the hills, often in steep surroundings, until curving east and crossing a river to reach an ideal campsite (c4800m: 15,748ft) situated between a rockface to the north and high mountains to the south. This is a hard day's walk of 8+hr from Tingri, but it brings you much closer to your goal. (By continuing south through the valley Cho Oyu Base Camp can be reached.)

The road continues eastward and rises up a hill to gain a small pass, over which it descends into a valley before rising again. From here you have a choice of passes, both known as the Lamna La. The track opts for the lower, northern pass, while the southern alternative (c5350m: 17,552ft) has no track over it and gives the aura of a very

View from the Lamna La (5340m). The head of the Tingri plain can be seen in the distance (Joe Williams)

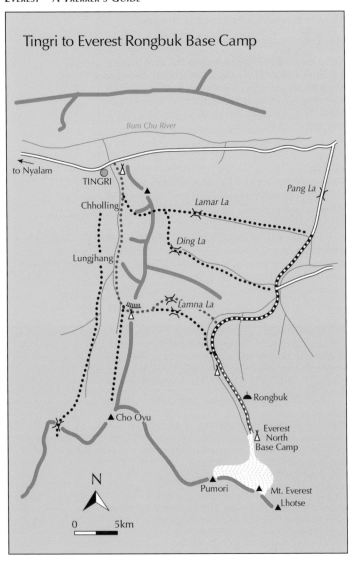

Tingri to Everest Rongbuk Base Camp

Bum Chu River

to Nyalam

TINGRI

Chholling

Lungjhang

Lamar La

Pang La

Ding La

Lamna La

Rongbuk

Cho Oyu

Everest
North
Base Camp

N

0   5km

Pumori

Mt. Everest

Lhotse

high crossing. By taking the northern Lamna La, the track descends past a village and enters the Rongbuk valley, and then follows the road to the Rongbuk monastery and North Base Camp. The southern crossing is among strange rock formations that shape the land underfoot, with a descent along a faint trail on the left-hand side of a small river; vegetation is seen once more, and after 1hr or so the vast Rongbuk valley is reached. Turn south here along a path, and soon a rickety bridge can be crossed to reach the road that leads to Base Camp. Follow this road for a while until a suitable camping area is found on the right. ▸

The road now moves south, with a gentle uphill gradient, until the North Face of Everest appears, and at last the Rongbuk monastery (Dza Rongphu) is reached at 4980m (16,339ft). Built on an historic site, the monastery is well worth visiting. It stands on the east side of the road with guesthouse accommodation and a small settlement adjacent. A short distance away, on the other side of the road, a half-built Chinese hotel stands ominously. The road continues through the moraines, and after a couple of zigzags arrives at Base Camp (5150m: 16,896ft), less than 2hr walk away.

The road to Base Camp was built for the 1960 Chinese Everest expedition which had 214 members, a third of them Tibetan; the summit was reached via the North-East Ridge on 25 May.

Above Base Camp

The Rongbuk Base Camp is usually much less busy than the Nepalese equivalent on the Khumbu glacier, and while from the latter Base Camp Everest cannot be seen at all, at Rongbuk the view of the world's highest mountain is simply stunning. The North Face – where all the pre-war attempts took place – can be seen rising majestically out of the Rongbuk glacier. Behind Changtse (the 'north peak' – now named Bei Peak) lies the North Col, with the North Ridge rising from that to the summit ridge (North-East Ridge).

Writing in 1938 of the view of Everest, Bill Tilman said: 'Seen from Rongbuk it looms up magnificently, filling the head of the valley. The final pyramid, with or without its streaming banner, is a glorious thing.'

Base Camp is located on the flat moraine at the tail-end of the Rongbuk (Rongpu) glacier, and about halfway

THE RONGBUK MONASTERY

Everest from the Rongbuk Monastery (Joe Williams)

The Rongbuk area was recognised as a site of religious importance around 300 years ago, and the first *gompa* built there as a Buddhist nunnery about 100 years later. By the end of the 19th century, however, there were just a few hermits living below the Rongbuk glacier, where the current Base Camp is sited. The present monastery was founded in 1902 by the great religious leader Dzatrul Rinpoche, described by General Bruce as 'a large, well-made man ... full of dignity, with a most intelligent and wise face and an extraordinarily attractive smile'. Dzatrul Rinpoche was also influential in the founding in 1916 of the Thyangboche monastery on the south side of Everest. When the first Everest reconnaissance expedition arrived at Rongbuk in 1921, the monastery supported some 20 lamas, while several hundred lay lamas or monks stayed for varying lengths of time; more hermits lived in caves and cells higher up the valley. Rongbuk was noted as a place for meditation, an exceptionally holy place, and at the time of the Chinese invasion of Tibet in 1950 it had almost 250 residents, most of whom were nuns. But the Cultural Revolution (1966–76) – which destroyed most of Tibet's monasteries – also brought destruction here. When Galen Rowell visited in 1983 he found the monastery 'without a single ceiling; just broken walls stretching a hundred yards up a hillside devoid of life, where hundreds of pilgrims and lamas once worshipped' (*The Mountains of the Middle Kingdom*). Some rebuilding has taken place since then; the new monastery stands on the site of Dzatrul Rinpoche's, and includes an image of Dzatrul as the central figure in the *lhakhang* or temple.

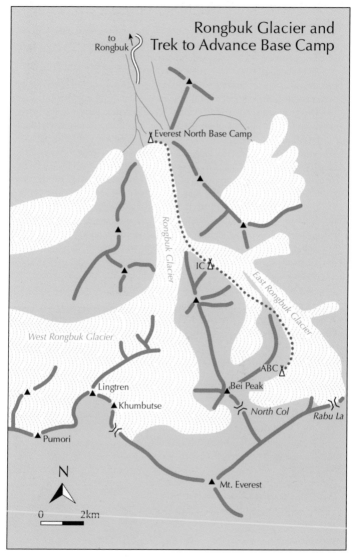

Rongbuk Glacier and
Trek to Advance Base Camp

to
Rongbuk

Everest North Base Camp

Rongbuk Glacier

IC

East Rongbuk Glacier

West Rongbuk Glacier

ABC

Lingtren

Bei Peak

Khumbutse

North Col

Rabu La

Pumori

N

Mt. Everest

0   2km

With several options
for continuing
beyond Base Camp,
you must be both
well acclimatised
and in good health;
the prospect of
developing AMS or a
related illness here is
not to be dismissed
lightly.

*Everest seen from
Rongbuk Base
Camp during a
Puja ceremony
(Joe Williams)*

along the plateau there's a Chinese building beyond which you are not officially allowed to pass without a permit. However, there's often no one there and you can continue without comment. ◄

The valley directly east of Base Camp provides an opportunity to gain height and superb views of the Rongbuk valley, while a short trek westward opens a view of Cho Oyu. If you continue south, along the west bank of the glacier, the West Rongbuk glacier can be followed as far as the Nup La, a 5850m (19,193ft) pass – but this is a high-altitude trek of several days.

The main objective should be to reach Advance Base Camp (ABC) at around 6200m (20,341ft) on the north slopes of Changtse, for this gives very impressive views of Everest's North Face. From Base Camp take the yak path heading south along the east bank of the Rongbuk glacier. The going is quite tough, along small paths on rough moraine, and you may have to dodge laden yaks along the way. Upon reaching the junction with the East Rongbuk (Dong Rongpu) glacier, turn east where steep slopes lead to a contouring path that comes to

Intermediate Camp (IC) at around 5760m (18,898ft). From here it's possible to continue the ascent southward, passing along the moraine, past ice towers, and over the 6000m mark to reach ABC. This camp is situated on the rocky moraine below Changtse and the North Col. The enormous expanse of Everest's North Face looms above, with the pinnacles of the North-East Ridge dominating the view. The summit is just beyond these.

Here the trekking stops. Any further upward progress requires climbing equipment. But the view is nothing less than spectacular.

THE KANGSHUNG VALLEY AND EAST FACE BASE CAMP

The Kangshung region is much more heavily vegetated than the arid approaches to Rongbuk, and more remote. From the administrative centre of Kharta a trek of 4–5 days leads to the East Face Base Camp site via the Langma La (5330m: 17,487ft), or in 5–6 days by way of the lower Shao La and the Kaama Tsangpo valley.

KHARTA, above the Phung Chhu or Arun river, is where Howard-Bury, leader of the first Everest reconnaissance expedition, made his base from which to explore the eastern side of the mountain in 1921. It is reached by a spur off the Rongbuk track built for the Chinese Everest expedition mentioned above, the turn-off for Kharta being at Phadruchi.

The **LANGMA LA** is enticingly described by Stephen Venables in his book *Everest: Kangshung Face*. He called it '. . . the most dramatic I have ever seen'. The trail over the **SHAO LA** (4970m: 16,306ft) is hardly less so, for it leads into what has been called 'one of the most beautiful valleys in the world'. Staggering high mountain scenery – including Everest, Lhotse and Makalu – underlines that beauty. It would be possible, of course, to make a circuit that includes both passes; one on the up-route, the other saved for the return from Base Camp, making a round trip of about 10 days – plus time to enjoy and explore the Base Camp area. Whatever the choice, trekkers are bound to have a memorable experience – the very stuff of dreams.

To aid these dreams see *Trekking in Tibet* by Gary McCue, and *Tibet: A Trekking Guide to Southern Tibet* by Bob Gibbons and Sian Pritchard-Jones.

APPENDIX A

SUMMARY OF TREKS

Trek	Time	Distance
Trek 1 Jiri to Namche Bazaar	7–9 days	94km (58 miles)
Trek 2 Namche Bazaar to Thame	2 days	10km (6 miles)
Trek 3 Namche Bazaar (or Khumjung) to Gokyo	3–4 days	22km (13½ miles)
Trek 4 Gokyo to Lobuche via Cho La	3 days	20km (12½ miles)
Trek 5 Gokyo to Lobuche via Phortse, Pangboche and Pheriche	3–4 days	35km (22 miles)
Trek 6 Namche Bazaar (or Khumjung) to Lobuche, Gorak Shep, Kala Pattar and Everest Base Camp	5–7 days	35km (22 miles)
Trek 7 Tingri to Everest Rongbuk Base Camp Via Lamna La	3–4 days	65km (40 miles)

APPENDIX B

THE STORY OF EVEREST

According to an oft-told story, an official of the Great Trigonometrical Survey of India burst into the office of the Surveyor General one day in 1852 and announced: 'Sir, I have discovered the highest mountain in the world!'

The height of Peak XV, as the mountain was then coded, was calculated as 29,002ft (8840m) – a remarkably near-accurate measurement considering the methods used at the time, and the fact that surveyors had not been allowed into Nepal to further their work. This measurement was generally accepted for over 100 years until it was increased to the height of 29,028ft (8848m).

Some 13 years after the supremacy of Peak XV had been discovered, it was named Mount Everest in honour of Sir George Everest. He was Surveyor General from 1830 to 1843, and the driving force behind the work of the Survey. Everest himself was unhappy about such a precedent, being firm in his opinion that mountains should bear the name by which they are locally known. However, despite the fact that the Tibetan name of Chomolungma was known to some members of the Survey, an excuse of ignorance was promoted as both Tibet and Nepal were then off-limits. The name Mount Everest stuck – and so it is known throughout most of the world today (although Chomolungma is becoming more widely accepted than hitherto).

Although the mountains of Nepal were firmly out of bounds to foreigners until after World War II, in 1907 an Indian surveyor, Natha Singh, was given permission to map the Dudh Kosi's valley. During his brief visit he almost reached the foot of Everest where he outlined the end of the Khumbu glacier, the first non-Sherpa to venture there.

The first Westerner to gain a reasonable view of the mountain was J. B. Noel who, in 1913, made a clandestine journey into Tibet, specifically to 'seek out the passes that led to Everest and if possible to come to close quarters with the mountain'. He got to within 40 miles (64km) of it and saw the upper pyramid rising through the shifting clouds. After lecturing on his travels to the Royal Geographical Society in 1919 a committee – formed jointly by the RGS and Alpine Club – began seriously to look at ways of climbing Everest. Little did they realise that their ambition would take more than 30 years to fulfil.

In 1921 the first reconnaissance expedition passed from Sikkim into Tibet and journeyed across the arid, windswept plateau to the base of the mountain. On the way one of the members, Dr A. M. Kellas, died of a heart attack at Kampa Dzong, from where the expedition caught their first sight of the peak. In the party was George Leigh Mallory who, with G. H. Bullock, that year discovered the route to the North Col.

The following year General Bruce led the first proper attempt and, by way of the East Rongbuk glacier and using oxygen, a height of 8320m (27,297ft) was reached on the North-East Ridge. Unfortunately the expedition was blighted when seven Sherpa porters were lost in an avalanche below the North Col.

On the 1924 expedition Lt Col Norton reached 8580m (28,150ft) without the use of supplementary oxygen, but the outcome of this expedition was overshadowed by the disappearance of Mallory and Irvine, last seen at about 8450m (27,723ft) 'going strong for the top'. Whether they reached the summit may never be known, but that unknown has been the source of much speculation. In 1975 a Chinese climber, Wang Hongbao, is said to have found a body at about 8100m (26,575ft). If true this could have been either Mallory or Irvine, but Wang died in an avalanche before anyone had an opportunity to question him closely about it. Mallory's body *was* discovered in May 1999, 75 years after he and Irvine disappeared, but the find did nothing to quell speculation as to whether he and Irvine had first made it to the summit.

A fourth British expedition set out in 1933 under the leadership of Hugh Ruttledge. Once again a height of about 8580m (28,150ft) was reached, and an ice axe found which could have belonged to either Mallory or Irvine. (Several other items of equipment from the 1924 expedition have been found at various times since.) Also in 1933 aerial photographs of Mount Everest were taken as light aircraft flew over the summit for the first time.

The next official expedition had to wait until 1935, but an unauthorised solo attempt was made in 1934 by Maurice Wilson, a survivor of Ypres in World War I.He entered Tibet in disguise and, with no more mountaineering background than a few scrambles in the Lake District to his credit, began to climb towards the North Col under the impression that willpower, fasting and faith would see him through. His body was found the following year at a height of 6400m (20,997ft).

The 1935 expedition was led by Eric Shipton, and among the Sherpa porters employed by him was one Tenzing Norgay, the man destined to reach the summit 18 years later. This expedition spent rather too much time exploring and mapping, and reached the mountain too late to mount a serious attempt to climb it. Both of the next two expeditions (1936 and '38) were hampered by an early monsoon, and little new was achieved. A year after Tilman's low-key 1938 attempt the world was at war, and more than a decade would pass before another official expedition could be mustered to look seriously at Mount Everest again. By that time Tibet would be out of bounds and mountaineers would need to examine the problem afresh.

But before the Chinese invasion effectively stifled mountaineering activity in Tibet, another clandestine visit was made to Mount Everest by the Canadian Earl Denman. Unlike Wilson, Denman had at least made an effort to learn something of mountaineering at altitude immediately after the war by climbing a number of peaks in East Africa, including Kilimanjaro. Kilimanjaro and the Virunga mountains were hardly adequate preparation for the highest mountain in the world, and it is no surprise to learn that his attempt failed just below the North Col – despite the fact that of the two Sherpas with him one was none other than Tenzing Norgay again, for whom 'the pull of Everest was stronger ... than any force on earth'.

After the war the forbidden kingdom of Nepal began to relax its closed-door policy at about the same time as Tibet was being invaded by the Chinese communist army. In 1948 a party of Indian scientists was given leave to explore the Bhote Kosi valley, during which they reached the Nangpa La on the borders with Tibet. Two years later Bill Tilman led a small expedition in the region of Manaslu and Annapurna, and before he could return to Britain was invited by the American Oscar Houston to join an informal party that had just received permission to visit Solu-Khumbu. Tilman, and Houston's son Charles (with whom he had climbed on Nanda Devi in 1936), pushed up to the head of the Khumbu valley and studied Mount Everest for the first time from the slopes of Kala Pattar. As far as a practicable route to the summit was concerned, Tilman was not impressed by what he saw. It would be left to his fellow explorer and lightweight expedition guru Eric Shipton to prove that a way did indeed exist into the Western Cwm by way of the Khumbu glacier, and through it would be found the key to the summit.

A remarkable effort was made in 1951 by a forceful Dane, Klavs Becker Larsen, who – with a number of Sherpas – crossed the Nangpa La into now-forbidden Tibet (the first Westerner to do so) and made his way round to Rongbuk. From there an unauthorised attempt was made to climb Everest by the known route to the North Col. On the way to the col Larsen's Sherpas refused to continue and he was forced to abandon his attempt. Dodging Chinese communist guards out looking for him, he eventually managed to return safely to Nepal.

In the same year the British had managed to secure permission to mount a reconnaissance expedition via the Khumbu valley. An impressive team under Shipton's leadership made a thorough exploration of the southern approach to Everest, during which they forced a way through the Khumbu Icefall far enough to know that it was possible to enter the Western Cwm. With Shipton were W. H. Murray, Tom Bourdillon, Michael Ward and two New Zealanders, Earle Riddiford and a tall, gangling beekeeper, Edmund Hillary.

Until now Mount Everest had been very much the preserve of the British, but the government of Nepal broke that monopoly by allowing the Swiss to mount two expeditions in 1952. On both of these Tenzing Norgay was the sirdar. On the pre-monsoon attempt the Swiss broke new ground by climbing through the Western Cwm and reaching the South Col. From a high camp on the col Lambert and Tenzing climbed to about 8595m (28,199ft) on the South-East Ridge before turning back. Later that year, during the post-monsoon attempt, weather conditions prevented movement above the South Col. Although they failed to make any gains on the previous high point, they had at least found a better way to the col itself.

The British were greatly relieved at the Swiss failures for they had booked the mountain for 1953, and in the spring a team of 14 climbers, physiologist, film-maker and reporter from *The Times*, plus 20 Sherpas and 350 porters, set up Base Camp at the foot of the Khumbu Icefall. Leading the expedition was John Hunt, an army officer with five Himalayan expeditions behind him, and an unquestionable flair for organisation. His team was among the strongest ever to be assembled, and included Ed Hillary – who had performed so well with Shipton in 1951 – and the highly experienced sirdar Tenzing Norgay, who by now knew the route to the South Col better than anyone. On 26 May Charles Evans and Tom Bourdillon gained the South Summit (8763m: 28,750ft), a great achievement that is often underplayed in reviews of the mountain's exploration. Three days later Hillary and Tenzing left their Camp IX at about 8504m (27,900ft), crossed the South Summit, and battled their way up what has since become known as the Hillary Step. At 11.30am on 29 May they became the first men to stand on the main summit, 101 years after it was discovered to be the highest mountain on earth. In Hillary's words: 'We knocked the bastard off!'

Unknown to organisers of the official '53 expedition, another group of climbers also planned to tackle Everest that year – the Creagh Dhu Club from Scotland. The Creagh Dhu were a tough bunch with little respect for the

Establishment. Their idea was to travel out to Nepal as cheaply as they could, trek up to Everest and wherever possible live off stores left behind by the Swiss the previous year, as they tackled the mountain from camp to camp. In the event only John Cunningham and Hamish MacInnes reached Nepal. They had neither sponsorship nor visas; in fact, no permission to be in the country at all. When they crossed the border from India they managed to fool officials by showing their passports and an airmail letter bearing an official-looking crest. According to one account they walked through Kathmandu at night to avoid the police, then trekked all the way to Namche Bazaar, hiring a Sherpa who refused to carry any baggage. That left Cunningham and MacInnes with loads of 140lb each, which they carried porter-style, using head-bands to ease the weight. However, by the time they reached Gorak Shep, Hillary and Tenzing had already climbed the mountain. Cunningham is said to have commented, 'We didn't fancy making the second ascent' so instead they made an attempt on Pumori – which failed.

Of course, the story of Everest does not end in 1953. The allure of the world's highest mountain seems not to have diminished one iota, for since Hillary and Tenzing's great achievement the momentum has increased by leaps and bounds. Every face and every ridge has been under assault. It has been climbed in winter, climbed without supplementary oxygen, climbed solo. It has been traversed, encircled, skied down, jumped off. In 1988 it was climbed from Base Camp to summit in 22½ hours by Frenchman Marc Batard, while in 1995 Italian guide Reinhard Patsheider recorded the fastest ascent on the northern side by climbing from Advanced Base to the top in 21 hours without bottled oxygen. These times were roundly beaten in 2000 by Babu Chhiri Sherpa who romped from Base Camp to summit in an astonishing 16 hours 56 minutes. Two Sherpas, Ang Rita and Appa Sherpa, have both to date reached the summit more than 10 times, while 33-year-old speed climber Babu Chhiri spent 21 hours camping there on the night of 6–7 May 1999 without supplementary oxygen. Sadly, Babu died two years later after falling into a crevasse in the Western Cwm while taking photographs. (He was the 168th climber to die on Everest, 48 of whom were Sherpas.)

Such record-breaking efforts may be remarkable achievements, but is this what mountaineering is all about?

Everest will still have the last word, as was proved in the tragic pre-monsoon season of 1996 when a bottleneck of mountaineers from five commercial expeditions was overtaken by a sudden storm high on the mountain. Eight climbers – professional guides and their clients – lost their lives in what proved to be the worst tragedy the mountain has seen. Sadly it will not be the last.

The story of Mount Everest has followed the fate of major peaks in Europe during the Victorian era, when a mountain was first claimed to be 'An inaccessible peak', then 'The most difficult climb in the Alps', then 'An easy day for a lady' (with apologies to women readers).

But perhaps that is unfair. Mount Everest will never quite be an 'easy day' – for ladies or for men. By the original South Col route the technical difficulties may not be as daunting as they once were; the psychological barrier of the unknown has disappeared, and advances in mountaineering technique and equipment have made a vast difference to the performance of climbers. But Everest will always be special, if only for the draining effects its great altitude inflicts on those who venture high upon it.

Surely no one can look upon that great wind-blasted pyramid – from the summit itself, or from the safety of Kala Pattar – without being deeply moved by it. Everest *is* special, because it is Everest. Sagarmatha, Chomolungma, 'Goddess Mother of the World'.

For the full story of man's involvement with Mount Everest up to 1999, Walt Unsworth's *Everest* makes compelling reading (see also other books recommended in the Bibliography).

APPENDIX C

TREKKING PEAKS IN THE SOLU-KHUMBU REGION

The term 'Trekking Peak' is somewhat misleading, for although the summits of such designated mountains are not among the most difficult to scale in the Himalaya, several on the list drawn up by the Nepal Mountaineering Association (NMA) involve serious climbing and are beyond the dreams or abilities of the majority of trekkers. Measuring between 5500 and 6600m (18,045–21,654ft) most of these peaks demand a certain expertise on snow and ice, and provide climbing adventure which falls somewhere between alpine and high peak expeditionary mountaineering. The list naturally includes some peaks that prove easier than others, and if tackled under good conditions may seem rather 'tame' to climbers with a few epic alpine experiences behind them. However, in the Himalaya (as in the Alps) conditions can vary enormously, and what might be a straightforward four-day ascent one week can easily turn into a nightmare of life-threatening proportions the next.

Trekking peaks, as opposed to full-scale expedition mountains, are subject to a minimum of formalities and expense, while the rules and regulations governing those who attempt them have been formulated by the NMA. Peaks are grouped according to height. Those of 6000m and above are in Group A, those under 6000m are listed in Group B.The royalty (climbing fee) for attempting those in Group A is double that for Group B, and is levied on expeditions of up to 10 people.

Although there are plenty of foreign and Kathmandu-based trekking companies offering the chance to climb several peaks within the area covered by this guidebook, it is quite feasible to organise your own expedition. A full list of rules and regulations is set out in a booklet available from the NMA, Sports Council Building, PO Box 1435, Kathmandu.

Application is first made to the NMA at the above address. On completion of a form and payment of a modest fee – in foreign currency or in travellers' cheques – a one-month permit is granted. A sirdar, registered by the NMA, must accompany the climbing party for the duration of the trek to and from the peak. The sirdar may also act as a climbing guide.

Those peaks accessible from the Solu-Khumbu region are detailed below. Bill O'Connor's book *The Trekking Peaks of Nepal* is highly recommended to anyone planning to tackle them. It is widely available in specialist bookshops in the West as well as in those of Kathmandu.

MERA PEAK (6476m: 21,247ft) stands in comparative isolation above the remote Hinku and Hongu valleys to the east of the Dudh Kosi, and is the highest of Nepal's official trekking peaks. It was first climbed by Jimmy Roberts and Sen Tenzing in 1953 while the British were busy on Everest. Views from the summit are extensive and include Everest, Lhotse, Makalu, Chamlang, Kanchenjunga and Cho Oyu. Because of its superior height Mera is one of the most popular trekking peaks, but the difficulties, even of reaching the mountain, should not be underestimated. The shortest route of approach is from Lukla by way of the Zatrwala La (4580m: 15,026ft), but to attempt this crossing without prior acclimatisation is to risk serious AMS. All other access routes – and there are several – have their own difficulties. At least three successful routes have been achieved on the mountain itself. O'Connor lists these as being via the Mera La, the West Face and South-West Pillar. The North Face glacier route (via Mera La) has also been climbed on ski.

KUSUM KANGGURU (6369m: 20,896ft) teases trekkers on the long walk-in from Jiri. A graceful, multi-summited mountain, it may be seen from several points along the trail, but none better than the brief glimpse it allows between Choplung and Ghat as the way crosses the entrance to the gorge of the Kusum Khola. One glance is sufficient to know that this is a very serious climbing proposition. Kusum Kangguru repelled four attempts to climb it before the first ascent was achieved in 1979 by a Japanese expedition. A number of different routes have subsequently been made. None could be considered easy.

LOBUCHE EAST (6119m: 20,075ft), sometimes spelt Lobuje, rises immediately above the lodges of Lobuche to provide a spectacular panorama of high mountains. Many parties content themselves with reaching a false summit rather than make a descent into a notch and climbing steep slopes from there to the true top. Few commercial groups attempt the actual summit. The South Ridge route is usually tackled from a camp situated near a small lake reached from the Duglha to Dzonglha trail, while attempts from the eastern side normally begin with a high camp reached directly from Lobuche's lodges. **Note:** There is also a separate peak named Lobuche (6145m: 20,161ft) to the northwest of Lobuche East. This is not included on a trekking peak permit.

POKALDE (5806m: 19,049ft) is one of the easiest and most accessible of trekking peaks in the Khumbu. It rises in a rough-crested wall above Pheriche, but is usually climbed from a camp sited among a cluster of tarns on the northern side. The Kongma La is just above these tarns, and it was from this pass that the mountain was first climbed by members of the successful 1953 Everest expedition as part of their acclimatisation programme.

MEHRA (5820m: 19,094ft), also known as Kongma Tse, is a near neighbour of Pokalde, from which it is separated by the Kongma La. Mehra and Pokalde form part of Nuptse's South-West Ridge, and as such are well seen from Gorak Shep and Lobuche respectively. Climbing Mehra from the south, groups usually have a base camp at the tarns below the Kongma La at about 5300m (17,388ft), and tackle the peak by way of a glacier which hangs down the southern flank.

ISLAND PEAK (6189m: 20,305ft) was aptly named by Shipton in 1952, although it has since been renamed Imja Tse. As with Pokalde, it also received its first ascent by members of the British Everest expedition of 1953. Island Peak stands near the head of the valley of the Imja Khola beyond Chhukhung and is moated by glaciers. Lhotse soars above it to the north, Baruntse to the southeast, Makalu well to the east. Summit views are magnificent. Not surprisingly it is a very popular trekking peak, although it is not as easy as it appears from below Chhukhung. The narrow North Ridge offers a classic route to the summit, but the South-West Ridge is the one usually taken. In addition to its tremendous summit panorama, Island Peak is also noted for strong winds and avalanche danger, especially following a heavy snowfall.

KWANGDE (6187m: 20,299ft) looks down on Namche Bazaar from its guardian position at the entrance to the Bhote Kosi valley. Many trekkers gain their first view of it from a Namche lodge early in the morning, its upper wall painted by dawn light, its lower reaches still black with night shadow. Also known as Kwange Ri or Kongde, this large mountain has a main ridge 5km long, and four summits. The highest summit, Kwangde Lho, was reached for the first time in 1975 by a Nepalese expedition. The route used was, like all other routes on the mountain, a serious one.

PARCHAMO (6187m: 20,299ft) overlooks the Trashi Labtsa, the pass which links the Khumbu region with Rolwaling, and actually forms part of the headwall of the Rolwaling valley. Shipton, Gregory and Evans made an attempt on Parchamo from the Trashi Labtsa in 1952, but it was not climbed until three years later when the Merseyside Himalayan expedition swept through the region, claiming no less than 19 summits on the way. The route from the pass is heavily crevassed.

RAMDUNG (5925m: 19,439ft), or Ramdang Go, belongs to the Rolwaling valley, but is included here because of its proximity to the Khumbu. First climbed in 1952 from the Yalung La, a pass to the north of the mountain, the route is over snow and ice slopes that adorn the North-East Face.

APPENDIX D

USEFUL ADDRESSES

1 Selected overseas missions of the Nepalese Government
Embassies
UK
12a Kensington Palace Gardens
London W8 4QU
Tel: 020 7229 1594

USA
2131 Leroy Place NW
Washington
DC 20008
Tel: 202 6674550

France
45 bis, rue des Acacias
75017 Paris
Tel: 01 46 22 48 67

Germany
Guerickestr. 27
10587 Berlin-Charlottenburg
Tel: 030 3435 9920
Consulates

USA
Suite 400
909 Montgomery St
San Francisco
CA 94133
Tel: 415 434 1111

Australia
PO Box 474
Edgecliff
NSW 2027
Tel: 02 9328 7062

Level 7
344 Queen Street
Brisbane
Queensland 4000
Tel: 07 3220 2007

Canada
Royal Bank Plaza
PO Box 33
Toronto
Ontario M5J 2J9
Tel: 416 865 0200

2 Selected foreign missions in Nepal
British Embassy
Lainchaur
Kathmandu
Tel: (1) 410583)
email: britemb@wlink.com.np
www.britishembassy.gov.uk/nepal

American Embassy
Pani Pokhari
Kathmandu
Tel: 411179/413890

Australian Embassy
Bansbari
Kathmandu
Tel: 371466/371076

3 Map suppliers
Edward Stanford Ltd
12–14 Long Acre
London WC2E 9LP
Tel: 020–7836–1321
email: sales@stanfords.co.uk
www.stanfords.co.uk

Cordee Ltd
3a De Montfort Street
Leicester LE1 7HD

The Map Shop
15 High Street
Upton-upon-Severn
Worcs
Tel: 0800 085 40 80)
www.themapshop.co.uk

Bradt Enterprises Inc
95 Harvey Street
Cambridge
MA 02140
USA

Note: There are also many booksellers in Kathmandu who stock trekking maps for the Everest region. Especially useful are the Himalayan MapHouse shops, with nine outlets in Thamel, Kathmandu; or contact Himalayan MapHouse Pvt Ltd, GPO Box 3924, Kathmandu (**maphouse@wlink.com.np www.himalayan-maphouse.com**).

APPENDIX E

GLOSSARY

Although it would be possible to trek the main trails of the Everest region speaking only English, a little effort to communicate with Nepalis in their own language will be amply repaid. If you are travelling with an organised group plenty of opportunities will arise to practise a few words and phrases with your trek crew and porters. Teahouse trekkers will find that some attempt to speak the language will be appreciated by lodge-keepers and owners of teahouses along the trail, while those who employ a porter-guide will discover that mutual language-exchange is a valuable bonus to the day-to-day pleasures of the trek. Nepalis who meet and work with Europeans are invariably eager to expand their vocabulary, and are usually happy to offer some instruction in their own language in return for help given in English.

The following glossary lists a selection of words that may be useful along the way. However, there are a few Nepali phrasebooks and dictionaries available that would be worth consulting, in addition to Stephen Bezruchka's highly recommended language tape and accompanying book, *Nepali for Trekkers* (The Mountaineers 1991). Lonely Planet publish a small, lightweight *Nepal Phrasebook* that would fit easily into a shirt pocket for instant use on the trail.

aaja	today	chaulki	police post
ama	mother	chini	sugar
ava	father	chiso paani	cold water
baato	trail	chiyaa	tea
baayaan	left (direction)	chorpen	temple guardian
banthanti	the place in the forest	chorten	Buddhist shrine, like an elaborate cairn
bazaar	market		
bhanjyang	pass	daahine	right (direction)
bhatti	traditional inn or guesthouse	daal bhat	staple meal of Nepal: rice with lentil sauce
bholi	tomorrow	danda	ridge
Bhot	Tibet	deurali	pass on a ridge
Bhotyia	Buddhist people of mountain Nepal	dhai	yoghurt
		dhara	waterspout
bistaari	slowly	dharmsala	pilgrims' resthouse
chang	home-made beer	didi	older sister, but also used to denote female lodge owner
charpi	latrine		
chautaara	trailside platform for resting porters' loads		
		dokan	shop (see also *pasal*)

doko	porter's conical load-carrying basket
drangka	stream
dudh	milk
ghar	house (see also khangba)
gompa	Buddhist temple
goth	herdsman's shelter
hijo	yesterday
himal	snow mountain
kang	mountain
kani	covered archway, decorated with Buddhist motifs
katha	ceremonial white scarf
khaana	food
khangba	house (see also *ghar*)
kharka	high pasture
khola	river
khukari	Gurkha knife with curved blade
kosi	river
kot	fortress
la	high pass
lama	Buddhist monk or priest
lekh	hill, or foothill ridge
lho	south
maasu	meat
maati baato	upper trail
mani	Buddhist prayer; from the mantra *Om Mani Padme Hum*
mani wall	stone wall carved with Buddhist mantras
mantra	religious incantation
momo	stuffed pastry
namaskar	more polite form of namaste
namaste	traditional greeting; 'I salute the God within you'
nun	salt
nup	west
paani	water (see also chiso paani, *taato paani* and umaleko paani)
panchayat	system of area council
pasal	shop (see also *dokan*)
phedi	literally 'the place at the foot of the hill'
phul	egg
pokhari	lake
rakshi	distilled spirit
ri	peak
Rinpoche	reincarnated priest
roti	bread
sadhu	Hindu ascetic
satu	flour
shar	east
Sherpa	ethnic people of Solu-Khumbu
sherpani	female Sherpa
sidha	straight ahead (direction)
sirdar	man in charge of trek crew
stupa	large *chorten*
suntala	orange (fruit)
taato pani	hot water
tal	lake
thanka	Buddhist scroll painting
thanti	place
thukpa	noodle soup
trisul	trident symbol of followers of Shiva
tsampa	roasted barley flour
tsho	lake
ukaalo	steep uphill
umaleko paani	boiled water
yersa	a collection of herdsmen's shelters or summer settlement

Days of the week

Aitobar	Sunday
Sombaar	Monday
Mangalbaar	Tuesday
Budhbaar	Wednesday
Bihibaar	Thursday
Sukrobaar	Friday
Sanibaar	Saturday

Numbers

1	ek
2	dui
3	tin
4	char
5	paanch
6	chha
7	saat
8	aath
9	nau
10	das
11	eghaara
12	baahra
13	tehra
14	chaudha
15	pandhra
16	sohra
17	satra
18	athaara
19	unnaais
20	bis
25	pachhis
30	tis
35	paitis
40	chaalis
45	paitaalis
50	pachaas
55	pachpanna
60	saathi
65	paisatthi
70	sattari
75	pachahattar
80	asi
85	pachaasi
90	nabbe
95	panchaanaabbe
100	ek sae
1000	ek hajaar

APPENDIX F

USEFUL PHRASES

Nepali grammar is not very complicated, but it may take practice before it flows naturally with daily usage. One of the main rules to remember is that sentences end with the verb, for example:

Haami (We) kukhoro (chicken) khaanchau (eat).

When asking a question, the structure is the same as for a statement, but is differentiated by intonation. For example, if you want to ask 'Which trail is going to Namche?', the emphasis is placed on the word 'which' with your voice making a rising tone at the end of the sentence.

Namche (Namche) jaane (going) baato (trail) kun (*which*) ho? (is?)

It is essential to avoid asking a direct question in relation to direction finding, such as 'Does this trail go to Namche?', for you will invariably receive a positive response, even if the way does not! Instead, ask 'Which trail goes to Namche?'

Emergencies and medical problems

Help!	Bachaau!
I am sick.	Ma biraami chhu.
I have altitude sickness.	Lekh laagyo.
My friend is sick.	Mero saathi biraami bhayo.
Please call a doctor.	Daaktarlai bolaaunuhos.

On the trail

Hello/Goodbye	Namaste
How are you?	Tapailai kasto chha?
How far is Namche?	Namche kati taadi chha?
How many hours does it take?	Kati ghantaa laagchha?
How much are the oranges?	Suntaala kati parchha?
I am going to Gokyo.	Gokyo maa jaane.
I am lost.	Ma baato haraayo.
I don't know.	Thaahaa chhaina.
I need a porter.	Ma kulli chaainchha.
I will stay two days.	Dui din baschhu.
Is it far from here?	Yahaa bata kati taadhaa chha?
Is the trail very steep?	Baato dherai ukaalo chha?
My name is . . .	Mero naam . . . ho.
Please give me a cup of tea.	Ek cup chiyaa dinuhos.
Take it slowly.	Bistaari jaau.
What is the name of this village?	Yo gaaunko naam ke ho?
What is your name?	Tapainko naam ke ho?
Where are you coming from?	Kata baata?
Where are you going?	Tapaai kahaa jaane?
Where have you been?	Kata pugera aanubhayo?
Where is a shop?	Pasal kahaan chha?
Which trail goes to Namche?	Namche jaane baato kun ho?

BIBLIOGRAPHY

There is no shortage of books on Nepal, but many of those listed below have specific interest to trekkers concentrating on the Everest region. Several have wider scope, of course, but all contain information relevant to users of this guidebook. Inevitably some are out of print and unobtainable in the West, except through public libraries or internet sites. However, many bookshops in Kathmandu stock an admirable selection of new, old and reprinted volumes, and will be worth investigating if you cannot obtain what you require at home.

1 General tourist guides

Insight Guide: Nepal edited by Hans Höfer (APA Publications) Expert contributions, both textual and photographic, give this regularly updated book an air of authority.

Nepal: The Rough Guide by David Reed (Rough Guides) and *Nepal – A Travel Survival Kit* by Hugh Findlay (Lonely Planet) Both offer lots of practical information on getting around Nepal, and include some trekking information. Regularly updated.

Nepal: The Kingdom of the Himalayas by Toni Hagen (Kümmerley and Frey 1980) Not a tourist guide as such, this large format coffee-table book is packed with an assortment of information and photographs gleaned from the author's wide-ranging travels throughout the country. Toni Hagen was the first man to be given the freedom to explore the whole of Nepal, and as such his knowledge of the country must be considered unique.

Mount Everest National Park – Sagarmatha Mother of the Universe by Margaret Jefferies (The Mountaineers 1991) A guidebook to the Sagarmatha National Park.

Kathmandu: Valley of the Green-Eyed Yellow Idol by Bob Gibbons & Siân Pritchard-Jones (Pilgrims Publishing 2005) Gives a colourful description of Kathmandu, its temples, history, legends and its valley, presented in a highly readable and idiosyncratic style.

2 Trekking

Most trekking guides that focus on Nepal attempt to cover as many areas as possible. Each one contains much of interest and practical use, but for the majority of trekkers – whose visit concentrates on one route or one region only – there will inevitably be large passages of unused material.

Trekking in Nepal by Stephen Bezruchka (Cordee/The Mountaineers – 7th edition 1997) The classic trekker's guide. Packed with information, it is a gem of a book. Sensitively written and regularly revised, the author's love of the country and his concern for the people is a shining example to all who follow in his footsteps. Anyone planning a visit to Nepal should study this book before leaving home.

Trekking in the Nepal Himalaya by Stan Armington (Lonely Planet – 8th edition 2001) A compact guide to five regions of Nepal including, of course, the trek to Everest. The author has spent many years leading trekking parties in the Himalaya and now lives in Kathmandu.

Trekking & Climbing in Nepal by Steve Razzetti (New Holland 2000) Written and beautifully illustrated by a well-known British trek leader, it naturally includes treks in the Everest region.

Trekking in Nepal, West Tibet and Bhutan by Hugh Swift (Sierra Club/Hodder & Stoughton 1989) Provides an interesting overview of trekking possibilities in these three countries. It seeks to cover too much territory to give precise detail, but makes enjoyable reading nonetheless.

Trekking in Nepal by Toru Nakano (Springfield Books – latest edition 1990) Has a strong photographic content, and some of the illustrations are particularly striking – serves as a reminder to take a camera and plenty of film.

Adventure Treks: Nepal by Bill O'Connor (Crowood Press/Cicerone Press 1990) Not a route guidebook as such, it consists of a series of personal narratives describing various treks, and manages to convey some of the magic – as well as some of the frustrations – of trekking in Nepal. Currently O/P.

The Trekking Peaks of Nepal by Bill O'Connor (Crowood Press 1991) This companion volume to *Adventure Treks* is, perhaps, of more value, even if you have no ambition to climb. Brief details of major trekking routes are given, as well as outlines of the possibilities for climbing on all 18 nominated trekking peaks.

Trekking in the Everest Region by Jamie McGuiness (Trailblazer Publications 4th ed. 2002) Covers the same area as the present book. Well researched and with lots of background information taking precedence over route details.

Trekking Mount Everest by Ryohei Uchida (Chronicle Books, 1991) Large format full-colour photographic guide to the trek from Jiri.

Trekking in Tibet by Gary McCue (Cordee/The Mountaineers 1991) Includes the northern side of Mount Everest. A very informative book, and worth having if you consider visiting Tibet.

Tibet: A Trekking Guide to Southern Tibet by Bob Gibbons & Sian Pritchard-Jones (Tiwari's Pilgrims Book House 1993) Published in Kathmandu, this slim guide gives route details for the treks to Everest and Xixapangma.

Classic Walks of the World edited by Walt Unsworth (Oxford Illustrated Press 1985) Includes a chapter on the trek from Lukla to Kala Pattar.

The Trekker's Handbook by Thomas R. Gilchrist (Cicerone Press 1996) Written in humorous style by an experienced trek leader, and packed with sound advice. Highly recommended, wherever you may plan to trek. Currently O/P.

The Mountain Traveller's Handbook by Paul Deegan (BMC 2002) Similar to Gilchrist's book above – but with a wider remit – this is for climbers as well as trekkers.

3 Mountains and mountaineering

There are far too many books describing expeditions (successful and otherwise) to Mount Everest to be included here, so the list is necessarily selective.

Everest by Walt Unsworth (The Mountaineers/Baton Wicks 1999) The definitive 'biography' of the mountain. Impeccably researched and intelligently written, the narrative unfolds the story of climbing activity up to 1999. A 'must' for all who have an interest in the world's highest mountain.

Nepal Himalaya by H. W. Tilman (Cambridge University Press 1952 – now contained in the collection of 'The Seven Mountain Travel Books' (Diadem Books/The Mountaineers 1983) Tilman was the first Westerner to visit the upper Khumbu valley in 1950, and his account of that journey is one of the best sections in this book, which also deals with his travels in Langtang and the Marsyangdi valley east of Annapurna. 'The Seven Mountain Travel Books' collection also contains his *Mount Everest 1938*.

The Ascent of Everest by John Hunt (Hodder & Stoughton 1953) This became an instant classic following the first successful ascent by Hillary and Tenzing in 1953. All the innocent beauty of Khumbu, as well as the drama of the build-up towards the summit attempt, remain intact. Worth reading.

The Alpine Journal 1993 (Alpine Club/Ernest Press 1993) Has a section celebrating the 40th anniversary of the first ascent of Everest, which contains a number of previously unpublished articles and letters of interest to Everest 'buffs'.

Everest: The Best Writing and Pictures by Peter Gillman (Little, Brown 1993) A superb anthology which contains many little-known gems.

Everest: Summit of Achievement by Stephen Venables (Bloomsbury/RGS 2003) One of many books published to celebrate the 50th anniversary of Everest's first ascent, this is a pictorial history with intelligent essays by various writers. Includes many fine historic photographs from the RGS archives never previously published.

Everest: 50 Years on Top of the World by George Band (HarperCollins 2003) Entertainingly written by a member of the successful 1953 expedition, this is a selective history of climbing on the world's highest mountain.

Everest: The West Ridge by Thomas Hornbein (San Francisco 1965, London 1971) Tells the story of the American expedition of 1963 that made the first traverse of the mountain and put six members on the summit.

Everest: The Hard Way by Chris Bonington (Hodder & Stoughton 1976) In 1975 Doug Scott and Dougal Haston became the first men to reach the summit via the huge South-West Face, where six previous expeditions had failed. Bonington was the expedition leader.

The Crystal Horizon by Reinhold Messner (Crowood Press 1989) Messner's second oxygen-less ascent of Everest, this time solo in 1980, from Tibet.

Everest: Kangshung Face by Stephen Venables (Hodder & Stoughton 1989) In 1988 Venables was part of a four-man expedition attempting to climb the East, or Kangshung, Face which overlooks Tibet. This book recounts the success of that expedition, as well as the horror of descent.

Mount Everest Massif by Jan Kielkowski (Explo Publishers, Gliwice, Poland) A guidebook describing no less than 124 routes on Everest and its immediate neighbours. No photographs, but scores of line drawings showing routes and attempted routes. Meticulously researched.

Tenzing: Hero of Everest by Ed Douglas (National Geographic 2003) A highly readable and authoritative biography.

4 Travel

Chomolungma Sings the Blues by Ed Douglas (Constable 1997/Robinson p/b 2001) Essential reading for anyone planning to trek in the Everest region, for it gives a realistic view of the sometimes damaging effects of adventure tourism.

Travels in Nepal by Charlie Pye-Smith (Aurum Press 1988) Gives some thought-provoking views on the question of aid to Nepal, as well as being a lively and entertaining travel book. He spends time in Jiri and Namche Bazaar, among others.

Footloose in the Himalaya by Mike Harding (Michael Joseph 1989) Both humorous and thoughtful. Harding describes trekking in Zanskar and Ladakh, in the Annapurna region, and also Namche to Kala Pattar.

First Across the Roof of the World by Graeme Dingle and Peter Hillary (Hodder & Stoughton 1982) An astonishing tale of a journey on foot from Kanchenjunga to K2 by two New Zealanders and a Sherpa. Some inspiring photographs will set you dreaming about other areas to trek in.

Himalaya by Michael Palin (Weidenfeld & Nicolson, 2004) Based on the popular BBC television series, Palin, in his easy-going style, describes the Rongbuk side of Everest during his journey along the Himalayan chain. With splendid photos by Basil Pao.

5 Anthropology and natural history

Birds of Nepal by Fleming, Fleming and Bangdel (Avalok 1984) A comprehensive field guide, richly illustrated.

A Birdwatcher's Guide to Nepal by Carol Inskipp (Prion 1988)

Concise Flowers of the Himalaya by Oleg Polunin and Adam Stainton (Oxford University Press 1987)

Butterflies of Nepal by Colin Smith (Tecpress 1989)

Wildlife of Nepal by T. K. Shrestha (Tribhuvan University)

People of Nepal by Dor Bahadur Bista (Ratna Pustak Bhandar – 5th edition 1987) Background information on a number of ethnic groups of Nepal.

Sherpas: Reflection on Change in Himalayan Nepal by James F. Fisher (University of California Press 1990)

The Festivals of Nepal by Mary M. Anderson (George Allen & Unwin 1971)

WANT TO HELP?

Not surprisingly many trekkers and mountaineers return from a trip to Nepal fired with enthusiasm for the country and its people, in the knowledge that they have had a life-changing experience. Hopefully you will too. And having received generous hospitality, care and consideration from materially poor – but resourceful and naturally cheerful – Nepalis, there is often a desire to give something back in the way of practical help and support.

Mountaineer Doug Scott has done just that through a charity which he co-founded with the aim of improving the infrastructure of villages in the Middle Hills, through the provision of schools and health posts, training in primary health care, clean water projects and other community-strengthening schemes, such as cottage industries.

Without favour towards any specific ethnic group, religion or culture, Community Action Nepal (CAN) works closely with village committees, and actively encourages local participation in each scheme in an effort to avoid donor dependency and to cultivate a sense of ownership and responsibility towards a project's success and development. CAN is currently supporting some 40 projects underway in the Middle Hills of Nepal.

All money gift-aided or donated to CAN goes directly to Nepal, without any deductions to cover UK administration costs, all of which are met by Community Action Treks, Doug Scott's trekking company that supports the charity as its trading arm.

Want to help? Want to give something back?

Community Action Nepal would welcome your support. Visit **www.canepal.org.uk** for further information, or contact:

Community Action Nepal, Warwick Mill, Warwick Bridge, Carlisle, Cumbria CA4 8RR (info@catreks.com tel: 01228 564488).

Perhaps you would like to do something positive to improve the lot of **Nepalese porters**? The International Porter Protection Group (IPPG) was formed as a direct result of the tragic death of a porter from AMS after being abandoned by his employers when falling sick above Manang in the Annapurnas. Started in 1997, IPPG focuses on the provision of protective clothing, shelter and medical care for working porters, and support for injured porters and/or their dependents. By supporting IPPG you can help make a difference to the lives of the often-forgotten men and women on whose backs (literally) much of the success of a trek often depends.